FROMMER'S

1985-86 GUIDE TO LISBON, MADRID & THE COSTA DEL SOL

by Darwin Porter

Published by Frommer/Pasmantier Publishers
A Simon & Schuster Division of
Gulf & Western Corporation
1230 Avenue of the Americas
New York, NY 10020

ISBN 0–671–52421–6

Manufactured in the United States of America

Motif drawings by Paul Berkow

*Although every effort was made to ensure the accuracy
of price information appearing in this book,
it should be kept in mind that prices
can and do fluctuate in the course of time.*

CONTENTS

Chapter I	An Introduction to Iberia	1
Chapter II	Getting Acquainted with Lisbon	4
Chapter III	Hotels in and Around Lisbon	14
Chapter IV	Restaurants in and Around Lisbon	31
Chapter V	Sightseeing in Lisbon	44
Chapter VI	Lisbon after Dark	66
Chapter VII	Shopping in Lisbon	74
Chapter VIII	The ABC's of Portugal	79
Chapter IX	Portugal in a Nutshell	88
Chapter X	Getting Acquainted with Madrid	96
Chapter XI	The Hotels of Madrid	107
Chapter XII	Late Dining in Madrid	122
Chapter XIII	The Attractions of Madrid	137
Chapter XIV	Madrid After Dark	150
Chapter XV	Shopping in Madrid	160
Chapter XVI	The ABC's of Spain	164
Chapter XVII	One-Day Trips from Madrid	174
Chapter XVIII	Spain in a Nutshell	185
Chapter XIX	The Costa del Sol	191
Appendix	The $25-A-Day Travel Club—How to Save Money on All Your Travels	219

MAPS

Portugal	6
Lisbon	11
Spain	98
Madrid	104–105
Central Madrid	110
Costa del Sol	195

Inflation Alert

It is hardly a secret that a wave of inflation has battered the countries of Europe, including those of the Iberian peninsula. The author of this book has spent many hours researching to ensure the accuracy of prices appearing in this guide. As we go to press, we believe we have obtained the most reliable data possible. However, we cannot offer guarantees for the tariffs quoted. In the lifetime of this edition—particularly its second year (1986)—the wise traveler will add *at least* 20% to the prices quoted.

Currency Conversions

The currency conversions from escudos to dollars and from pesetas to dollars, which appear in parentheses throughout these pages, were prepared on the basis of 133 escudos = $1 and 154 pesetas = $1, respectively. These rates may not be accurate by the time you travel, as they do change from day to day, depending on the relative values of both currencies on world markets. Use our currency conversions, therefore, only as a gauge of what you'll be spending and check with a banker before you leave for Iberia to determine what the actual rates of exchange are at that time.

Chapter I

AN INTRODUCTION TO IBERIA

AS YOUR JET descends over the port of Lisbon or sweeps above the golden plains of Castile on its way to Madrid, you'll be embarked on a unique travel adventure—the conquest of Iberia.

Long isolated from mainstream Europe by nature and man—the Pyrenees mountains and the Moors—Iberia developed and grew in its own very individual, very distinct way. Exotic is the word for it. Where else in Europe will you come across anything like the bold, sensuous rhythm of flamenco, the mournful wailing strains of fado, or the truly long, lazy siesta? And above all, the colorful and fascinating sport of bullfighting.

These are aspects of Iberia every person has heard of or seen, but to experience them firsthand is something else, something no traveler should miss. But Iberia is much more than this—indeed, it is a continent in miniature.

SPAIN—QUEEN OF A LOST EMPIRE: Castles, mostly in ruins, dot the Spanish countryside, hollow reminders of Spain's Golden Age, when she dispatched her fleet to conquer the New World and return with its riches. Columbus sailed to America, Balboa to the Pacific Ocean. Cortés conquered Mexico for her glory and the glory of the Church; Pizarro brought her Peru.

The conquistadores too often revealed the negative side of the Spanish soul, the brutality in the name of honor and glory, but they also embodied the positive side, the belief that "the impossible dream" was possible—Don Quixote's chasing windmills on the plains of La Mancha, and often conquering them.

It's difficult to see Spain today without recalling its golden past, for there are many, many reminders. Spain today is a perfect mixture of the old and the new, and its images constantly float by you—silvery olive trees in the south; mantilla-wearing Carmens in Andalusia; Moorish palaces; harsh Basque fishing villages along the northeast coast; the luxurious sandy beaches from the Costa de la Luz to the Costa Brava, thronged with bikini-clad tourists; the orange groves of Valencia; the hard-working industrial city of Barcelona, the largest of the Mediterranean ports; the elegance and serenity of Madrid.

So how can a traveler in Spain go wrong? Here you'll have the glories of the past and the excitement of the present.

AND PORTUGAL—IN ITS OWN RIGHT: Portugal suffers from one of the most widespread misconceptions in European travel: that it's really "another Spain." This completely erroneous judgment exists even today, because Portugal is still relatively unknown and unexplored by the mass of foreign travelers, who, at best, know only Lisbon and the famous resort of Estoril.

Victorian guidebook writers called Portugal an "island," even though it's obviously connected to Spain. The marriage of this Iberian couple, which lasted for 60 years, was never successful. Spain was too large, too dominant, too intent on protecting its own interests, which conflicted with those of its reluctant bride. Although ruled by their powerful neighbor, the Portuguese staunchly maintained their identity during the captivity and zealously waited for the moment they could throw off the yoke and reassert their independence.

Despite its small size— only 140 miles in width, 380 miles in length—Portugal is one of the most rewarding adventures on the European docket. Exploring its towns, cities, villages, and countryside takes far longer than expected, because there is so much richness, such variety, along the way.

The people are the friendliest in Europe. The land they inhabit is majestic—almond trees in the African-looking Algarve; cork forests and fields of golden wheat in Alentejo; ranches that raise the brave black bulls in Ribatejo; the narrow, winding streets of the Alfama in Lisbon; ox-drawn peasant carts crossing the plains of Minho; apron-clad *varinas* (the wives of the fishermen) carrying baskets of wiggling eels on their heads; and the vineyards of Douro.

Azaleas, rhododendrons, and canna grow for miles on end; the sound of fado drifts out of small cafés; windmills clack in the Atlantic breezes; rare, intricate *azulejos* (tiles) line churches and buildings; sardine boats bob in the bay; gleaming whitewashed houses; and the sea . . . always the sea.

Kaleidoscopic scenery, sandy beaches, mild climate, and unique man-made attractions much as Manueline architecture, have contributed to the recent tourist boom in Portugal. But what made the land initially popular with its many English visitors—and later the German multitude pouring into the Algarve—is its low tariffs, not only in its hotels and restaurants, but in its shops as well. Portugal charges some of the lowest prices in Western Europe. Inflation, however, is the rule here too, and the people are hard pressed. Nevertheless, Portugal is still a soothing breeze to those who've been to Rome and Stockholm lately.

Focusing on the unique features of each of these two countries is one goal of this guide. The other is finding those special hotels and fine restaurants that will make your trip to Iberia memorable.

Fisherman mending net

Chapter II

GETTING ACQUAINTED WITH LISBON

NARROW, COBBLESTONED STREETS . . . pastel-washed houses . . . cable cars clacking down to the river . . . a black-shawled *fadista* singing of unrequited love . . . floodlights illuminating an ancient castle . . . boats loaded with fresh seafood . . . mosaic sidewalks . . . ferryboats plying the Tagus . . . laundry flapping in the wind . . . the crowing of a rooster early in the morning.

This is Lisbon, an ancient city, whose people fancifully like to claim Ulysses as their founder. If this legendary figure did indeed possess a character of "experience, tenacity, and intelligence," then he is the appropriate father symbol for Lisbon, Europe's westernmost capital, sprawling across seven hills on the right bank of the Tagus.

HISTORY IN BRIEF: Those cynical of the Ulysses legend claim (no history backs them up) that the seafaring Phoenicians founded Lisbon. In time, the Carthaginians sailed into the port. Romans occupied the city from the beginning of the third century B.C. to the fourth century A.D., during which time it was known as "Felicitas Julia." After Rome's decline, Lisbon was a Visigoth stronghold, then a Moorish city before it was liberated by the Catholic Portuguese from the north in 1147. But it wasn't until 1256 that Afonso III felt safe enough to move his court there, forsaking Coimbra, now a university city.

During the Age of Exploration some of the greatest names, such as Vasco da Gama and Magellan, embarked from Lisbon on their voyages of discovery. Like Ulysses, the captains of those long-ago crews had to contend with widely held beliefs that their ships would be consumed by huge sea monsters, or else be swallowed up by the fiery mouth *(boca)* of Hell.

In time, the discoveries and exploration, the opening of new worlds to the west and east, created a mother city of Lisbon, called in its Golden Age the "eighth wonder of the world." Ivory and slaves from Africa; spices, silks, rubies, pearls, and porcelain from China and the East Indies; ginger and pepper from the Malabar Coast—all these riches were funneled through the thriving port of Lisbon. Shopkeepers literally had more money than they knew how to spend. Their wives hired servants more for ostentation than need. The sea captain's spouse wore finery fit for a princess.

And then came the earthquake. At the peak of Lisbon's power, influence, and wealth, it suffered one of the greatest earthquakes of all time. Two-thirds of the city was destroyed. At 9:40 on the morning of November 1, 1755, most of the city's residents were at church, celebrating an important religious observance, All Saints' Day, when the earthquake struck. In minutes, the glory that was Lisbon became a thing of the past. The great earthquake was felt as far north as Scotland, causing damage even in North Africa. Ambassadors and slaves, merchants and sailors, courtesans and priests added to a death toll estimated at 20,000 to 60,000 persons. A fire raged for nearly a week, destroying much that the quake left undamaged, but thankfully sparing the heart of the Alfama district.

After the ashes had settled, the Marquês de Pombal, the prime minister, ordered that the dead be buried, the city rebuilt at once. To accomplish that ambitious plan, the king gave him the power of a virtual dictator.

What Pombal ordered constructed was a city of wide, symmetrical boulevards leading into handsome squares dominated by fountains and statuary. Bordering these wide avenues would be black-and-white mosaic sidewalks, the most celebrated in Europe.

LISBON TODAY: The mixture of the old (pre-earthquake) and the new (post-earthquake) was done so harmoniously that travelers consider Lisbon one of the most beautiful cities on earth.

Despite its sprawling size and population near the one-million mark, a shopkeeper laments, "It's really a village—everybody knows everybody else. You can't even look at a pretty girl without your wife finding out."

PORTUGAL
VALENÇA
MONÇÃO
P. DA BARCA
BRAGANÇA
CHAVES
VIANA DO CASTELO
BRAGA
GUIMARÃES
VILA REAL
PORTO
T. DE MONCORVO
VIZEU
AVEIRO
VILAR FORMOSO
CURIA
GUARDA
BUSSACO
FIGUEIRA DA FOZ
COIMBRA
COVILHÃ
CASTELO BRANCO
LEIRIA
SEGURA
NAZARÉ
BATALHA
TOMAR
S.
MARTINHO DO PORTO
FÁTIMA
MARVÃO
ALCOBAÇA
PORTALEGRE
C. DA RAINHA
SANTAREM
T. VERDAS
ELVAS
MAFRA
V. FRANCA DE XIRA
SINTRA
ESTREMOZ
CASCAIS
LISBON
MONTEMOR O NOVO
ESTORIL
SETÚBAL
ÉVORA
CACILHAS
ALCACER DO SAL
S. LEONARDO
FERREIRA DO ALENTEJO
SANTIAGO DO CACEM
BEJA
V. VERDE DE FICALHO
ODEMIRA
S. BRAZ DE ALPORTEL
LAGOS
V. REAL DE STO ANTONIO
SAGRES
PRAIA DA ROCHA
FARO

Many who don't know Lisbon from actual fact know it well from all those World War II spy movies. It would be only natural, you'd assume, to see Hedy Lamarr slinking around the corner any moment. In World War II, Lisbon, officially neutral, was a hotbed of intrigue and espionage. It was also a haven for thousands of refugees. Many of those—such as deposed royalty —remained, settling into villas in Estoril and Sintra.

THE DISTRICTS OF LISBON: As conceived by the Marquês de Pombal, the gateway to Lisbon is the **Praça do Comércio** (Commerce Square), also known as the *Terreiro do Paço* (Palace Grounds) in memory of the days when the royal court was located here before the earthquake destroyed it.

However, in the past century, the English dubbed this same square **Black Horse Square,** and the name stuck (even some Portuguese refer to it in this way). The appellation is derived from the equestrian statue on the square of King José I, dating from 1775, the work of Machado de Castro, the leading Portuguese sculptor of his day. It was on this square in 1908 that the king, Carlos I, and his son, Prince Luís Filipe, were killed by an assassin's bullets.

To the east of the square lies the sector known as the **Alfama,** the ancient Moorish district of Lisbon spared from the earthquake. It is crowned by *St. George Castle,* once a Visigoth stronghold, although the present structure dates from the 12th century. This eastern quarter of Lisbon consists of narrow streets (some really stairways) and medieval houses, where neighbors could, if they wanted to, reach out and shake hands with the people next door. Old street lanterns and flower-draped balconies, barefoot children, and fishwives selling the latest catch from the sea add to the local color.

To the north of Black Horse Square lies the **Rossio,** more formally known as *Praça Dom Pedro IV.* A riot of neon, it draws the devotee of the sidewalk café, who sits talking, getting a shoeshine, and sipping the black, aromatic coffee of Angola. Again, tourists have bestowed a nickname on it: *Rolling Motion Square.* The undulating patterns of the black-and-white mosaic sidewalks certainly do give that impression.

A statue there honors Pedro IV, emperor of Brazil. The *Estaçao do Rossio,* the railway station on one side— one of the most bizarre in Europe—is built in what many have described as

"Victorian Gothic" or "neo-Manueline." Also opening onto the square is the *Teatro Nacional Dona Maria II.*

Proceeding north, you arrive at the *Praça dos Restauradores,* with an obelisk commemorating the Portuguese overthrow of Spanish domination in 1640.

Beginning here is Lisbon's main boulevard, the **Avenida da Liberdade** (Avenue of Liberty), dating from 1880. Graced with gardens, palm trees, ponds with swans, it is often compared to Paris's Champs-Élysées or New York's Fifth Avenue. But those suggestions are misleading, as the Portuguese avenue maintains a distinctly original flavor. Along this most fashionable, mile-long promenade, you'll encounter many outdoor cafés, airline offices, restaurants, and shops.

Crowning the avenue is the *Praça Marquês de Pombal,* a heroic monument honoring the 18th-century prime minister who rebuilt Lisbon after the earthquake. Directly to the north is the magnificently laid out *Parque Eduardo VII,* commemorating the visit of the English king to Portugal. It's one of the most attractive spots in all of Lisbon. In the northern section of the park is the *Estufa Fria,* one of the best greenhouses in Europe.

The commercial district ("downtown" Lisbon) is **Baixa,** a sector which is centered mainly between the Rossio and the Tagus. Its three principal streets are the *Rua do Ouro* (Street of Gold), *Rua da Prata* (Street of Silver), and the *Rua Augusta.* All three streets lead to the *Praça do Comércio.*

West of Baixa is the **Chiado,** higher up and considered more fashionable. Its main street is known as the *Rua Garrett,* in honor of a Portuguese poet, an appropriate commemoration, as this street has been the traditional gathering place for the literati. Today it contains some of the city's finest stores.

Looking down over the Chiado is **Bairro Alto** (the upper quarter). When many visitors see the laundry flapping in the wind, the fishwives, the narrow, cobblestoned streets, they think they're in the Alfama. Not so, but much of this district was, like the Alfama, spared from the destruction of the earthquake. It is of interest today because of its excellent fado cafés.

The western quarter of Lisbon is known as **Belém** (Bethlehem). In reality, it's a suburb, characterized by its world-famous landmark, the *Tower of Belém,* the point from which the explorers set out in the age of discovery (at Belém, the Tagus—after a long run beginning in Spain—pours into the sea). Opening onto the *Praça do Império* (Square of the Empire) is the *Jeróni-*

mos Monastery, and down the street, on the Rua de Belém, is the *Coach Museum.*

Lisbon is connected to the working-class district, **Cacilhas,** which lies on the left bank of the Tagus, by the *Ponte 25 de Abril.* Built at a cost of $75 million, it is the longest and most expensive suspension bridge in Europe. Before it was opened, Lisbon was cut off from the south, except by ferryboat connections. The bridge is 7473 feet long, its towers rising to a height of 625 feet. A herculean statue of Christ, his arms stretching out to the sky, stands watch over the southern banks of the Tagus. Tourists and Portuguese alike, by the way, visit Cacilhas because of its seafood.

THE CLIMATE: The climate of Portugal is most often compared to that of California, with the rainfall occurring mostly in the winter, the summers tending to be dry. Where the border touches Spain's Galicia, Portugal is on the same latitude as New York—but there the resemblance ends, thanks to the mitigating force of the Gulf Stream.

For most tastes, spring through autumn is the best time for a Portuguese vacation. But many visitors head to the Algarve in the south in winter. At Madeira, winter is high season.

From November through March, the average temperatures in Lisbon and Estoril range between 46 and 65 degrees Fahrenheit. June through August, the range is 60 to 82 degrees Fahrenheit.

THE CURRENCY: Portugal is one of the most inexpensive countries in which to travel in Europe. But first-time American visitors often panic at price quotations because Portugal uses the same dollar sign ($) to designate its currency. The Portuguese *escudo* is written as 1$00—the dollar sign between the escudo and the centavo. Bank notes are issued for 20, 30, 50, 100, 500, and 1000 escudos. In coins of silver and copper, the denominations for escudos are 1, 2.50, 5, 10, and 20. In *centavos* (100 to the escudo), the denominations are 10, 20, and 50.

It is possible, by the way, to exchange your money at your arrival at Portela Airport; the bank there is open all the time.

FLYING TO LISBON: If you wish to fly directly to Lisbon from North America, as most visitors will, there are two major airlines which do so: TAP (the Portuguese international airline), and **Trans World Airlines.**

As part of my continuing policy to travel on many airlines and report on the services of dozens of national carriers, I recently chose Trans World Airlines for my flight from New York to Lisbon. In a companion edition on Portugal, I report on the services of TAP.

TWA has been a pioneer in international routings since it was founded in 1929. It was the first commercial airline to fly between Europe and North America in the aftermath of World War II, and in 1961 it became the first carrier to make exclusive use of jet engines for flights across the Atlantic. It has flights which go nonstop from New York's JFK airport to Lisbon every day in summer, with slightly reduced service in winter. Easy connections can be made from most major points throughout North America.

The cheapest fare offered is a midweek APEX (Advanced Purchase Excursion) ticket (departing Monday through Thursday inclusive). Passengers can travel on one of those days in both directions. TWA requires a reservation period of 14 days advance purchase, with stopovers lasting from 7 to 180 days.

There is also a regular APEX fare, requiring 21 days' advance purchase, with a stopover of 7 to 180 days.

Yet another ticket, the excursion fare, differs from APEX fares in that no advance purchase or reservation is necessary. This fare, however is costlier. It allows a 30-day minimum stay or a maximum of one year.

Of course, if you don't qualify—or don't want the limitations —of either the APEX or excursions fares, you then must pay the regular coach fare. Businesspeople generally gravitate to the more expensive Ambassador Class, and those savoring the most of luxury—at the greatest expense—book a first-class ticket. All flights are on 747s or L-1011s.

GETTING AROUND LISBON: If all the attractions lay on the Avenida da Liberdade, getting around Lisbon would be easy. As it is, many of the most charming nooks lie on streets too steep or too narrow for automobiles. Thus, a good pair of walking shoes is essential for the explorer who really wants to get to know Lisbon.

Lisbon is suitably endowed with a quite adequate public transportation system that is cheap if not always convenient. At any rate, some form of public or private transportation is necessary, as most of the major attractions of Lisbon are in such suburbs

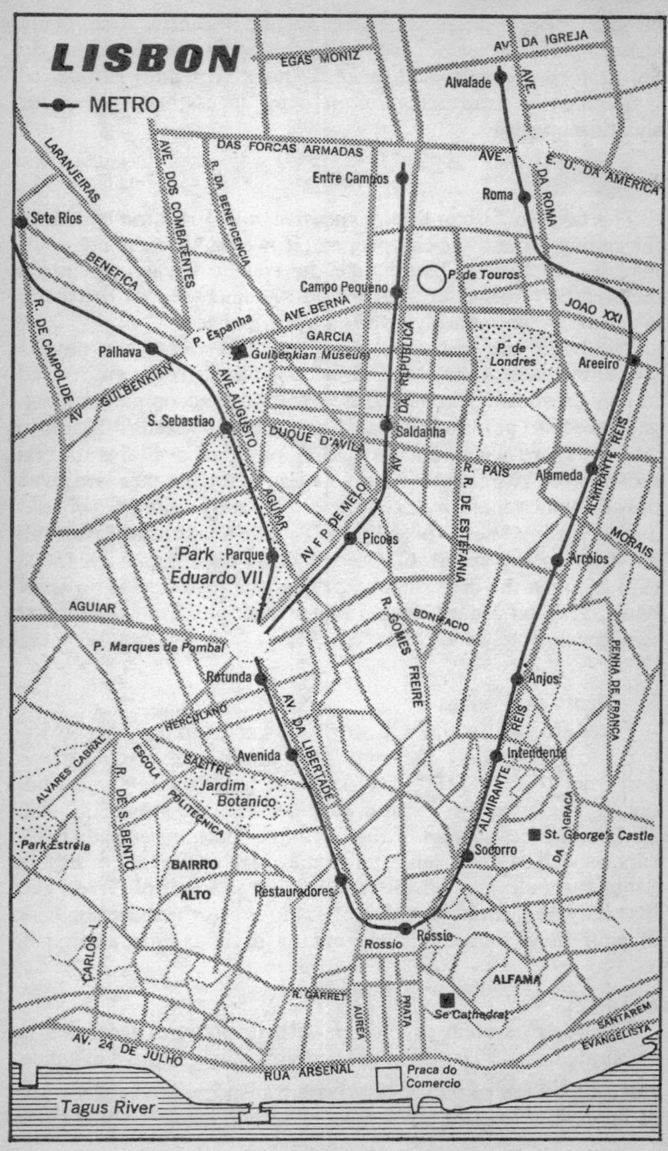
LISBON
METRO
EGAS MONIZ
AV. DA IGREJA
AVE.
Alvalade
LARANJEIRAS
DAS FORÇAS ARMADAS
AVE.
E. U. DA AMERICA
Entre Campos
DA ROMA
Sete Rios
Roma
BENEFICA
AVE. DOS COMBATENTES
R. DA BENEFICENCIA
R. DE CAMPOLIDE
Campo Pequeno
P. de Touros
JOAO XXI
AVE. BERNA
Palhava
P. Espanha
GARCIA
P. de
Londres
Areeiro
AV. GULBENKIAN
Gulbenkian Museum
AVE. AUGUSTO
DA REPUBLICA
S. Sebastiao
DUQUE D'AVILA
Saldanha
Alameda
ALMIRANTE REIS
AGUIAR
R. PAIS
R. R. DE ESTEFANIA
MORAIS
AV F P DE MELO
Picoas
Arroios
Park   Parque
Eduardo VII
R. GOMES FREIRE
BONFACIO
PENHA DE FRANÇA
AGUIAR
P. Marques de Pombal
Rotunda
Anjos
HERCULANO
REIS
ALVARES CABRAL
ESCOLA POLITECNICA
SALITRE
Avenida
AV. DA LIBERTADE
Intendente
R. DE S. BENTO
Jardim
Botanico
ALMIRANTE REIS
DA GRAÇA
St. George's Castle
Park Estrela
BAIRRO
Socorro
ALTO
Restauradores
CARLOS-L
Rossio
Rossio
ALFAMA
R. GARRET
AUREA
PRATA
Se Cathedral
SANTAREM
EVANGELISTA
AV. 24 DE JULHO
RUA ARSENAL
Praca do
Comercio
Tagus River

or neighboring centers as Belém, Queluz, or Sintra. Also, many visitors prefer to anchor into hotels along the nearby Costa do Sol (Estoril, Cascais) and make frequent trips into Lisbon, so mastering the transportation network is essential—even for short-time visitors.

Taxis

The taxis in Lisbon are inexpensive, and I recommend them for getting around the city proper. (However, if you're commuting, say, to Estoril, better take the train.) Always get into a metered cab (most likely a Mercedes)—and see that the meter is turned down before you begin your journey.

The basic fare begins at 40$ (30¢). Thereafter you pay 3$ (2½¢) for each additional 142 meters. The driver is authorized to levy an additional charge of 50% if your accompanying luggage needs to go into the trunk, provided it exceeds 30 kilos in weight. There is a surcharge of 20% on the above fares for taxi service from 10 p.m. to 6 a.m. Note also that these fares are given only for your general guidance, and will surely undergo increases during the lifetime of this edition. To take a taxi from Lisbon all the way to the resort of Cascais costs approximately 1500$ ($11.25). Tip the driver about 20% of the regular fare on short hauls, 15% on longer treks—as, for example, from the airport to a beach hotel at Estoril.

Streetcars and Buses

Fares are inexpensive. On streetcars expect to pay from 16$50 (12¢) to 32$50 (24¢). Depending on where you're going, buses cost from 16$50 (12¢) to 50$ (38¢), the latter for an express bus ticket. The buses are green double-deckers, the streetcars gold. To obtain a description of the routing of both buses and streetcars, as well as a timetable, go to the kiosk at the foot of Eiffel's Santa Justa elevator off the Rua do Ouro (Street of Gold). But it's really best, certainly simpler, to inquire at the reception desk of your hotel before striking out on a sightseeing excursion.

Subways

The Metro system of Lisbon, with its stations decorated in elaborate mosaics, is still in the fledgling stage. From a distance, you can spot the stops by a large "M" sign, lit at night. The Metro charges a flat rate of 27$50 (21¢), but if you buy a series of 10 tickets for 180$ ($1.35), tickets cost only 25$ (19¢) each, regardless of the distance.

Electric Trains

These provide the most efficient and cheapest method of reaching destinations in the environs. Go to the **Cais do Sodré** station on the Tagus to make connections for resorts such as Estoril or Cascais along the Costa do Sol. There is only one class, the fare from Lisbon to Cascais or Estoril costing 65$ (49¢).

To take the train for Sintra, you must go to the **Estaçao do Rossio** station, in the center of the city. The above fare also applies between Lisbon and Sintra.

Ferry or Bridge

From the **Praça do Comércio** (Black Horse Square), you can catch a ferryboat that will take you to the left bank of the Tagus (and particularly to the working-class district with its seafood specialty restaurants) for 30$ (23¢). If you're taking your car over, the one-way fare ranges from 60$ (45¢) to 105$ (79¢), depending on the size of the car.

However, most motorists prefer to drive over the **Ponte 25 de Abril**. This suspension bridge, described earlier, charges from 30$ (23¢) to 100$ (75¢) for a large vehicle such as a Mercedes. The bridge provides the quickest link to the left bank of the Tagus and the towns of the south, including Sesimbra and Setúbal.

Car Rentals

You'll have to decide whether you want a car on a straight daily or weekly basis, with a kilometer charge, or an unlimited-mileage arrangement. Unfortunately, some agencies do not offer the choice. One firm that does is **Avis**, a worldwide firm with 100 depot stations on the Portuguese mainland, in Madeira, and on the Azores. In Lisbon, Avis has offices at the airport; the Sheraton Hotel, the Ritz Inter-Continental Hotel, the Penta Hotel, the Tivoli Hotel, and at 12-C Avenida Praia da Vitória (tel. 56-11-77), which is the main office. In making a reservation in the United States, you can call a toll-free number—800/331-2112.

Hertz is also well represented in Portugal. Before leaving America, you can make international reservations by calling, toll free, 800/654-3134.

Chapter III

HOTELS IN AND AROUND LISBON

IN SEARCHING FOR A HOTEL, it's best to think of the Portuguese capital as "Greater Lisbon." For Lisbon differs from most European capitals in that it can be visited on a day trip (or several day trips) from one of several attractive resorts along the Costa do Sol, such as Estoril or Cascais. Few capitals in Europe offer such resort-style accommodations so close to metropolitan life.

If you're arriving anytime between April 1 and October 1 and planning a fairly long stay, you may want to find an attractive resort hotel on the sea, venturing into Lisbon only for sightseeing excursions, fado singing, shopping, or whatever. If your stay is for only two or three days, you'll want to stay in Lisbon proper, as it takes more time to adjust to life in a resort hotel. And if your visit is in off-season, you'll doubtless prefer a city lodging.

When staying along the Costa do Sol, the matter of transportation to Lisbon is easily taken care of by either renting a car or using the electric train system running from Cascais along the coast to Lisbon.

GOVERNMENT-CONTROLLED PRICES: In my selections—the majority of which are within Lisbon city limits—I have mainly kept to establishments the Portuguese government rates as "first-class." First-class hotels in Portugal, however, are moderate in price. Many would even be considered "budget" by some. In some cases, there is a slight distinction made between a first-class "A" hotel and a first-class "B" hotel. But often this is only a legal, technical difference that's of interest more to badge-wearing bureaucrats than tourists.

At the reception desk of your hotel, you'll see (or should see) a sign on which the official tariffs are quoted. In Portugal, the Directorate of Tourism regulates the price a hotel owner may charge clients. To that official rate, a 10% charge is added for service, plus an additional 3.1% "tourist tax," which is another way the government has of earning a bonus from the influx of foreign visitors.

OFF-SEASON DISCOUNTS: Off-season visitors find that the government requires hotels or inns along the coast—and especially in the southern province of the Algarve—to give you a reduction of at least 15% on room charges. Off-season is November to February. Many establishments, of course, grant greater reductions than this, often extending the time limit from mid-October to April 1. From November to March, hotels in Estoril grant reductions that average around 15%. Few Lisbon hotels grant off-season discounts; rates are the same year round.

The recommendations in this guide include a few of the older, more established lodgings, but generally the hotels are products of the 1960s and early 1970s, and come complete with modern equipment and furnishings.

If the expense of a first-class accommodation is too much for a lean budget, you have an ample choice of smaller hotels and pensions (listed further on) where you can live inexpensively, the more so if you take all three meals at your lodging place.

Lisbon—Deluxe Hotels

The **Ritz Inter-Continental**, 88 Rua Rodrigo da Fonseca (tel. 68-41-31). You can't lose with a name like "the Ritz," especially when such a hotel lives up to its tradition. This is Lisbon's most prestigious accommodation, now a part of Inter-Continental Hotels Corporation. "The Ritz, please," is all you need to tell your cab driver. Close to everything, the 12-story modern structure faces the capital's Edward VII Park, and its clientele is chock full of diplomats, tycoons, and movie stars.

The suites, naturally, are top drawer, furnished extravagantly with antiques such as fringed canopy beds, fine Italian and Portuguese wood pieces, inlaid desks and chairs.

The conventional doubles and singles, however, are . . . well, more conventional; some are done in ocean-liner blond modern. All rooms are absolutely comfortable, spacious, and well kept, and contain color TV, radio, and mini-bar.

Singles range from 10,500$ ($78.75) to 15,000$ ($112.50);

doubles from 12,500$ ($93.75) to 18,000$ ($135), the higher priced twins decidedly luxurious and fronting Edward VII Park. Service and taxes are included. Suites, including a sitting room and boudoir, rent for far more, of course. Whichever your room, you'll have your own breakfast terrace and an all-marble bathroom, with a separate shower, as well as air conditioning and soundproofing.

The lobbies here are refined, with magnificent tapestries. The Grill Room deserves its high culinary ranking, and the Ritz dining room is a favorite of many.

In this rarefied atmosphere of poodles and minks, the skilled management will not only quote special tariffs for your chauffeur, but also for your dog.

Lisboa-Sheraton, 1 Rua Latino Coelho (tel. 57-57-57), is the tallest building in Portugal, rising 30 stories. Opened in the autumn of 1972, the hotel boasts 400 bedrooms in a fine position on a prominent boulevard near Edward VII Park. The bedrooms are compact but not crowded—air-conditioned, with marble-topped chests and desks, plus small sitting areas. Singles range in price from $59 (U.S.) to $75. Two persons pay from $75 to $90 for a twin-bedded room with a continental breakfast, these prices including tax and service. Crowning the tower is a panoramic restaurant and cocktail lounge (the view of the hills of Lisbon is stunning). All meals are à la carte. The Alfama Grill downstairs provides regional Portuguese dishes. Among the numerous facilities are a health club, an open-air heated swimming pool with a snack and refreshment area, a shopping arcade, beauty parlor, and barbershop.

Altis, 11 Rua Castilho (tel. 56-00-71), a deluxe hotel on a tree-lined street, it has mezzanine lounges big enough to shelter a small army and the Herald Bar with piano music. Although it appears geared for groups, the individual traveler can also find comfortable accommodations here. The rooms are brightly decorated—cheerful colors offset by white. Singles go from $58 (U.S.); doubles, $70. Some rooms open onto a view over the old part of the city. All rooms have self-regulated air conditioning, music, televisions on request, and double sinks in the tiled baths. Typically Portuguese dishes are featured in both the Girassol Restaurant and in the Don Fernando Grill overlooking the city. Sometimes fado and folklore entertainment is presented. You can enjoy before- or after-dinner drinks in the São Jorge Bar.

Lisbon—First-Class Hotels

The **Tivoli**, 185 Avenida da Liberdade (tel. 53-01-81), and the **Tivoli Jardim**, 7-9 Rua Júlio C. Machado (tel. 53-99-71), are two sister hotels in the heart of Lisbon. They are, by far, the most popular all-around hotels in the capital. Right on the main boulevard, the five-star, maximum-comfort Tivoli is more deluxe and has more facilities. Its center of action is a glassed-in, two-story courtyard lounge. The air-conditioned rooms are streamlined, some opening onto terraces fronting the avenue, others facing the garden in the rear and a side parking lot. Furnishings are semimodern, with a liberal use of bold colors. Singles rent for $60 (U.S.), doubles for $68, including a continental breakfast. For a sweeping view of Lisbon, try the charcoaled specialties on the top-floor O Terraço. Even if you aren't into astrology, you may prefer a meal in O Zodiaco, with its zodiac tapestry.

Set back from the street, the newer, fully air-conditioned Jardim is a better buy. It has that rarity in Lisbon, a spacious parking lot. And you'll see the rows of bedroom balconies. Zippy elevators and an efficient staff whisk you to the large bedrooms. Singles here rent for $53 (U.S.), doubles from $60, including a continental breakfast. The public rooms carry out a theme of maximum comfort in a rather glamorous atmosphere. The tiled and marbled front lobby, with its two-story-high wall of glass, is a blaze of color—peacock blue, emerald green, autumnal gold, and bright orange. An opera-red carpeted staircase leads to a mezzanine and bar where you can relax ensconced in black leather chairs. For a leisurely meal, costing $15, the hotel provides a garden-style dining room and a breezy breakfast room and snack-bar.

Príncipe Real, 53 Rua da Alegria (tel. 36-01-16), is that intimate and highly personalized little hotel the traveler hopes to find in every big city. One *Los Angeles Times* newspaper columnist called it ". . . one of the finest small hotels in Europe." It's in the neighborhood of the Botanical Gardens, in the center of Lisbon.

The Príncipe Real is the personal world of Mrs. Maria C. Rezende, an ingratiating woman who brings her eclectic taste to the furnishings and running of the hotel. Her living room evokes a villa home, with a wood-burning fireplace, comfortable armchairs, and a windowseat nook. Well-selected antiques and reproductions—gathered by Mrs. Rezende on "scouting" expeditions—have been discreetly placed throughout the hotel.

Tiles, gilt and woodcarvings, ecclesiastical figures, an Empire lamp, a pieces-of-eight chest, an Oriental rug—all create the comfortable ambience. The little wood-paneled bar with its black leather chairs and red tiled tables is one of the coziest spots in Lisbon for a predinner drink. The owner says simply and honestly: "I have good things here." Among her "good things" is a superbly trained staff—one of the friendliest and most helpful you're likely to encounter.

When you see the bedrooms, you'll understand why the Ritz sometimes sends overflow guests here. Each room has its own personality. Although each is compact, everything desirable seems to be there: unusual older-style beds, coordinated printed or solid fabrics at the windows and on the beds, tall mahogany swivel mirrors, an inlaid desk—all backed up by a well-maintained private bathroom. The high-season rates are $55 (U.S.) in a single: $80 in a double; $85 in a triple, all with continental breakfast, taxes, and service included. The morning meal is served in the picture-window room on the top floor, with a slanted beamed ceiling, red velvet chairs, and a mahogany jewel box at the entrance.

Hotel Flórida, 32 Rua Duque de Palmela (tel. 57-61-45), suits those desiring a first-class anchor in the center of Lisbon life, convenient to boutiques, shops, restaurants, and discos. From the restaurant, you look out onto the circular Praça de Marquês de Pombal, with its statue of the 18th-century prime minister and a bronze lion guarding the top flank of the Avenida da Liberdade.

Totally modern, the Flórida is decorated with vibrant, primitive colors which have been daringly used to bring warmth and vitality to every room. For example, the main lounge—with walls of glass and a checkerboard floor of Portuguese marble, orange and royal blue sofas—draws constant lobby devotees.

The 120 bedrooms—each with private bath, radio, air conditioning, and telephone—are ingeniously designed and dramatically colored. A double room runs from $40 (U.S.); a single, $32; service, breakfast, and taxes included. There are two bars and a large lounge on the second floor—even a winter garden.

Hotel Lutécia, 52 Avenida Frei Miguel Contreiras (tel. 80-31-21), is in a fast-rising center of Lisbon, in the direction of the airport. This 12-story structure incorporates every kind of contemporary comfort. There is air conditioning in its 151 rooms and suites, each unit has a private bath, and every guest has a private balcony.

Twin beds are set against walls of fine-grained wood paneling, and the rooms are filled with all sorts of "built-ins." The stream-lined baths are tiled, the draperies soft and filmy, the furnishings chic and up-to-date. Singles average 5000$ ($37.50); doubles 5800$ ($43.50); including a continental breakfast, taxes, and service.

The reception area is spacious and smartly designed, as are the public rooms. The preferred place to dine is the rooftop lounge, with its grand vista; select one of the chef's specialties, cheese or meat fondues, or perhaps the smoked swordfish. Those in a hurry gravitate to the attractive snackbar on the second floor.

Hotel Mundial, 4 Rua Dom Duarte (Tel. 86-31-01), is a modern hotel in the heart of Lisbon, close to the Alfama. The hotel is properly manicured and serviced by a capable staff.

The bedrooms (those on the upper floor sport private balconies) are good, with restrained, contemporary dignity enhanced by color coordination. A room with a gold-and-white-striped bedcover, for example, might have yellow draperies and a matching headboard wall to blend with herringbone parquet floors. Each of the 147 rooms is equipped with a fully tiled bath, telephone, radio, and air conditioning (a TV set will be provided for a small daily charge). Double rooms cost 6800$ ($51); singles, 5600$ ($42); including a continental breakfast and all taxes. The most expensive rooms have private terraces.

On the top floor is a dining room (some alfresco tables in summer), offering a panoramic view of Lisbon, with St. George Castle in the background. The skilled chef prepares a four-course dinner for $14, including, perhaps, gazpacho, grilled swordfish, braised veal tongue in Madeira wine, and dessert.

Hotel Flamingo, 41 Rua Castilho (tel. 53-21-91), is a neat and moderately priced little modern hotel in the heart of Lisbon, not far from the Ritz. It's an air-conditioned structure, with a wide window façade that allows the sun to pour through, making for well-lit and cheerful bedrooms. The owner, Luís Nobre Sequeira, speaks English well.

The rooms he offers are small, but efficiently laid out, with mahogany built-in headboards, bedside lights, desks, and armchairs. For single rooms, he charges from 3500$ ($26.25) to 4100$ ($30.75) nightly; for double rooms, 3900$ ($29.25) to 4300$ ($32.25). A continental breakfast and taxes are included.

The dining room (chef's specialty: smoked duck), lounge entryway, and a Flamingo Bar open one onto the other—all modestly furnished. The most delightful spot is the rear garden terrace, with its striped canopy and lush growth of semitropical vines and flowers.

Lisbon—Other Top Choices

Dom Manuel I, 187-189 Avenida Duque d'Avila (tel. 57-61-60), is for those who desire a high standard of living at a reasonable price. Its location is a little off center, but not its taste level. A little hotel, it has a rear lounge styled as in a fine private home, with an Aubusson tapestry, a raised fireplace, and sofas and armchairs. A window looks out onto a planter of subtropical greenery. The intimate mezzanine cocktail lounge, with decorative brass fixtures, overlooks the living room. The lower-level dining room is in the typically Iberian style, with leather armchairs, tall candle torchères, and a large stained-glass rose window. The bedrooms, although small, are consistently winning. Singles go for 4200$ ($31.50); doubles, 5400$ ($40.50). A continental breakfast is included in the rates. The accommodations contain many built-in features and unusually fine bedcovers, color coordinated.

Hotel Dom Carlos, 121 Avenida Duque de Loulé (tel. 53-90-71), is a cool and inviting choice, set back from a busy boulevard and separated from the street by a small garden in which canna and daisies bloom. An all-modern, 73-room, glassed-in structure, the Dom Carlos lies just off Marquês de Pombal Square, in the center of Lisbon. Around the corner is a service station and a garage belonging to the hotel.

A favorite spot is the cozy mezzanine bar, ideal for a rendezvous or meeting new people. The staff and management are attentive and courteous. The hotel no longer operates a restaurant. However, arrangements can be made for its guests to have lunch or dinner at a nearby dining room, a complete meal going for about 950$ ($7.13).

The bedrooms are distinctively paneled with a reddish South American wood. Cleverly compact, the rooms utilize built-in pieces well and come with air conditioning, TV, and radios. Doubles start at 4200$ ($31.50), singles at 3500$ ($26.25). These prices include a continental breakfast.

Hotel Fenix, 8 Praça Marquês de Pombal (tel. 53-51-21), lives in the shadow of the Ritz. From its perch at the top of the Avenida da Liberdade, it offers a location in the heart of Lisbon. This eight-story hotel is owned by the Torralta chain.

Most of the bedroom windows open onto views of Parque

Eduardo VII. Each of the 112 rooms is air-conditioned and has a private bath with shower. The rooms are compact and cozy, with built-in headboards, push-button service, and telephone. For double- or twin-bedded rooms the charge is 5800$ ($43.50), and for singles, 5000$ ($37.50) daily. All taxes are included.

There's a two-level reception lounge, with a hideaway mezzanine nook for drinks. On the ground floor is a rustic-style restaurant, the Bodegón, specializing in international food.

Hotel Jorge V, 3 Rua Mouzinho da Silveira (tel. 56-25-25), wraps up comforts and little amenities and ties them with a ribbon of modest prices. Just off the Avenida da Liberdade, in the heart of the shopping district, the George V is up to date. Built in 1963, it provides balconies for some of the rooms. Light sleepers may prefer the quieter chambers in the rear.

You enter into a miniature reception lobby and a combination lounge-drinking bar dotted with chairs and sofas in flashy colors.

Each bedroom is comfortable, and you'll find all the necessities: soft beds, built-in wardrobes, bedside tables and lights, air conditioning, and a small tiled bath. Singles rent for 3500$ ($26.25). Doubles are 4500$ ($33.75). A continental breakfast, taxes, and service are included.

Hotel Rex, 169 Rua Castilho (tel. 68-21-61), has one thing in common with the Ritz: both open onto views of Edward VII Park. Its 11 floors of 68 rooms (and nine suites) have front-view balconies, and the hotel is crowned by a rooftop panoramic restaurant. However, the public is invited to dine in the Rex's rustic tavern, the Cozinha d'El-Rey, which offers an à la carte menu. All bedrooms are well maintained, each having a private bath, central heating, air conditioning, TV, Frigo-bar, four-channel music, and functional furnishings. Singles cost $45 (U.S.); doubles, $50.

Hotel Presidente, 13 Rua Alexandre Herculano (tel. 53-95-01). On a convenient, central corner near the Avenida da Liberdade and Edward VII Park, the Presidente is so clean-cut and modern that the effect is stark. Small enough to avoid staffs that overpower and intimidate, it contains but 59 rooms, all with private bath, central heating, air conditioning, and telephone.

The rooms are compact, with chestnut-paneled walls and furniture more functional than stylish. Single rooms rent for 3700$ ($27.75); doubles, 5000$ ($37.50). A continental breakfast, the only meal served, is included.

Hotel Príncipe, 201 Avenida Duque d'Avila (tel. 53-61-51), an establishment a quarter of a century old, is a favorite of visiting Spanish and Portuguese matadors. All of its large rooms have private baths, and most of them open onto private balconies. A single room costs 2700$ ($20.25); a double, 2000$ ($15) per person. A continental breakfast is included. Full-board rates are also available—and those matadors do seem to like the Príncipe's dining room and bar.

Lisbon—Budget Lodgings

Residência Caravela, 38 Rua Ferreira Lapa (tel. 53-90-11), near the U.S. Embassy, is great for bargain hunters. This recently renovated 45-room, three-star hostelry charges just 1400$ ($10.50) for a single, 2200$ ($16.50) for a double. Breakfast is extra. Each accommodation comes complete with a private bath or shower, telephone, and central heating in winter. The well-maintained, modern hotel is cozy, with tasteful, somewhat smallish rooms, the halls are dignified by reproductions of French furniture.

Residencia Imperador, 55 Avenida 5 de Outubro (tel. 57-48-84), not far from the center, provides rooms with private bath for 3000$ ($22.50) for two persons. The front entryway, designed in Portuguese pinewood, is barely large enough for one's suitcase; however, the bedrooms and upper lounge are adequate in size. Opening onto balconies, the front bedrooms face a tiny private garden. The units are contemporary in concept, neatly planned with built-in beds and simple lines. Muted colors are used on the walls and in the fabrics. The owner provides a personalized service. On the top floor is an airy public room and terrace with a glass front where breakfast is served. Tram 1 or 21 and the Metro (Saldanha station) can whisk you into the city center.

Belém—Moderate Prices

Now a suburb of Lisbon, Belém once had its own share of greatness. Here the Portuguese built the ships to sail on their voyages of discovery. Today Belém still has its share of charm. It's an attractive little town in its own right, filled with colorful restaurants serving regional food. And since it happens to be the site of the major sightseeing attractions in the Portuguese capital, it is rarely missed by visitors.

Few know, however, of the fine hotel Belém possesses. It's the **Hotel da Torre,** 8 Rua Dos Jerónimos (tel. 63-62-62), near the estuary of the Tagus. The three-story inn is modest, but the

A Converted Convent

York House, 32 Rua das Janelas Verdes (tel. 66-24-35), a convent built in the 16th century, was skillfully restored by a French lady, Mme Andrée Goldstein—and it has been savored by discerning guests ever since. The location is on one of the tree-shaded streets up from the Tagus, next to the National Art Gallery. A great many professors, painters, and writers from both America and England wouldn't stay anywhere else.

You enter on a lower level, passing through iron gates, ascending steps past trailing vines and pepper trees into the patio where guests relax under fruit trees. The rooms overlook either this courtyard or else the river below, with its parade of ships and tugs. Madame has ambitiously installed private baths in all rooms except the six student accommodations. Each room has its own architectural shape and personality and its own share of antiques.

Those who request demi-pension or full board are given preference on the reservation list—and I'd advise so doing, not just to better your chances of staying here, but because the French-Portuguese cuisine is most appetizing. The cost for two in a room with private bath is $42 (U.S.). A single with bath is $34. A luncheon or dinner in the restaurant begins at $8.

The dining room has coved ceilings and whitewashed walls, enhanced by a touch of gilt wall sconces. There are several living rooms furnished in a personal manner, with old furniture, rare prints, high-backed leather and velvet armchairs, brass-studded chests, and fresh flowers brought in daily from the market. The most popular room is the two-level bar-lounge, with its open fireplace, carved wooden figures, bronze chandeliers, coats-of-armor, and lamps made from handcarved gilt candelabra.

Good news to York House patrons is the annex across the street. It's a fine old town house, which has been renovated and restored to create a comfortable pension.

The lounge of the annex is predominantly red, chic Victorian, turn-of-the-century Lisbon. Over the fireplace is a grotesque portrait of Alfonso, the former king of Spain, as a child. The bedrooms have a unified color theme and antiques—and tiled baths.

> ### On Top of Old Monte
> **Albergaria da Senhora do Monte**, 39 Calçada do Monte (tel. 86-28-46), is perched on a hilltop belvedere in the Graça section, at a spot where knowing Lisboans like to take their guests for a view of their city. Once a small rambling apartment house, the hotel has been converted to provide unique guest bedrooms, each with a sense of style. Multilevel corridors lead to the rooms; a few have private terraces. Knowing decorator touches abound, as reflected by the grass cloth walls, the attractively tiled baths (one with 18th-century *azulejos* rescued from an old villa), and solid bronze fixtures. A single rents for 2500$ ($18.75), a twin for 3500$ ($26.25), a continental breakfast included. Suites are also available, costing 4500$ ($33.75). The combination reception area and lounge is intimate, containing a few fine antiques—note the monumental rosewood sofa. On the lower level is a drinking lounge.

facilities are contemporary, and the decor is both cheerful and colorful. Singles cost 2400$ ($18); doubles, 3500$ ($26.25), a continental breakfast included. The public rooms are air-conditioned, the restaurant attractively styled in a provincial manner. There's a wood-paneled bar, with black plastic lounge chairs; the main lounge presents a refreshingly white contrast, with armchairs grouped for conversation.

Carcavelos—Moderate Rates

Hotel Praia-Mar, 16 Rua do Gurué (tel. 247-31-31), is a modern resort hotel in Carcavelos, 9½ miles west of Lisbon en route to Estoril. (The electric train station to Lisbon is only a two-minute walk from the hotel.) This nine-floor building was constructed so that every guest gets a good—or better—view: more than half of its bedroom balconies face the hills and fields of Sintra; the others overlook the front swimming pool and ocean. The rooms combine modern with traditional, with an emphasis on the Portuguese provincial style, which you'll note in some of the chests, chairs, armoires, and headboards. The terraces of the more expensive rooms are decked out with ornate white wrought-iron furniture. Depending on the view, singles range in price from $55 (U.S.) to $60; doubles, from $60 to $65. Rates include a continental breakfast. The dining room fills the entire top floor of the hotel. You sit on heavy chairs with thick leather and brass studs, enjoying the good food and view. Adjoining is a spacious, wood-paneled bar. You can swim in the oval pool on the front terrace or traipse down to the ocean (changing cabins for rent). There is a playground for children.

Estoril

About 15 miles west of Lisbon, Estoril—with its splendid, cabana-studded beaches—is one of the most fashionable resorts of Europe. Raymond Postgate wrote that it has "everything Cannes has except a film festival. . . ."

Much of the history of Estoril is associated with Fausto Figueiredo and his deluxe Hotel Palácio. His vision of a chic seaside resort in Estoril predated World War I. And in the 1930s, with the opening of the hotel, Estoril began attracting a steady stream of international visitors—such as the Crown Prince of Japan and his bride on their honeymoon. During World War II, spies—both Allied and Nazi—thronged through the rooms of the Palácio and the nearby Casino.

Since rebuilt, the Casino remains a potent attraction. In the center of the resort is the Parque Estoril with its sweep of palms and carefully tended subtropical gardens extending from the Casino to the shore road. But to many the major attraction of Estoril is its golf course (see Chapter V).

Monte Estoril, with its many hotels, is a satellite sprawling across the slope of a hill, offering vistas of the Bay of Cascais.

A DELUXE CHOICE: The **Hotel Palácio do Estoril,** Parque Estoril (tel. 268-04-00), won its fame as a haven for royalty, a "court away from home," so to speak. The longtime dream of one man, Fausto Figueiredo, whose heirs own the hotel today, the hotel has been known as one of the finest in all Europe since it opened its doors in 1930. At the height of World War II, it was a hub of espionage and intrigue with international spies and counterspies everywhere. One night the swastika might be hoisted for a Nazi cocktail party; the next night the Stars and Stripes would hang in the lounge as the Allies took command of the drinks.

The two-story entrance hall is grand indeed, with handsome furnishings, handwoven carpets, and fine paintings. You walk along a series of intimate salons, with Wedgwood paneling, large chandeliers glittering with sparkling prisms, fluted pilasters, and arched windows opening onto the large garden and lawn. The main drawing room, with its classic columns and black-and-white marble floors, is a stately yet friendly place for after-dinner coffee accompanied by soft piano music. The dining room is a proper backdrop for impeccable service and good-tasting food. There is also the Grill Four Seasons, an outstanding à la carte restaurant, where both Portuguese and French cuisine are served in an atmosphere of class and distinction. The center of predinner life is the bar, also in neoclassic decor. On the pool terrace, under a border of shaped bougainvillea, guests gather for breakfast or a buffet lunch.

The bedrooms are traditional in style, some with brass beds, a dressing table, and a double wardrobe. Many of the rooms have sun balconies with a view of the pool. In high season (April through October), bed-and-breakfast rates for singles are in the $95 (U.S.) range; doubles go for anywhere from $110 to $130, service and taxes included. Of course, the air-conditioned duplex suites overlooking the pool cost more. From November 1 to February 28, all tariffs are lowered. Everything is run expertly, supervised by the general manager, Manuel Quintas.

The bonus—for golfers—is the 9- and 18-hole course in the foothills of Sintra, bordered by pine woods, about a three-minute drive from the hotel. Guests of the Palácio are granted a temporary membership; those on the *en pension* plan can take their lunch at the clubhouse. A further attraction is the seven tennis courts, three floodlighted for night games, located immediately next door to the hotel.

Fronting Estoril Park, the hotel is but a short walk from either the water or the Casino.

THE MIDDLE BRACKET: Hotel Alvorada, 3 Rua de Lisboa (tel. 26-00-70), is a tastefully modern little hotel, directly opposite the grand entrance to the Estoril Casino. What makes staying here so special is the very attractiveness of the rooms, plus such facilities as a solarium and a private garage. The decor combines modern with provincial: carved country-style pieces, simple wall colors, wooden screens used as dividers, lounge chairs, and coffee tables. For all this you pay 5500$ ($41.25) double. The Alvorada is as well a pleasant place at which to entertain.

Monte Estoril—Budget

Zenith, 1 Rua Belmonte (tel. 268-02-02), is a modern, six-story hotel, right in the center of this hillside resort, just high

Luxury Living in a Fortress

Hotel do Guincho, Praia do Guincho (tel. 285-04-91), is a unique resort hotel, the remake of a 16th-century fortress, standing high on a rocky coast, near Cabo da Roca on the westernmost tip of the European continent. The Portuguese regard it as a honeymooner's hotel, and, as such, it is not recommended for singles. Its stark white exterior in no way reveals the opulence and high-fashion taste reflected inside. The inner courtyard is encircled by a colonnade of stone arches, with potted subtropical plants and flowers. Inside, the stone coved ceilings, the Romanesque arches, the curving staircases, the heavy beams, the baronial fireplaces have been preserved. Added were furnishings and trappings both handsome and harmonious to the ambience. These include large gilt ecclesiastical sculptures, Portuguese tapestries, oil paintings, and handwoven rugs. The bedrooms, all with private baths and many with loggias, are equally tasteful, with beautiful fabrics. High-season rates remain in effect from early spring until October 31. With breakfast included, doubles cost from $75 (U.S.) daily, with half-pension costing an extra $12 per person. The suites cost the same whether occupied by one or two persons. Even if you can't stay here, try to visit for a meal. The spacious ocean-view dining room has a regal touch, with hand-embroidered draperies, high-backed red chairs, and overscale antique armoires. The food is impeccable, the service the same. Watching the maître d'hôtel flambé a peach is worth the trek up from Lisbon, which, incidentally, is 20 miles away.

enough up from the coast to provide a view of the ocean and of the rooftops of villas, palm trees, sunrises, and sunsets. A drink on the rooftop cocktail lounge at twilight is a treat. The Zenith's small wood-paneled lounges are intimate and especially comfortable, done with attractive furnishings. There's even a wood-burning fireplace for nippy evenings. Each of the bedrooms contains a private bath, radio, and telephone. Those on the seaside have little balconies; others contain bay windows. The furnishings are tasteful and restrained. In high season, singles rent for from $25 (U.S.); doubles for $32. Rates include a continental breakfast, and from November 1 to April 1, a reduction is granted. English is spoken here. A good-size swimming pool is a special feature.

Taking Flight in Cascais

Estalagem Albatroz, 100 Rua Frederico Arouca (tel. 28–28–21), is an exclusive seaside villa, which in the past catered to such discerning guests as Cary Grant or Chief Justice Warren Burger. Named after that bird of gliding flight, the Albatroz is a stately white inn, recently restored, with a red tile roof that was originally created during the 19th century for the neoclassical home of the Duke of Loulé.

Today it has 37 beautifully appointed rooms, each with a private marble bath. Its bedrooms either face the sea or else open onto a quiet garden. Antiques and Portuguese handicrafts adorn the public rooms. The rate in a single ranges from $45 (U.S.) to $66 daily; in a double from $53 to $114, and in a triple from $66 to $140, depending on the season. Facilities include a saltwater swimming pool and a deluxe restaurant serving a French-Portuguese cuisine (see my dining recommendations). Reservations can be made through the office of Marketing Ahead, 515 Madison Ave., New York, NY 10022 (tel. 212/759-5170).

Cascais—Upper Bracket

Estoril Sol, Parque Palmela (tel. 28-28-31), is a showcase resort hotel, facing the ocean on the edge of Cascais. It is the most elaborate and all-encompasing in the area. Everything here is outsize: not only is the hotel the largest in Portugal (it and the Lisboa-Sheraton have 400 rooms each), but the dining room of the Estoril Sol is the largest on the Costa do Sol. Twenty floors of superb and serviceable bedrooms, each with marble bath, await the visitor. The chambers open onto balconies with views of ocean or hills. In high season, standard singles range in price from $80 (U.S.) to $100; regular doubles, $100 to $120. Warning: The lower rooms facing the sea reflect the coastal traffic—so ask for a lodging on a higher perch. Facilities abound, including radios, color TV, in-house movies, and Frigo-bars in the bedrooms, an elegant grill room, a coffeeshop, a health center, squash courts, at least five bars, a boîte, even a swimming pool with a five-level diving board and adjoining café. The management doesn't look askance if you slip away to the Estoril Casino for a late-night supper or show. The Estoril Sol family clan built it and run it, too.

Cidadela, Avenida 25 de Abril (tel. 28-29-21), is a gem. It is set on a knoll, with six floors of balcony bedrooms overlooking an enclosed garden and swimming pool. The lounges and dining room have been furnished with both restraint and good taste, plus a sense of the best of Portuguese decor. You may never make it to the beach once you discover the thatched bar and poolside restaurant at one end of the garden. Two blocks from the center of Cascais, the "Citadel" offers rooms, suites, or apartments. From July to September, the highest tariffs are charged—5000$ ($37.50) in a single, 6500$ ($48.75) in a double. Suites and apartments are more expensive, of course. Full pension costs 6500$ (48.75) per person.

A Converted Palace in Seteais

Palácio dos Seteais, Seteais (tel. 923-32-00), is a small palace converted in 1956 into an elegant hotel. Lodged in the hills adjoining Sintra—it is approached by an encircling avenue of shade trees and a clipped yew hedge—its twin formal buildings are linked by an ornate towering gate. The estate was built at the end of the 18th century by a Dutch gildemeister, then restored by the fifth Marquis de Marialva, who used it for lavish parties and receptions. Even its gardens are appropriate for its regal interior.

A lightness, a sense of quiet joy, pervades the interior—there's nothing stuffy about this palace. You enter a long galleried hallway, with white columns and a balustraded staircase leading to the lower-level drinking salon and the L-shaped dining room. Along the corridors are several tapestries, groupings of antiques, and handwoven Portuguese carpets.

Unfolding before you are a music salon, a sedate library, and a main drawing room overlooking the countryside so beloved by Byron. There are only 18 rooms, so reservations are imperative. But even the simplest chamber has antiques or reproductions. In high season, the tariffs, including breakfast, range from 15,000$ ($112.50) in a single, from 16,000$ ($120) in a double, service and tax included.

Meals are events here; many Portuguese travel for miles just to dine here. See my restaurant chapter immediately following. Full-pension rates are quoted, although you may order your meals separately.

Cascais—The Middle Bracket

Estalagem Senhora da Guia, Strada do Guincho (tel. 28-92-39) is on the Quinta da Marinha estate, just five minutes from the center of Cascais. It's named after a nearby lighthouse which gives the region its name. Owned and directed by members of the Orellas family, this charming Portuguese inn is housed in a stately stone-built manor, whose wrap-around terrace affords a view of the sea, with a saltwater swimming pool and flower gardens below.

The 18 accommodations, including three suites, are furnished with private bath and are beautifully appointed with fine antiques. There is access to a nearby golf course, tennis courts, and riding stables. Meals are served family style in the inn's elegant dining room. This is one of the newest hotels along the Costa do Sol, having opened during the summer of 1984. It plans to keep its prices low through the early stages of its operation, but may raise them during the lifetime of this edition.

At present, count on spending from $52 (U.S.) daily in a double or else from $46 in a single. There are some triples at $67 daily, and the already mentioned suites rent for $78. These prices include a continental breakfast, although lunch or dinner is another $10 per person. Reservations can be made through Marketing Ahead, 515 Madison Ave., New York, NY 10022 (tel. 212/759-5170).

Cascais—Budget Choice

Albergaria Valbom, 14 Avenida Valbom (tel. 28-65-801), is a modern 42-room hotel. It offers pleasant accommodations with private baths. Singles range in price from 2800$ ($21); doubles, 4000$ ($30).

Chapter IV

RESTAURANTS IN AND AROUND LISBON

EARLY BRITISH VISITORS spoke contemptuously of the Portuguese diet they encountered. They claimed the Portuguese sustained themselves on cod, but thrived on their dreams. Codfish, in fact, is the national dish, prepared in hundreds of ingenious ways. For instance, there's . . .

Bacalhau (salted codfish). This is most often served boiled, accompanied by potatoes and greens. The true connoisseur tosses in olive oil and vinegar as well, but this is an acquired taste. Appearing commonly on menus—in both upper-grade restaurants as well as low taverns—are such variations as bacalhau à Brás (Brás-style); bacalhau no forno (baked in the oven); and bacalhau à gomes de sá (with eggs and onions, flavored with garlic).

When you see the different ways it is cooked and how it's savored by the locals, then you'll know why the Portuguese speak of bacalhau as *o fiel amigo* ("faithful friend").

Another Portuguese specialty is caldeirada, described to visitors as a "fishermen's stew" or the "Portuguese bouillabaisse" if someone is trying to be fancy. This savory kettle of goodness is made with at least four different types of fish, even in simple establishments, although I know of one Portuguese chef who uses a dozen different kinds of fish. The fish is cooked with onions and tomatoes, but many contain nearly 12 different vegetables.

Portuguese sardines, packed in tins with olive oil, are shipped around the world. One publicist for the sardine industry claims that they are "the ideal health, strength and beauty food." This is not disputed, except to say that one woman reported after such a *típico* meal she was trailed by half the cats in the Alfama that afternoon. Sardines are best when you see the menu listing sardinhas assadas (grilled). In the Alfama, housewives cook the sardines over an open brazier in front of the doorways to their houses.

As you've gathered by now, the item to order in Portugal is fish. Even in the simplest tavern, it's likely to be fresh and abundant—that is, all except shellfish. Portuguese lagosta (crayfish), for example, is justly famous. Once it was served commonly throughout the land, almost as a side course. But in recent years catches have yielded less and less, and foreign markets in such countries as Italy and France have demanded more and more. Because the price of crayfish varies from day to day and it's quite expensive, it is rarely set forth on the menu, so inquire about that price before ordering or eating it.

Meat tends to be inferior in Portugal, especially beef and veal. However, acorn-fattened porco (pork) is tender and packed with flavor. A real banquet is porco Alentejano (pork in the style of the province of Alentejo—that is, fried and coated with a savory sauce of clams and mussels, often accompanied by bay-leaf-flavored tomatoes and onions). Another good dish, popular in taverns with beer, is bife na frigideria (steak with mustard sauce, but it's suggested that you forgo its usual accompaniment, a fried egg).

Many a peasant has staved off hunger with tripe cooked with fat white beans and flavored with bits and pieces of pungent sausage. Iscas is also good—calf liver thinly cut and coated with onions and served (most often in an earthenware dish) along with fried potatoes.

A Portuguese specialty, with infinite regional variations, is cozido (a boiled dinner including beef and pork as well as cabbage, bacon, sausages, potatoes, and other greens—almost anything the chef has in abundance). Lamb is poor, but a savory treat is cabrito (roast kid), especially when it's prepared in the style of the province of Alentejo.

Portuguese dining hours have less in common with the country's Iberian neighbor—and are more related to hours in the United States—that is, between 1 and 2 p.m. for lunch, between 7:30 and 9 p.m. for dinner. Of course, meals are served both earlier and later at most establishments. For example, many visitors dine between 10 p.m. and midnight in the fado cafés of Lisbon.

WHERE TO DINE: Whether you're seeking regional or international fare, the restaurants of Lisbon offer a rich, imaginative banquet of choices. To give you the widest possible sampling, I've selected restaurants that have exceptional appeal, not only because of their well-prepared cuisines, but often because of their *típico* decor or atmosphere.

I'll lead off with:

Lisbon—Deluxe Choices

Restaurante Aviz, 12-8 Rua Serpa Pinto (tel. 32-83-91), for many years reigned supreme as the most prestigious—and the finest—restaurant in Portugal. Clement Freud once proclaimed it "the best restaurant in Europe," which put it in heady company. Today, its position has been seriously challenged by other fast-rising establishments, and many readers have complained about the service, food, and prices. Nevertheless, it should be noted that many respected food critics still consider it the Número 1 choice in Lisbon.

The Aviz was once part of Lisbon's special hotel of the same name, catering to the whims of the greats of Europe. When the hotel was torn down, its restaurant operation was rescued.

Today, you encounter an old-world aura as you enter the reception lounge for a predinner drink. You plan your meal with deliberation while munching from a bowl of roasted slivered almonds from the Algarve. You look around and find yourself in a private club atmosphere of green marble columns, deep, tufted black leather chairs, crystal chandeliers, and a pair of paintings of respectable nudes reclining in bed.

As you glance into the glittering dining room, you see three communicating salons, their walls paneled or covered with grained silk, gilt sconces, even a life-size statue of an American Indian girl, with a brief skirt of tobacco leaves (known as "Miss Tobacco Leaf of 1800" by the waiters). The two smaller rooms are more intimate, the larger one more animated.

To begin your meal, try, if featured, the espadon fumé, razor-thin slices of smoked swordfish served with half a lemon wrapped in white gauze to prevent seeds from falling on the fish. Its delicacy is memorable. My most recent duck had an orange sauce that was bittersweet with shredded orange peel, and the dish was accompanied by light, crisp potato croquettes. Crêpes Suzette is a popular dessert. Sipping Portuguese coffee from tiny Vista Alegre cups is an appropriate way to conclude.

Your bill is discreetly presented in a leather folder. That final charge is likely to be 4000$ ($30) or a whole lot more. The restaurant is closed on Sunday.

Tagide, 18 Largo da Biblioteca Pública (tel. 32-07-20), has had a prestigious past, and now it is a distinguished place to dine in the Chiado. Its situation is colorful—up from the docks, on a steep hill on a ledge overlooking the old part of Lisbon and the Tagus. Once the town house of a diplomat, then a leading nightclub, it is now one of Lisbon's leading restaurants. Some gourmets say it serves the finest food in town.

It's very old, with a museum look to it. You go up marble steps with shiny brass balustrades. The dining room has view windows, overlooking moored ships and the port. Set into the white plaster walls are overscale figures made of blue and white tiles, each depicting a famous queen. The chairs are provincial and the tablecloths have hand-crocheted edges. Glittering above are crystal chandeliers.

Both Portuguese dishes of quality as well as selections from the international repertoire are featured and are beautifully served. For an appetizer, try the salmon pâté or the cream of shrimp soup, or perhaps the soufflé Tagide. Other well-recommended dishes include rabbit, Minho style, along with duck liver with fresh mushrooms or sautéed quail. I'm also fond of the pork coriander. Expect to spend from 4000$ ($30) up for a complete meal. The restaurant is closed for Saturday lunch and all day Sunday, and it's important to reserve a table.

Lisbon—Other Top Restaurants

Escorial, 47 Rua Portas de S. Antao (tel. 36-44-29), has an exclusive club aura, rich in wood paneling from South America, opera-red carpets and tablecloths, plus sedate, but attentive, service. Near the Rossio, it offers excellent Portuguese cookery, attracting a steady clientele of business people and out-of-towners, even owners of fashionable villas out at Cascais. The English menu helps the foreigner. A good opener is steamed clams in the Cataplana style, followed by sea bass cooked "the Portuguese way." If you want something more festive, you can order a barbecue of lamb or spring chicken on the spit. It's good to finish off with a peach Melba. Expect to pay from $30 (U.S.) for a dinner here. Try to reserve a table for this centrally located establishment, right in the heart of the city.

Michel, 5 Largo de Santa Cruz do Castelo (tel. 86-43-38), is

Lisbon's Oldest Restaurant

Restaurante Tavares, 37 Rua da Misericórdia (tel. 32-11-12), is a concentrated nugget of glamour that serves one of the finest cuisines in Lisbon. It's a prestigious star, favored since the 18th century by gourmet-minded politicians, diplomats, authors, and exiled royalty drawn to its personalized cooking and service. In a reception lounge, diners gather for a meal.

The preferred street-level dining room is a salon of mirrors, with panels of ecru and gilt, crystal chandeliers, and sconces. You dine on Louis XV-style armchairs, enjoying a small bouquet of roses (or the flowers of the season) on your finely set table. The Tavares is the oldest restaurant in Lisbon, founded in 1784 by Nicolau Massa (nicknamed "O Talao"). In the 19th century, it became the property of two Tavares brothers.

For an appetizer, you can choose presunto de Chaves (Chaves ham). The chef does a velvety vichyssoise. Among the main dishes are santola (crab) recheada à Tavares, linguado (sole) Newburg, and the special beef of the house. At the start of your meal, you can ask the chef to whip up an Alp-high soufflé as a finale. Then top it off with a café filtro, and lean back, reflecting on an unforgettably fine meal and experience. For this quality cuisine, your final bill is likely to cost from 3000$ ($22.50) to 4000$ ($30) for a complete meal. Closed Saturday and for Sunday lunch.

the most fashionable restaurant in the Alfama. On a tiny plaza near St. George's Castle, this popular first-class restaurant serves a continental cuisine prepared under the watchful eye of Michel da Costa, the restuarant's Moroccan-born owner and chef. Tempting continental specialties include smoked swordfish, seaweed sea bass, and black bass Don Fernando. A recommendable main dish is green-pepper duck. For dessert, the apple tart Michel is favored. Michel also specializes in his own version of the "new cuisine," as exemplified by a prosciutto-like specialty made from goose with a well-seasoned salad, or blinis with swordfish. The cost of a regular meal ranges from 2500$ ($18.75) to 4000$ ($30). The restaurant is open Monday through Saturday from noon to 3 p.m. and 8 to 11 p.m. Reservations are necessary.

Sua Excelência, 40-42 Rua do Conde (tel. 60-36-14), is the creation of Francisco Queirós, who was a travel agent in Angola before he returned to Portugal. In Lisbon he has created his little dream restaurant, with a refined, sedate atmosphere, attracting a discerning clientele. Outside you'll see no sign. There is only a large heavy door with a bell which you ring to announce your arrival. The patron will greet you with personalized hospitality. The atmosphere he has created is modish, somewhat like a fashionable drawing room, with colorful round tables containing cloths that reach to the floor. There's a hushed quiet among the appreciative diners.

The cuisine is French-Portuguese. Try, for example, an order of beef bourguignon or tender squid. The patron will be heartbroken if you're not tempted by his dessert display. All the baking is done on the premises. The cost of a regular meal (soup/appetizer, main course, dessert, wine, and coffee) ranges from 1800$ ($13.50) to 2500$ ($18.75). The restaurant is just a block up the hill from the entrance to the National Art Gallery, so it could be visited on a tie-in museum/luncheon adventure, although its ambience is more charming in the evening.

Lisbon—Moderately Priced Restaurants

What follows is a selection of restaurants in the Portuguese capital that serve good food at moderate prices. Of course, if you order shellfish, such as lobster, you can expect to pay a lot of money.

Restaurante O Faz Figura, 15-B Rua do Paraíso (tel. 86-89-81), is one of the best and most attractively decorated dining rooms in Lisbon. Part of its atmosphere is a veranda where you can order both lunch and dinner overlooking the Tagus. When reserving a table, ask for a choice perch there. The restaurant lies in the heart of the Alfama, and it offers faultless service and typical Portuguese food along with international specialties. A complete meal will cost around $18 (U.S.). You are given a warm reception and then shown to your table, unless you want to stop first for a predinner drink in the handsome "international cocktail bar." The restaurant serves daily from 12:40 to 4 p.m. and from 8 p.m. to midnight. It is closed on Sunday.

Gambrinus, 25 Rua das Portas de Santo Antao (tel. 32-14-66), is an establishment whose stature among Lisbon's leading restaurants is justified. Intimate dining rooms are clustered around an open blue-tile kitchen, where expert chefs in starched white hats prepare fine meals, using large copper pots and a charcoal grill. The location is a breeze for those who want to dine in the heart of the city, off the Rossio, near the railway station, and on a little square near the National Theater.

You can have your meal while sitting on leather chairs in the rear under a cathedral-beamed ceiling, or else select a little table beside a fireplace upon the raised end of the room. All is dominated by an impressionistic tapestry along one wall. There is also an alcove with a stained-glass enclosure, all primitively modern. The walls of the back room are sedate with paneling, not unlike a country lodge. For before-dinner drinks, a front bar beckons.

Although there is a diversified à la carte menu, don't fail to check the *especialidades do dia.* The soups are good, everything from bisque of shellfish to onion. Fish dishes range from conha com mariscos à thermidor (conch with shellfish) to tobalo (bass) minhote. A Germanic meat dish is frankfurters with sauerkraut. Another specialty is rumpsteak Gambrinus. The restaurant offers elaborate desserts, including a vanilla soufflé and crêpes Suzette. Coffee with a 30-year-old brandy complements the meal perfectly. Expect to spend from 2200$ ($16.50) up for a meal here. It's open seven days a week from noon to 2 a.m.

Chester, 87 Rua Rodrigo da Fonseca (tel. 68-78-11), near the Ritz Inter-Continental, is an attractive restaurant and bar, with a good cellar. Its specialty is grilled steaks. The pepper steak is tempting, as is the rib steak for two. Entrecôte with whisky sauce is hearty, and the fondue bourguignonne is prepared only for two persons. The tab is likely to range from 1800$ ($13.50) to 3000$ ($22.50) for a complete meal for one. The restaurant is upstairs, and a cozy little bar lies below. Service is friendly, and reservations are suggested. Chester is closed on Sunday.

Pabe, 27A Rua Duqúe de Palmela (tel. 53-56-75), is the Portuguese name for pub, and that's what this cozy English-style place is. Convenient to the Praça do Pombal, the pub has done its best to emulate English establishments. There's soft red carpet on the floor, mugs hanging over the long bar, a beamed ceiling, coats-of-arms, and engravings of hunting scenes around the walls. Two saloon-type doors lead into a wood-paneled dining room, where you can sup on meat specially imported from the U.S. A châteaubriand for two is about the most expensive dish. If you prefer local fare, start off with a shrimp cocktail, then Portuguese veal liver or chicken breast with mushrooms, and finish with a sherbet, all for a cost of 2000$ ($15) to 3000$ ($22.50). The crowd tends to be a well-groomed Portuguese set as well as resident Yanks and Britons. It is closed on Sunday.

Casa da Comida, 1 Travessa de Amoreiras (tel. 68-93-86), has steadily gained in popularity. If you're in Lisbon between December and March, when the winters are mild, but gray and rainy, this is among the best choices for dining in the city. A roaring fire will greet you and warm you. Not only is the atmosphere most pleasant (at any time of the year), but the food is impeccably served and good-tasting. You enter, exchanging greetings with a large parrot, before going into a step-down garden. The sole is delectable, and the meat, especially veal, is well prepared. Dinners begin at 2500$ ($18.75). Closed Saturday at lunchtime and Sunday.

A Palace at Seteais (near Sintra)

The **Palácio dos Seteais**, Seteais, in the vicinity of Sintra (tel. 923-32-00), provides a background for one of the finest meals you're likely to be served in Portugal. The exquisite 18th-century palace—reached only by car or taxi—is also recommended highly as a place at which to stay.

Lunch or dinner is served in the lower dining room, overlooking the hillside of villas and orchards. However, you may want to have a predinner drink in the loggia or the salon at the bottom of the grand staircase. Once seated, you are apt to have a bouquet of pink hydrangeas placed at your table. Serving stewards are skillful and polite.

For 3000$ ($22.50), you can order a four-course meal which begins with your choice of any or all of the 20 different kinds of hors d'oeuvres, such as shrimp, Russian salad, fish mousse, egg in a gelatin pâté. The next course is fish, say, turbot Florentine (creamy with spinach and browned in the oven). Your following meat course will be abundant and tasty, with a wide choice of fresh vegetables. When a cart is brought to your table, you'll be tempted by all of the creamy, fruit-stuffed pastries and cakes. In spring, the fresh strawberries from Sintra are the best in the world.

Lisbon—The Budget Restaurants

Except for the A Quinta, the restaurants described below are patronized mainly by Portuguese and one characteristic that these restaurants have in common, other than their low prices, is that the chefs are generous with their helpings. Added economy tip: Look for the chef's *prato do dia* (plate of the day)—invariably inexpensive and fresh. And some Portuguese restaurants save you more by still persisting in offering reductions for double portions which are shared.

A Quinta, 251-3 Rua do Ouro (tel. 36-55-88), basks in its own tradition. It's just a short ride up the ornate Eiffel-designed Santa Justa elevator (reached from the Street of Gold, near Sarmento jewelers). A colorful little place, "The Farmhouse" is usually crowded with travelers from Idaho to New York, who know they can find well-cooked food, enjoyed all the more if they get one of the tables at the cliff edge, overlooking the hills of Lisbon.

The atmosphere is friendly, the service prompt. The menu still reflects the Russian background of the former owner, although there are many Portuguese specialties offered as well. Thus, A Quinta offers the national soup of Portugal, caldo verde, as well as a bowl of Russian borscht. Or you might begin your meal with charcoal-broiled sardines from Nazaré. Tempting main dishes include Lisbon sole, boned and stuffed with shrimp, the chef's specialty; Hungarian goulash; and beef Stroganoff. Desserts include a Russian "royal Romanoff" cake. The cost of a regular meal ranges from 950$ ($7.13) to 1500$ ($11.25). Closed Sunday and holidays.

O Funil (Funnel), 82-A Avenida Elias Garcia (tel. 76-60-07), is recommendable for its *cozinha Portuguêsa*. You almost never find a free table at mealtimes. It's that popular—and with the Portuguese who know they can get good home cooking at reasonable prices here. The dining rooms are on two levels, the street-floor one in the tavern style, funnel-like, with the tables leg to leg. Most habitués, however, gravitate to the lower level, with its adjoining tiny bar. This is the kind of place where you ask for the *vinho de casa,* and it comes in three different sizes of pitchers. Or you may want to try the red-bottled Valpaços. The three male owners have set down-to-earth prices. Special and typical dishes include clams (ameijoas) and cabrito assado (roast goat). The chef does a special chicken—called frango à Funil. An almond tart makes a nice finish. A complete meal costs from 1000$ ($7.50) to 1500$ ($11.25).

António Restaurante, 63 Rua Tomás Ribeiro (tel. 53-87-80). Just outside the center of the city, the air-conditioned António lies only a few blocks from Edward VII Park, in back of the Lisboa-Sheraton. Special touches here include pewter service plates, a blue-and-white tile motif, and an English menu. Each day the chef features a different soup, and clams are always a favorite opener. A Portuguese regional dish worth recommending is pork with a savory clam sauce, or try the chicken with clams. I'd also suggest the fresh sole and the swordfish. A very special dessert is António pudding. Expect to pay about 2000$

($15) for a really filling meal.

Seafood in Cacilhas

Floresta do Ginjal, 7 Ginjal (tel. 275-00-87), is on the left bank of the Tagus, reached by frequent ferryboat service. You can board ferries at Cais do Sodré. The two-level restaurant opens onto unobstructed views of ships and the river scene of Lisbon. You ascend to the dining rooms via a staircase that's a veritable tunnel of assorted sea shells imbedded in the wall, a proper introduction to the array of fresh and well-prepared fish that will be set before you.

Family-owned and -run, the restaurant attracts a largely Portuguese trade drawn here to sample such regional dishes as coldeirada—the national dish. Other specialties include grilled sole. For dessert, a good Portuguese cheese is queijos serra (from the hills or farm). Fresh cheese and almond cake is another favorite dessert. A complete meal here begins at about 1500$ ($11.25).

In the "Kitchen" at Queluz

Cozinha Velha, Palácio Nacional, Queluz (tel. 95-02-32), is housed in the former kitchen of the 18th-century Queluz Palace. A luncheon here can easily be tied in with a sightseeing jaunt to the palace. You enter through a small patio garden. The high, vaulted ceiling with wide stone arches is intact, as is the tremendous walk-in central fireplace.

The cook's 15-foot marble table is still in use, although it's now laden with ready-to-serve delicacies: hors d'oeuvres, salads, fish mousse, assorted cheese, along with abundant flower arrangements. The ladderback chairs, torchier lights, 15-foot-high front door, the well-trained waitresses in regional dress, plus the superb food, make it well worth the trip. The restaurant is open from 12:30 to 3 p.m. and from 7:30 to 11 p.m.

You must order from an à la carte menu, which includes the house specialty, linguado (sole) Cozinha Velha. Other courses include a filet mignon with a béarnaise sauce, or the more traditional bife à Portuguêsa. A good meal is likely to cost from 2200$ ($16.50) to 3500$ ($26.25). Reserve a table.

THE FOREIGN CORNER: The sun has now set over much of the Portuguese empire, but the memory lingers on in a handful of its restaurants which brought the cuisines of other lands back for the home folks to sample. A good one is **Velha Goa,** 41-B Rua

Tomás de Anunciação (tel. 60-04-46). India forcibly annexed this Portuguese colony in 1961. Against a backdrop of Oriental decor, Indian dishes are served at this pleasant, friendly restaurant where English is spoken. Typically Goanese dishes include curries—prawns, chicken, Madrasta, and other specialties. But pork chops and beef are also served. All dishes are prepared according to the taste of the clients—that is, mild, pungent, and very pungent. Expect to pay about 1000$ ($7.50) for a meal in the dining hall. The restaurant is open from noon to midnight, although final orders are taken at 10:30 p.m. You can also visit the bar, which is open from 6 p.m. to 1 a.m., enjoying a drink in a pleasant atmosphere (you can also order food here). Jazz musicians frequently entertain. A beer costs from 75$ (56¢), a whisky from 250$ ($1.88).

A Gondola, 64 Avenida de Berna (tel. 77-04-26), is Lisbon's "Little Italy," serving what are perhaps the finest Italian specialties, such as ravioli and cannelloni, in town. The restaurant offers indoor dining as well as alfresco meals in the courtyard. Although the decor isn't inspired, the food makes the restaurant worth the trip out of the center. It's best reached by taxi (the street on which it sits crosses the Avenida da República). A full dinner is offered for about 1500$ ($11.25) and up. This is quite a buy when you realize what you get. A first-course selection might include Chaves ham with melon and figs or liver pâté. For a second course, you're likely to face a choice—say, filet of sole meunière or grilled sardines with pimientos, even red mullet. This is followed by yet another course, ravioli or cannelloni in the Roman style, perhaps veal cutlet Milanese. The banquet is topped off by fruit or dessert.

Oitavos

Restaurante de Oitavos, Estrada do Guincho (tel. 285-02-21). A winding road leads to this restaurant and teahouse, sitting on a plateau with an awesome view of the entire coastline, including the hills of Sintra. It's housed in a modern building, with all-glass walls except for the kitchen and serving area. Those exiles of the Costa do Sol long ago discovered it (the former king of Italy has even staked out his favorite table). Food lovers from Lisbon happily make the trek here. The food is, of course, typically Portuguese. You might want to begin with a shrimp cocktail, although the true native prefers the grilled sardines. Fish dishes are the items to order here, including sole prepared in a number of ways. If you're seeking something really local—and really hot—then order frango (chicken) à piri-piri. The desserts are good, especially the recently sampled bananas flambés. A complete meal begins at 1200$ ($9).

A Portuguese Beer Hall

Cervejaria Trindade, 20-B Rua Nova de Trindade (tel. 32-35-06), is one of the oldest beer halls in Lisbon—owned by the makers of Sagres beer. Along with those steins of beer, you'll be given quite good small steaks, smothered in a mountain of crisp french fries. Also featured are clams (ameijoas) in a savory sauce. You'll be tempted to have more than one of the accompanying beers. Every day a different typical Portuguese dish is featured, including açorda de marisco (bread, panada, and seafood), carne de porco à Alentejana (pork and clams), and presunto de Chaves (ham from Chaves, a town near the northern border of Portugal). If the day is sunny, then head for the open-air terrace. The cost of a regular lunch or dinner, featuring the typical dishes and including a large-size mug of beer, costs about 1000$ ($7.50). *Note:* This beer hall was once a convent, and it survived the great earthquake of the 18th century.

A Snackbar

Ritz Snackbars, 77C Rua Castilho (tel. 56-14-44), are in the Ritz compound, but reached by a separate entrance on a street bordering Edward VII Park. The maître d'hôtel of the Ritz Grill constantly and grandly redirects visitors who wander into his domain by mistake to the snackbars. The three snackbars are bright and attractive counter-dining rooms, each on a different landing. In season, they tend to be so popular with visiting Yankees that it's hard to find a seat.

The separate rooms specialize in different cuisines—Portuguese or Italian. But actually you can have any of the offerings, regardless of the level on which you land. The prices are low, as reflected in the sopa de marisco (shellfish soup). From the Italian kitchen, you can select a pizza, pasta in a Bolognese sauce, or lasagne. A hamburger plate is the most popular feature. On a lengthy dessert menu, you'll find such ice-cream concoctions as a Volcano and a Himalaya. Ordering is easy: just select the number that corresponds to the color photograph on the menu. Count on spending from 1000$ ($7.50) up.

Cascais

Estalagem Albatroz, 100 Rua Frederico Arouca (tel. 28-28-21), is the most elegant choice, the kind of place where Prince Rainier used to bring Princess Grace. The location is winning, right at the edge of town, on a promontory with windows allowing diners to enjoy sunset views over the Atlantic. The dining room is just a part of this exclusive inn, the remake of a ducal waterside villa. It's customary to have a predinner drink in the lounge. The food is exceptional. A complete meal in this elegant restaurant costs 3500$ ($26.25). Reservations are necessary.

The most preferred "middle bracket" restaurant is **Reijos,** 35 Rua Frederico Arouca (tel. 28-03-11). Your hosts are Portuguese-born Tony Brito and an American, Ray Ettinger, a purser for a transatlantic airline (he often brings in hard-to-get items by air, including curry from India and soy sauce from Hong Kong). The cuisine represents a blending of their two countries. For example, Reijos is the only place in Cascais where you can get baked Virginia ham. Portugal is represented by a codfish casserole à Reijos, which requires a 30-minute wait (and it's worth it). A delightful prelude to any meal is the shrimp pâté. The menu includes such items as an excellent roast beef as well as roast loin of pork served with rice and beans. The chef also is proud of his fresh seafood, featuring a "catch of the day." Usually sea bass, turbot, or red mullet are served. The restaurant has one of the most varied menus in town, right down to the homemade chutney and assorted condiments served with their authentic curries. The cost of a regular meal ranges from 1200$ ($9) up. The recent redecoration has produced an Oriental effect. Be sure to reserve your table, as this one's popular.

Modest tabs are also rung up at **Costa Azul,** 3 Rua Sebastião José de Carvalho e Melo (tel. 28-11-40). If a local in Cascais were to recommend a restaurant to his visiting Portuguese cousin, it would probably be the "Blue Coast." It has good regional fare, the daily specials announced on a blackboard out front. It's always crowded, and with good reason. The decor is most typically Portuguese, with onions, pineapples, garlic, and sprigs of bay leaf hanging from the ceiling. Try the clam soup. Also good is the cabrito (roast kid). Perhaps the most typical dish is bacalhau (codfish) à Costa Azul. This is the type of place to which you may want to return. You can dine very well here for about 1200$ ($9). It's open all week.

Chapter V

SIGHTSEEING IN LISBON

MANY VISITORS think seeing the sights of Lisbon can be accomplished by one quick visit to the Coach Museum in the parish of Belém. Not so, and if you limit yourself to just this one sight you'll be missing quite a lot. Lisbon is chock full of sights, attractions you'll be glad you took the time to see, and which will give you a greater feeling and knowledge of this very individual country, Portugal.

Those on the strictest of schedules should really try to visit the following at least: (1) the Coach Museum; (2) the Jerónimos Monastery; (3) the Alfama; (4) the Castle of St. George (for the view if nothing else); (5) the National Art Gallery; and (6) the Gulbekian Center for Arts and Culture.

However, if your time is so tight that you've allowed only one day for sightseeing in Portugal, head for the museum-filled area of Belém in the morning, then spend the afternoon enjoying Sintra.

For our exploration of all the major sights (and many esoteric but worthwhile ones), we'll begin in the old quarter . . .

The Alfama
(A Walking Tour)

The most *típico* district of Lisbon lies to the east of Black Horse Square. It's the old Moorish quarter of the city, the Alfama, partially spared by the earthquake of 1755, because its foundation was more solid than that of the rest of the capital. Here narrow, cobblestoned streets stretch down to the Tagus from St. George Castle, crowning the hill.

Today, the Alfama is the traditional home of stevedores, sailors, and fishermen. But in days gone by, it was the aristocratic sector. Even today you can see coats-of-arms of noble families imbedded in the façades of some of the houses.

Allow at least two hours for your walking tour of the Alfama.

The streets are rarely suitable for a car; at times, you must walk up steep stone stairs. A good point to begin your tour is the **Largo do Salvador** (a taxi can drop you off there), housing a 16th-century mansion that once belonged to the Count of Arcos. From there, turn down the **Rua da Regueira,** which leads to the **Beco do Carneiro,** the "cul-de-sac of rams." The lane couldn't be narrower. Families live in houses literally four feet (if that much!) apart. "Our lips easily meet high across the narrow street," wrote poet Frederico de Brito.

At the end of the alley, circle back via a flight of steps to your left to the **Largo de Santo Estevao,** named after the church on the site. Round the church and from the back proceed to the **Patio das Flores,** via a flight of steps, where you can see some of the most delightful little houses fronted with characteristic Portuguese tiles *(azulejos).* Walk down the steps to the **Rua dos Remédios,** cutting right to the **Largo do Chafariz de Dentro,** where you're bound to see the Alfama housewives busily gossiping in front of an old fountain and often walking with jugs of fresh water balanced on their heads.

From the square, you connect with the **Rua de São Pedro,** which is perhaps the most animated street in the Alfama. Strolling deep into the street, you'll probably eventually attract a trail of children, and will come upon women squatting on the street, bartering furiously with a rough-faced, barefoot *varina* (fishwife) over slices of giant swordfish.

Some local taverns will pass before you, and the most adventurous sightseers will venture inside to sample a glass of *vinho verde* (green wine). Later, your head reeling from several glasses, you'll step out onto the narrow street again, where you'll be virtually knocked down by an old fisherman with saffron and brown nets draped over his shoulder.

The Rua de São Pedro leads into the **Largo de São Rafael,** which convinces you the 17th century never ended. You pass a *leitaria* (dairy), which now sells milk in the bottle instead of via the old-fashioned method (cows were kept right inside, as the women of Alfama wanted to make sure their milk was fresh).

Right off the square is the **Rua da Judiaria,** so called because of the many Jews who settled there after escaping the Inquisition in Spain.

Go back to the Largo de São Rafael, crossing it to rejoin the Rua de Sao Pedro. Walk down that street to the intersection, forking left. You enter the **Largo de São Miguel,** with its church richly adorned with baroque trappings. From there, walk up the

Rua da São Miguel, cutting left onto the **Beco de Cardosa,** where from some flower-draped balcony overhead, a *varina* is bound to scream down hell and damnation to her street urchin son if he doesn't come inside immediately.

As you pass the doorways, you'll see black-shawled old women grilling Setúbal sardines on braziers. The armies of cats who reside in the Alfama will easily devour any bones or heads left over. At the end of the alley, you connect with the **Beco Sta. Helena,** a continuation, which leads up several flights of steps to the **Largo das Portas do Sol.**

On this square is the **Museum of Decorative Art,** handsomely ensconced in one of the many mansions that used to grace the Alfama.

One of the most favored belvederes in the city opens onto the square. Called the **Santa Luzia Belvedere,** it's really a balcony to view the sea, overlooking the houses of the Alfama, as they sweep down in a jumbled pile to the Tagus.

Although best explored by day, the Alfama takes on a different spirit at night, when street lanterns cast ghostly patterns against medieval walls and the plaintive sound of the *fadista* is heard until the early morning hours in the traditional cafés.

Castle of St. George

Known as the "cradle" of Lisbon, the present castle is of Visigoth origin; before that, the site was most likely used for a Roman fortress. The castle is named after St. George in honor of the Portuguese and English alliance of 1386. Around the periphery of the fortress is a district of much interest, looking as if it were removed intact from the Middle Ages.

Before entering the grounds, pause at the **Castle Belvedere,** known as the "ancient window" looking out over the city below. In the distance, you can see the best view of the "Bay of Straw," the hills of Monsanto and of Sintra, the Ponte 25 de Abril, the rusty red rooftops of Lisbon, and Black Horse Square. The statue is of Afonso Henriques, the first king of Portugal, who is said to have lived here after he liberated the city from the Moors.

Inside the grounds, you can walk along in cool shade or in sunlight, watching the swans gliding by in the moat, peacocks craning their long necks, olive and cork trees fluttering in the wind. Pink flamingos, weeping willows, and oleander create a dreamy feeling until you stumble upon a cannon, reminding you of the castle's bloody history, the lives lost in battles on this hill.

In the only room left of the ancient Royal Palace, the Alcáçova, you can wander in, and study the details of Roman and Islamic tombstones.

The admission-free castle is open daily from 9 a.m. till sunset.

The Cathedral (Sé)

As European cathedrals go, this one is not wealthy with great art, but it does remain an enduring landmark. Its twin towers give it a fortress-like look and the present structure is a mixture of architectural styles ranging from Romanesque to Gothic to neoclassic. Actually, the cathedral is a little bit of everything, having been changed and modified considerably after it suffered damage from two different earthquakes—one in 1344, the other in 1755.

It is said to have been built on the foundation of a mosque. After King Afonso Henriques liberated the city in the 12th century, the church was built as a triumphant gesture, the establishment of a Christian bastion. Lisboans speak of it as their mother church, the oldest one in the city.

Inside, the most interesting features are a rose window; the Gothic-style chapel of Bartolomeu Joanes dating from the 14th century; a "crib" by Machado de Castro, the leading Portuguese sculptor of the 18th century; the original nave and aisles; and the 14th-century tomb of Lopo Fernandes Pacheco. The church, at the Largo da Sé, within walking distance of Black Horse Square, may be visited from 9 a.m. to 6 p.m.

Belém

This western parish of Lisbon is forever linked to the glory of the Age of Exploration. Here, at the mouth of the Tagus, Vasco da Gama set out to blaze a new trail to India, Ferdinand Magellan to circumnavigate the globe, and Días to round the Cape of Good Hope, even if he didn't know it at the time.

At the point where the caravels, inspired by Henry the Navigator, were launched on their historic missions, Manuel the Fortunate erected:

THE TOWER OF BELÉM: Built between 1515 and 1521, the quadrangular tower is the most distinctive landmark in Portugal. It was designed by Francisco de Arruda, in a Manueline style that incorporates Gothic and Romanesque features, also betraying the debt the architect owed to the Moors during his years of work in Morocco. One historian claimed that the tower "seems to epitomize the hybrid yet highly original character of Portugal's people."

If you climb the stairs to the ramparts, you'll have a panoramic view of the Tagus, as well as the handsome villas in the hills. To reach the entrance door, you walk across a drawbridge. Inside, the rooms are sparsely furnished, except for a few antiques that include a circa 1500 throne-armchair with carved finials and an inset paneled with pierced Gothic tracery. Along the balustrade of the loggia are stone crosses symbolizing the Portuguese crusaders. On the tower is the coat-of-arms of **Manuel I.**

Fronting the Praça do Império is the **Fonte Luminosa** (Luminous Fountain), standing majestically between the Memorial to the Discoveries and the Jerónimos Monastery. Erected in 1940, the fountain attracts motorists from Lisbon who come out at night to watch the floodlit waterworks. To see the entire show takes nearly an hour, as there are about 75 original "liquid designs" from the water jets.

On the Avenida Marginal, it is open daily, except Monday and holidays. From April 1 through September 30, hours are 10 a.m. to 7 p.m. and during the rest of the year, times are from 10 a.m. to 5 p.m. only. The admission charge is 40$ (30¢)

THE MEMORIAL TO THE DISCOVERIES: The Portuguese speak of it with pride as their Padrão dos Descobrimentos. Standing in the river, the monument was designed to simulate the effect of a prow of one of the legendary caravels. Along the ramps of either side you'll see some of the more memorable explorers, such as Vasco da Gama. But occupying the most prominent position, at the meeting point of the ramps, is Henry the Navigator.

This memorial was unveiled in 1960 on the fifth centennial of the prince's death. Symbolized in the frieze are sailors, mapmakers, monks (always taken along on the missions of exploration), a kneeling Philippa of Lancaster (mother of Henry the Navigator), artists, cosmographers, and a man holding a flag with a cross representing the crusaders. At the highest point on the memorial is the 15th-century "arms of Portugal."

Dominating the Praça do Império is:

JERÓNIMOS MONASTERY: The extravagant, flamboyant architecture of Renaissance Portugal reached its pinnacle in this monastery. Traditionalists assert it was ordered built by Manuel the Fortunate to celebrate the opening of the route to India by Vasco da Gama. Certainly, it was paid for by the flourishing spice trade with the East.

Gothic elements romp with exotic Manueline motifs. The total effect was summed up by Howard La Fay: "Here, frozen forever in stone, is the blazing noontide of empire. Stylized hawsers writhe in the arches. Shells and coral and fish entwine on every column. Sanctuary lamps glow red above carved African lions."

Originally, a modest chapel founded by Henry the Navigator stood on these grounds; then the monastery was ordered built in 1502. Damaged but not destroyed by the earthquake of 1755, it was subsequently restored—the restoration a subject of controversy among architectural critics.

You enter through a magnificently sculptured doorway. To the right in the abbey are the tombs of Vasco da Gama and Luís Vaz de Camões, Portugal's greatest poet, whose fame rests on his *Os Lusíadas* ("The Portuguese"). In that heroic work, he spoke of the accomplishments of his countrymen and their triumphs over the enemies of Christ. With typical Portuguese individuality, he evoked pagan deities in his tome to Christianity. He also wrote of Vasco da Gama's discovery of the sea route to India. Franz Villier was skeptical of the claims made by the tombs: ". . . instead of Vasco, an unknown Gama was buried here by mistake, and the error had to be discreetly rectified, while for a long time people had quite forgotten where on earth Camões might be, and only tourists and illiterates really believe that this is the grave of the author of the Lusiads."

Also allegedly buried here are the kings of Portugal's Golden Age, such as Manuel the Fortunate and Sebastian. The latter was a mystic and religious fanatic who perished with his army in a mad attempt to lead a crusade against the Mohammedans in Morocco in 1578. (Actually, even though he was killed, many of his countrymen refused to accept the proof of his death. Thus arose "Sebastianism," a cult religion based on the belief that the king would return to Portugal. Four impersonators were unsuccessful in their attempt to claim the title.)

The most outstanding of the Romantic writers of Portugal, J. B. de Almeida Garrett (1799–1854), is also said to be entombed here.

The cloister is of exceptional style and beauty, and it's the most exciting part of a visit to the abbey. As you head down the corridors—observing that each pillar is sculptured in a different and original style—you'll be walking across the unmarked tombs of long-forgotten people. Later, you can climb to the second tier where monks of old paced in meditation. Opening onto the cloisters are the cells of the monks (seven feet long, four feet wide).

The monastery is open daily from 8 a.m. to 7 p.m.; no admission is charged.

In a wing of the abbey is the:

ETHNOLOGICAL MUSEUM: This establishment is sometimes referred to as the "museum of Dr. Leite de Vasconcellos," in honor of the man who wanted to create a showcase of Portuguese culture. The ages of Portugal are peeled away as you wander from room to room, exploring the artifacts of the centuries—from prehistory to more recent times. Floors of ancient mosaics, some discovered in the Algarve, evoke the Roman epoch. You'll also find the beginnings of the cork products that were to become one of Portugal's major industries.

Human figures, painted on a wall in ocher, were discovered in the north of Portugal and brought here. The coffins (some from Roman days) are extremely interesting—one depicts a mirthful skeleton having the last laugh. The ceramics on display are extensive—some designs still being reproduced in Portugal today. Greek and Roman terracotta vases, a small Egyptian collection, including some mummies, classic jewelry, and prehistoric stone tools round out the exhibits.

In several salons is an outstanding doll collection, the figures dressed in both regional and period costumes. Look for a dollhouse with everything designed in miniature, right down to the pea-size pewter plates. The museum is open daily, except Monday, from 10 a.m. to 12:30 p.m. and from 2 to 5 p.m., and charges 30$ (23¢) admission, except on Saturday, Sunday, and national holidays when it is free.

Next door to Jerónimos Monastery is:

THE NAVAL MUSEUM AND PLANETARIUM: At the Museu de Marina, Praça de Império, the glory of a maritime nation lives on in this remarkable museum that recalls in artifacts, ship models, full-size state barges, and traditional Portuguese fishing and traffic boats Portugal's dependence on the sea. As a historical maritime museum, it has navy, merchant marine, fishing, and pleasure craft sections. There is obvious glamor, of course, such as that in the Royal State Barges Hall, displaying an outstanding collection of magnificent barges built from the early 18th century up to the middle of the 19th century. The largest and most impressive one, displayed with 80 wax dummy oarsmen in gold and red jackets, was put into actual use during a state visit of Queen Elizabeth II of England to Lisbon in 1957. Also displayed are models of ships of Portugal's golden age, including the *caravela,* which were the most important ships of the discoveries, and *São Gabriel,* the flagship of Vasco da Gama, the great Portuguese navigator who discovered the sea route to India.

A special hall displays Queen Amélia's lodgings removed from the royal yacht of Carlos I, the king who was assassinated along with his son in Black Horse Square in 1908. In another hall can be seen a remarkable display of 16th- and 17th-century Portuguese charts, mostly replicas of originals which were taken out of the country.

There are also exhibits from the Portuguese Fleet Air Arm which was in operation from 1917 until the early 1960s, when an independent Portuguese Air Force was created. On display is the seaplane *Santa Cruz,* and other mementos which recall the feat of naval aviators Sacadura Cabral and Gago Coutinho, who in 1922 made the first crossing of the South Atlantic by air with astronomical navigation made possible by use of a modified sextant invented by Gago Coutinho. The sextant is in the museum. By that flight, the Portuguese were the first Europeans to arrive in Brazil by air, some 400 years after their forebears were the first to arrive by sea in the fleet of Pedro Alvares Cabral.

The museum (tel. 61-25-41) is open daily, except Monday and holidays, from 10 a.m. to 5 p.m. Admission is 40$ (30¢) for adults; 20$ (15¢) for children under 15.

In the same building stands an 82-foot domed **Planetarium,** in whose sky theater astronomical performances can be viewed. The entrance fee for the Planetarium is 40$ (30¢) for adults, 20$ (15¢) for children. Visitors are admitted only on Saturday and Sunday, either at 4, 5, or 6 p.m. from March 1 to September 30 and at 4 or 5 p.m. from October 1 to February 28.

MUSEUM OF POPULAR ART: This museum, on the Avenida Marginal, condenses Portugal into a nutshell, displaying its regional crafts grouped according to provinces. Contemporary artists painted the walls, and blowups of photographs provide intimate glimpses of the life, costumes, and customs of the country people.

The museum is open daily except Monday from 10 a.m. to 5 p.m. Admission is 30$ (23¢). Buses 12 and 14 go there.

Sun clocks, chests, embroidered waistcoats, harnesses, gold jewelry, elaborate feather fans, glazed ceramic plates of the past century, handpainted provincial beds, and spinning wheels are displayed from the verdant Minho district and from Douro, the region which grows the grapes from which port wine is made.

From the austere mountains of Trás-os-Montes is exhibited a collection of musical instruments of the wine makers, along with carts, fire blowers, and masks. The southern province of Portugal, the Algarve, looks like the landscape of North Africa. From this region come flowers made of paper, baskets of palm fronds, saddle bags, and "lime cut" chimneys.

Gathered from the flat coastal region of Beiras is an assemblage of such items as glazed earthenware, handpainted harnesses, wooden slippers, embroidered ware, and Aveiro boats. The wide plains of Alentejo and the popular tourist region of Estremadura (Nazaré, Obidos, Alcobaça, Batalha, and Fátima) turn out a unique popular art, as reflected in pottery, handpainted dolls, a covered cart from Elvas used on pilgrimages, wooden and cork works, a wax figure modeling the apparel of a *campino* (a Ribatejo cowboy), and the sweaters worn by the fishermen of Nazaré (you can purchase similar designs and styles in shops in Lisbon).

THE COACH MUSEUM: This is Lisbon's Number One sightseeing attraction. In what was once a riding academy attached to the royal residence at Belém, Queen Amélia, seeing many of Portugal's greatest old coaches falling into disrepair, started the nucleus of the collection. But poor Amélia used a yacht—not a coach—when she fled with her son, Manuel II, following the collapse of the monarchy in Portugal.

Gathered here are the magnificent coaches, some royal, ranging from the 17th through the 19th centuries. Far superior in the scope and style of its collection to that of the Palacio Real in Madrid, the **Museu Nacional dos Coches** is acclaimed as the world leader.

At Praça Afonsô de Albuquerque, the museum (tel. 62-80-22) is open from 10 a.m. to 6:30 p.m. from June through September.

During the rest of the year, hours are from 10 a.m. to 5 p.m. The entrance fee is 40$ (30¢) except on admission-free Sunday.

Among the more intriguing coaches is a 17th-century vehicle that the Hapsburg monarch, Philip II, rode to Lisbon in the era of Spain's domination. The most lavish trio—a collection of elegant gilded baroque carriages—was built in Rome for the Portuguese ambassador to the Vatican of Pope Clement XI in 1716. Less celebrated—but of much interest—is a *berlinda* belonging to the queen, Maria I. On the second floor, you'll find a collection of harnesses, saddles, armor, stirrups, and portraits from the deposed House of Bragança.

Other Museums of Lisbon

For art lovers, the two most important museums are the National Art Gallery and the newer Calouste Gulbenkian Museum.

NATIONAL MUSEUM OF ANCIENT ART: Although drawing fewer visitors than the Coach Museum, this is actually Portugal's greatest museum. It is the country's major showcase for both Portuguese and foreign paintings, exhibited along with an assemblage of French, Iberian, and Flemish tapestries; antiques (many from the 15th century); a remarkable collection of gold and silver jewelry; porcelain, pottery, and Oriental carpets. The museum, 95 Rua das Janelas Verdes (tel. 66-41-51) is open from 10 a.m. to 5 p.m. (from 11 a.m. to 7 p.m. Sunday), except Monday and holidays. The charge for admission is 30$ (23¢), except Sunday, when it's free.

The most celebrated painting here is *The Temptations of St. Anthony* by Hieronymus Bosch, which was restored in the early 1970s by the José de Figueiredo Institute for the Examination and Preservation of Works of Art. In the west building, the best-known Portuguese work is the 15th-century polyptych painted for the convent of St. Vincent de Fora by Nuno Gonçalves. These panels were the masterpiece of Gonçalves, Portugal's painter who, for a time, worked at the court of Afonso V.

Notable foreign paintings include a *St. Catherine* and a *Salomé* (with the head of John the Baptist resting on a platter) by Lucas Cranach; plus works by Anthony Van Dyck, Sir Joshua Reynolds, Velázquez, Raphael, Andrea del Sarto (a remarkable self-portrait), Tiepolo, Guardi (a small Venetian scene resting on an easel), Poussin, Zurbarán (a whole room), Murillo, Ribera,

Dürer (seek out his *St. Jerome*), Hans Holbein *(Virgin and Saints)*, Memling, Pieter Brueghel *(Charity Work)*.

The collection is rich in Portuguese works, including canvases by Frey Carlos, a well-known artist of the Flemish-Portuguese School. The jewelry collection here stuns—everything from a processional cross from the Monastery of Alcobaça to a *custódia* removed from the Monastery of Belém. This latter monstrance was said to have been made in 1506 by Gil Vicente from the first gold brought back from the East by Vasco da Gama.

From the 18th century, a silver plate, the work of the Germain family, is considered the finest in the world. Weighing more than a ton, it was ordered by King Joseph I. The miracle is that this group was never melted down to fill up some later king's sagging treasury.

Among sculptural exhibits are works by Machado de Castro, the leading Portuguese sculptor of the 18th century and a master of terracotta relief.

CALOUSTE GULBENKIAN MUSEUM: Opened in the autumn of 1969, this museum houses what one critic called "one of the world's finest private art collections"—deeded to the state by the Armenian oil tycoon, Calouste Gulbenkian, who died in 1955. The multimillion-dollar modern center, at 45 Avenida de Berna, is in a former private estate which belonged to the Count of Vilalva. It is open on Tuesday, Thursday, Friday, and Sunday from 10 a.m. to 5 p.m.; on Wednesday and Saturday from 2 to 7:30 p.m. (closed Monday and holidays), from June 1 to October 31. During the other months of the year, it's open every day except Monday and holidays from 10 a.m. to 5 p.m. The admission is 20$ (15¢), except on weekends, when it's free.

The collections cover Egyptian, Greek, and Roman antiquities, a remarkable set of Islamic art including ceramics and textiles of Turkey and Persia, Syrian glass, books, bindings, and miniatures, Chinese vases, Japanese prints, and lacquer work. The European displays include medieval illuminated manuscripts and ivories, 15th- to 19th-century paintings and sculpture, Renaissance tapestries and medals, important collections of 18th-century French decorative arts, French impressionist painting, René Lalique jewelry, and glassware.

In a move requiring great skill of negotiation, Gulbenkian managed to make purchases of art from the Hermitage at Leningrad. Among his most notable acquisitions are two Rembrandts:

Pallas Athene and *Portrait of an Aging Man.* Two other well-known paintings are a portrait of *Helene Fourment* by Peter Paul Rubens and Renoir's *Madame Claude Monet Lounging.* The French sculptor, Jean Antoine Houdon, is represented by a statue of *Diana.* Much of the collection of 18th-century silver—said to be the finest in the world—came from the sales by the Soviet government during their cash-raising activities of the 1920s. Much of it belonged to Catherine the Great, although many pieces from the French monarchs are also displayed.

As a cultural center, the Gulbenkian Foundation sponsors plays, films, ballet, and musical concerts, as well as a rotating exhibition of works by leading Portuguese and foreign artists.

CENTER FOR MODERN ART: Centro de Arte Moderna, Rua Dr. Nicholau de Bettencourt (tel. 73-51-31), around the corner from the entrance to the Gulbenkian Museum, is the first major permanent exhibition center of modern Portuguese painters to open in Lisbon. The center shares parklike grounds with the Gulbenkian Foundation, and was, in fact, a gift left from the legacy of the late Armenian oil magnate.

Housed in a British-designed complex of clean lines and dramatically proportioned geometric forms, with a Henry Moore sculpture in front, the museum houses a collection of some 500 paintings. It displays the works of many modern Portuguese artists, some of which enjoy world famous reputations, including Armando Basto and Carlos Botelho. Some of the paintings on exhibit were considered aggressively iconoclastic at the time of their execution.

Admission is 20$ (15¢) but free on Sunday. Hours are from 10 a.m. to 5 p.m. on Sunday, Tuesday, Thursday, and Friday, and from 2 to 7 p.m. on Wednesday and Saturday. The museum is closed on Monday.

MUSEUM OF DECORATIVE ART: The decorative arts school museum, Fundação Ricardo do Espírito Santo Silva, 2 Largo das Porta do Sol (tel. 86-21-83), is a foundation established in 1953 through the vision and generosity of Dr. Ricardo do Espírito Santo Silva, who endowed it with items belonging to his private collection and set up workshops of handicrafts in which nearly all activities related to the decorative arts are represented. The handsomely furnished museum is in one of the many mansions of the aristocracy that used to grace the Alfama. The principal aim of the foundation is the preservation and furtherance of the decorative arts by maintaining the traditional character and developing the craftsman's skill and culture. In the workshops, you can see how perfect reproductions of pieces of furniture and other objects are made in the purest styles. The foundation also restores furniture, books, and Arraiolos rugs. The workshops may be visited on Wednesday.

The museum has been given the character of an inhabited palace through placement in the mansion, in order to enhance the esthetic value of the objects on display by setting them in appropriate surroundings. Visitors can have a fairly accurate picture of what might have been the interior of a posh Lisbon home in the 18th and 19th centuries. There are particularly outstanding displays of furniture of the 17th through the 19th centuries; Portuguese silver of the 17th through the 19th centuries; and Arraiolos rugs of the 17th, 18th, and 19th centuries.

The museum is open daily except Monday between 10 a.m. and 1 p.m. and 2 to 5 p.m. Admission is 50$ (38¢); free on Sunday. Visitors must wait downstairs in the entrance hall, where an old coach sits, for a guide to show them through the three floors of rooms.

Close to the museum is a boutique with fine articles produced by the foundation and other Portuguese crafts products, as well as a bar where visitors can have a rest, snacks, or a drink. To reach the museum and the foundation, take tram 10 or 28 to the Graça stop right at the door.

CHURCH OF MADRE DE DEUS: Lisbon, past and present, lives on in its churches. The earthquake of 1755 destroyed many of them completely. Others were reconstructed, more or less well according to the times. The most intriguing one is the Church of Madre de Deus. Queen Leonor founded this *convento* in 1509; today it contains some of the most precious *azulejos* (glazed tiles)—virtually a museum of them—of any church in Lisbon. The Manueline façade hardly reveals the lush decorations inside. At 4 Rua Madre de Deus, the church may be visited from 10 a.m. to 1 p.m. and from 2:30 to 5 p.m. daily except Monday. There is no admission charge, but you should tip the guide who shows you around.

Leonor was the queen of João II. To her meager chapel were added a church and cloisters by King João III, a 16th-century monarch. João V further embellished the church, but his reign ended five years before the great earthquake of 1755, which left much of the church in ruins. The task of rebuilding fell to the lieutenants of José I in the 18th century.

As you enter into the church, you see walls lined with glazed tiles in clear blues and whites, the effect crowned by oils framed in lavish baroque gilt.

The guide will show you through the two-tiered cloisters. The rooms opening off the cloisters are lined with remarkable 16th- and 17th-century tiles, many from Delft (why anyone wanted to import tiles from Holland to *azulejo*-rich Portugal remains a mystery). Seek out the chapel dedicated to St. Anthony and don't miss the choir, with its delicately carved stalls from the 18th century.

PANTHEON CHURCH OF ST. ENGRÁCIA: When a builder starts to work on a Portuguese house, the owner often chides him, "Don't take as long as St. Engrácia." Construction on this Portuguese baroque church began in the 17th century and it resisted the earthquake. Nevertheless, it was only completed in 1966. The church is so well planned and built that relief and architectural idiosyncrasies would have been welcomed. It is graced with a quartet of square towers. The completed product appears pristine and cold, and the state has fittingly turned it into a neoclassic Pantheon, containing memorial tombs to Portuguese greats as well as heads of state.

Memorials honor Henry the Navigator; Luís Vaz de Camões, the country's greatest poet, author of *Os Lusíadas,* an epic poem of Portugal's world history; Pedro Álvares Cabral, discoverer of Brazil; Afonso de Albuquerque, viceroy of India; Nuno Álvares Pereira, warrior and saint; and Vasco da Gama, of course.

Also entombed in the National Pantheon are presidents of Portugal: Sidónio Pais, assassinated in 1918; Marshal António Óscar de Fragoso Carmona, under whose government António de Oliveira Salazar began his climb to power; and Téofilo Braga, first president of the provisional government after settling of the Republic. Several Portuguese writers are also interred here, including Almeida Garrett, the country's most outstanding writer of the 19th century; João de Deus, lyric poet; and Guerra Junqueiro, also a poet.

The National Pantheon is closed on Monday and holidays. Otherwise, it is open to the public from 10 a.m. to 5 p.m. Admission is 40$ (30¢). Ask the guards to take you to the terrace for a beautiful view over the river.

A visit to the Pantheon can be combined with a shopping trip to the Flea Market (walk down the Campo de Santa Clara, heading toward the river).

ST. ROQUE CHURCH AND MUSEUM. The St. Roque Church (tel. 36-03-61) was founded in the closing years of the 16th century by the Jesuits. To reach it, head for the Largo Trindade Coelho any day between 10 a.m. and 5 p.m., except on Monday, when it closes at 4 p.m. The museum is open daily from 10 a.m. to 5 p.m. and charges a 30$ (23¢) admission (free on Sunday). Take bus 37 from the Rossio.

The St. Roque Museum is visited chiefly for its collection of baroque jewelry. A pair of gold and silver torch-holders, weighing about 840 pounds, are considered among the most elaborate in Europe. The gold embroidery from the 18th century is a rare treasure, as are the vestments. The paintings are mainly from the 16th century, including one of a double-chinned Catherine of Austria, another of the wedding ceremony of King Manuel. Look for a remarkable 16th-century *Virgin (with Child) of the Plague,* and a polished conch shell from the 18th century that served as a baptismal font.

The church, with its painted wood ceiling, contains a celebrated chapel honoring John the Baptist by Luigi Vanvitelli. The chapel was assembled in Rome in the 18th century with such precious materials as alabaster and lapis lazuli, then dismantled and shipped to Lisbon, where it was reassembled. It was ordered by the Bragança king, João V, nine years before the end of his reign in 1750. The marble mosaics look like a painting.

You can also visit the Sacristy, rich in paintings illustrating scenes from the lives of the Society of Jesus saints. The Jesuits held great power in Portugal, at one time virtually governing the country for the king.

ST. VINCENT OUTSIDE THE WALLS. This outstanding Renaissance church houses the Pantheon of the House of Bragança, the dynasty that ruled Portugal beginning with the collapse of Spanish domination in 1640 and lasting until 1910. A former convent, the church contains an estimated one million *azulejos* (glazed earthenware tiles). The Sacristy is graced with Portuguese marble, jacaranda woodwork from Brazil, and an 18th-century ivory Christ from Goa.

When St. Vincent was first built between 1582 and 1627, it was outside the walls of Lisbon—hence, its name. The earthquake of 1755 caused its cupola to collapse. At Largo de S. Vicente, it is open daily from 10 a.m. to 6 p.m., charging 30$ (23¢) for admission. It is closed on Monday.

In the burial chamber are entombed the twice-married Maria II, who ascended to the Portuguese throne at the age of 15. Dom Carlos I is buried near his son, Luís Felipe, the latter only 19 when both were assassinated at Black Horse Square in 1908. Manuel II, who ruled for only two years, lived a life of exile in England, dying there in 1932, at which time his body was returned home to Lisbon.

The House of Bragança also ruled Brazil from 1822 to 1889. The coffin of Dom Pedro, the first emperor of that country (he abdicated in 1831), rests in this Pantheon. Finally, because there was no native burial ground for him, Michael, the last king of Rumania, was placed here in a handsome sarcophagus. King Michael of Rumania was forced to abandon his throne in the closing hours of 1947, and he lived in exile in Portugal until his death in 1953.

Queluz Palace

For most visitors, Queluz is the first stop of their venture into the suburbs of Lisbon. And what a fortunate choice. One writer called it ". . . the prettiest pink palace in the world, as well as the most important and charming example of Rococo architecture in Portugal." The Portuguese government is so proud of the little 18th-century nugget that it houses foreign dignitaries in its Pavilion of Dona Maria I (former guests have included General Eisenhower and Elizabeth II).

Queluz is most often described as Portugal's Versailles, but so lofty a comparison detracts from its true character. Essentially, it's a palace of faded pink walls that stands quietly in the bright sunshine, looking out over beds and beds of mauve-colored petunias. Its character has always been that of a summer residence, whose façade is rather simple and classic, although the interior is rich and ornate, overlooking beautiful gardens and ponds.

The palace was an adaptation of an old hunting pavilion of the Marquis Castelo Rodrigo, which came into the possession of the royal family in 1654. King Pedro III, husband of Maria I, liked it so much he decided to turn it into a summer residence, enlarging it and having it decorated with lavish interiors. What you see now is not the way it was, as the palace suffered greatly during the French invasions. Almost all the belongings were sent to Brazil with the royal family at the beginning of the 19th century.

Maria I was a well-educated princess who became queen at a troubled time. She had so many problems and suffered so much during her life that near the end she became insane. Before going mad, she was a bright, intelligent, and brave woman who did a fine job as ruler of her country. Her husband was her uncle, who became king by marrying her. A fire swept over the palace in 1934, but it has subsequently been restored. The glassy Throne Room intrigues visitors the most, although you can stroll under the watchful eye of a guard through the dressing room of the queen, through the Don Quixote Chamber, and into the Music Salon, with its grand French piano and 19th-century harp.

The furnishings and general accoutrements are eclectic: Venetian chandeliers, Empire antiques, Florentine marbles, Delft plates, Macao screens, Austrian porcelain, Portuguese Chippendale and tapestries, and pieces made of jacaranda wood from Brazil.

After a royal tour, you can wind down by strolling through the handsomely laid out gardens, with their lily-studded fountains, earthenware tiles, beds of flowers, and 18th-century statuary.

The palace is generally open from 10 a.m. to 5 p.m., except on Thursday. (On the grounds is the Cozinha Velha, or old kitchen, described in the preceding restaurant section.) Admission to the palace is 50$ (38¢), only 20$ (15¢) if you wish just to visit the gardens.

Queluz lies on the road to Sintra, about 9½ miles from Lisbon. To reach it by public transportation, take a train at Rossio Station in Lisbon; a one-way fare costs 35$ (26¢).

Sintra

Ancient Sintra, on the rugged slope of the Serra de Sintra, is the town Byron dubbed "glorious Eden." John Cam Hobhouse and Byron came this way in 1809 on their grand tour, and later Byron was to write his autobiographical poem, *Childe Harold,* in which he included his praise of the beauty of Sintra. Thus, Sintra became a focus for a host of English visitors.

Byron and Robert Southey, another English poet, didn't discover the wonders of this remarkable oasis. Its praises were sung centuries before by Luís Vaz de Camões poem, *Os Lusíadas.*

Even before Portugal's Golden Age, Sintra was favored by the Moors, who selected it as a site of one of their greatest castles which stands in ruins today crowning a hilltop. The castle fell to the Christian crusaders in 1147.

Today, Sintra is virtually a suburb of Lisbon, favored by the aristocracy, even exiled royalty, who inhabit the elaborate villas —often compared to birthday cakes—studding the hills. The most famous resident is the Count of Paris, the pretender to the French throne. In a story in the *New York Times,* Charlotte Curtis wrote: "He is a gentleman farmer whose dairy supplies the best tables in Lisbon. On a good day, he may be found in his barn, milking the cows."

Sintra lies about 17½ miles northwest of Lisbon, and is reached by private car, on an organized tour, or else by frequent train service, about a 45-minute ride from the main railway station at Rossio in Lisbon. But connections are possible from such Costa do Sol resorts as Estoril and Cascais.

Much of Sintra's charm comes from its luxurious vegetation— camellias, ferns, mimosa, eucalyptus, lemon trees, strawberry beds, pink bougainvillea, red geraniums, pine trees (and more lizards crawling up more damp tiled walls than in any other place in Portugal).

One publicist summed up the charm of the town quite well by saying, "It is indeed a fairytale setting and gives one the feeling that this is where Sleeping Beauty must have rested all those years."

When you arrive in the central square, your main destination will be:

THE NATIONAL PALACE: This royal palace was constructed primarily during the reign of two Portuguese kings: João I (1385 –1433) and Manuel I (1469–1521, known as "the Fortunate"). Subsequent additions were made in later centuries, and the palace continued to function as a royal palace until 1910 when Manuel II fled to exile in England.

Portuguese kings and queens summered here. Although the original Moorish palace that stood on this spot was torn down, the Moslem influence lived on when it was reconstructed. The introduction of the bastardized Gothic or Manueline style makes for a bizarre effect. Be sure to note the painted *azulejos* (tiles) which line many of the rooms, these are considered the finest in Portugal.

The palace has been intimately linked to the lives and legends of many members of the Portuguese royal family. For example, Afonso V, king of Portugal from 1438 to 1481, was born at Sintra. He was named king only six years later. But to a later king, Afonso VI, the palace was a gloomy prison. Imprisoned by his brother (later Pedro II), he lost not only his throne but his wife. The ill-fated Afonso endlessly paced his cell until his death in 1683.

The Room of the Swans was favored by João I, part of its window decoration coming from what is now Spanish Morocco (Ceuta). One of the most interesting legends of the palace revolves around João I, who married Philippa of Lancaster (they were the parents of Henry the Navigator). As the oft-repeated tale goes, Philippa discovered her husband making love to one of her fair ladies-in-waiting. Although the English queen forgave her errant spouse, gossips speculated at length. Enraged, the king ordered that the room be redecorated, its ceiling adorned with magpies, these noisy birds symbolizing the chattering court. Hence, the nickname Room of the Magpies.

For many visitors, the Stag Room—also called the Heraldic Room—is the most expressive, with its coats-of-arms of the noble families of Portugal and scenes from the hunt. The Room of the Mermaids (sometimes known as Sirens) is also graceful. In the old kitchen are the original tiled stoves.

From many of the salons, there are excellent vistas opening onto the hills surrounding Sintra. Tapestries, paintings, sheltered patios, softly falling water, potted plants, and long, dark corridors evoke the faded life of another era.

Tickets to the palace cost 30$ (23¢), except on national holidays, when one is admitted free. Purchase your ticket downstairs at a counter on the left, then walk up the stairway to the right and ring the bell to be let in. The palace is open daily, except Tuesday, from 10 a.m. to 5 p.m.

THE PALACE OF PENA: Some have called this the most romantic scenic spot in all of Portugal. The palace was built on a peak. about 1500 feet high, overlooking the Moorish castle on the opposite hill. Pena Palace (tel. 923-02-27) majestically looks down on Sintra from its regal throne. (Some actually walk it from the town square, but others take a taxi or drive their own car.)

The *National Geographic* labeled Pena Palace a "soaring agglomeration of towers, cupolas, and battlemented walls." A fantasy in the sky it truly is, constructed to the specifications of Ferdinand of Saxe-Coburg-Gotha, the consort of Queen Maria II. When she died in 1853 at the age of 34, leaving 11 royal offspring, one of her sons, the ill-fated Pedro V, was named king. But the German consort served as regent until Pedro was of age.

Helping Ferdinand achieve his dream was Baron Eschwedge, a German architect. The baron attempted to re-create the aura of the Middle Ages; in some respects he succeeded, but it's "merely the mock." On a rock in the vicinity of the castle is a statue of the baron, in the costume of an armed soldier. The present castle was built on the grounds of a monastery ordered erected in the early 16th century for Jerónimos monks by Manuel the Fortunate. What remains of the monastery is a cloister and a tiny ogival chapel (see its alabaster panel and stained-glass window).

Most critics satirize the interior of the palace, suggesting that it is Wagnerian or lacking in taste. Actually, it's quite fascinating, as it's been left almost intact since it was last occupied by the royal family in 1910. It was from this palace that the mother of Manuel II gathered her jewelry and most valuable possessions on a long-ago autumn day and was driven on a wild ride to Mafra, where she collected her son, the king, to flee with him into exile. Around the top of the hill is the **Parque de Pena,** mapped out between 1846 and 1850 under the direction of Ferdinand. It's acclaimed as one of the most majestic landscapes in Europe. Climb to the **Cruz Alta** for a panoramic view.

Tickets cost 50$ (38¢), except on national holidays when the palace is free. The hours are from 10 a.m. to 5 p.m. daily, except Tuesday, when it's closed.

A Bullfight Spectacle

Portuguese bullfights, of course, differ from the Spanish in that the matador doesn't kill the bull. This tradition dates from the 18th century when the son of the Duke of Arcos (bullfighting was then a nobleman's sport) lost his life in the arena. His father jumped into the ring and personally killed the bull. The dictator prime minister, Marquês de Pombal—worried about manpower needed to rebuild Lisbon after the earthquake—decreed that that was the last life to be sacrificed in the ring. From that day forth, the horns of the bull were bound with leather bandages known as *emboladas.*

The prohibition against killing the bull is always under fire from certain critics. For example, Jaime Saraiva, a commentator in Lisbon, was quoted in the press as saying, "a bullfight without a kill is a great lie; it is not serious." But don't let his words keep you from attending a spectacle. The fight may not be "serious," but it is what Marvine Howe termed "one of the most beautiful equestrian displays in the world."

Bullfighting in Portugal doesn't enjoy the number of fans it has in Spain. It's estimated that only one-quarter of the populace attends the *corridas,* as opposed to three times that number in neighboring Spain.

Opening the corrida, the matadors parade in wearing their colorful suits, many unchanged in design for 200 years. They are followed by *cavaleiros,* the horseback-riding men who place darts in the bull, and the *forcados,* the troupe of men who tackle the bull. Traditionally, the latter wear jaunty green caps with red bands on their heads. They are attired in gold jackets and olive trousers, with a red sash around their waist, white stockings covering their calves.

At the sound of a trumpet, the gates open and out comes the cavaleiro on a horse he's most likely trained from its birth. The trick is to lead the galloping horse into the pathway of a rampaging bull—only to get the steed to swerve in time to prevent a head-on collision (which has happened). Darts are thrust into the bull's neck at this point to weaken him.

In Portugal, the bull is tackled by hand, the action known as a *pega.* A phalanx of eight forcados advances on the bull. One takes the angry animal by the horns; another may latch onto his tail; still another may grab the flesh hanging from the bull's chest, and so forth until the matador enters and finishes up the show.

The "season of the corridas" runs from Easter until early autumn, and in Lisbon, bullfighters are presented at the Moorish-style **Campo Pequeno,** reached by the subway. Alternatively, you can attend the **Monumental de Cascais** (tel. 28-31-03) at one of the leading resorts on the Costa do Sol. Fights are usually scheduled for Thursday night and Sunday afternoon.

Seats are sold in three different categories: *sombra* (shade); *sombra y sol* (a seat in the sun for part of the fight, in the shade for the rest); and *sol* (a seat in the sun during the entire fight).

Naturally, the shady seats are the most expensive. Bullfight tickets range from 400$ ($3) to 2000$ ($15).

Organized Tours

Many travel agents in Lisbon offer organized tours for those who want to have all the arrangements, including transportation, made for them. One of the largest agencies is **Star**, the representative for American Express at 4-A Sidónio Pais (tel. 53-98-71). In high season, from March 1 to October 31, most major tours are operated daily, except Monday and holidays, departing from the Praça Marquês de Pombal.

Lisbon is broken into several different sections, each one highlighting a particular cultural, historic, or scenic sight, such as St. George Castle or the Jerónimos Monastery at Belém. Most of the city tours last three hours. The **Cityrama Tour** by sightseeing bus, for example, lasts three hours, departing at 9:45 a.m. and again at 2:15 p.m. However, another tour departs at 5 p.m. from April 1 to September 30 only.

The most heavily booked excursion to the environs is to **Queluz, Sintra,** and **Estoril,** with a luncheon stopover at Sintra.

Tower of Belém, Lisbon

Chapter VI

LISBON AFTER DARK

FADO SINGING is Portugal's most popular and important art form, originating as it does in the hearts and experiences of every Portuguese, whether a fisherman from Nazaré, a cork grower from the plains of Alentejo, or a metropolitan Lisboan. Every Portuguese has a point of view about fado: either he or she sings it, or else has a favorite artist whose particular style speaks to him or her directly.

Fado ("fate" in Portuguese) is the true folk song of the people, not superimposed on them in the name of art or culture. It's in their blood. The songs are poignant, from the core of the heart—sometimes tragic, sometimes wistful, even joyful at times, but usually melancholic, filled with nostalgia. The sound originates in Portugal, combining the Arabic "wail" with the throaty, almost guttural voice of the peasant.

Even if you don't understand the Portuguese language, fado speaks vibrantly for itself. Translations aren't really necessary, as the word images are lyrical and powerful. Traditionally, fado is sung to the accompaniment of one or two guitars. These songs of sorrow have been heard for more than a century. The most famous singer of the 19th century was a beautiful gypsy, Maria Severa. Originally from the province of Ovar, she migrated to Lisbon, where her electric and dynamic style won the attention of all the city, especially the Count of Vimioso, who loved her, defiantly making her "the toast of Lisbon."

Her style of singing stimulated others and sparked a host of imitators. Upon her death, the reverence for her was so great, the respect so lasting, that every female *fadista* to this day drapes herself in a black shawl in memory of Severa. This story is legendary, of course, and many knowledgeable fans of fado tend to discount it as "fanciful."

North Americans first heard fado in New York City in a chic club, La Vie en Rose, when Portugal's best known *fadista*,

Amália Rodrigues, appeared. She rose from a lowly beginning—a barefoot urchin of the streets of Lisbon selling fruit to Alfama housewives—to fame and fortune, and an international reputation.

There are more than 20 restaurants or cafés where fado is sung in Lisbon. Fado is rapidly becoming popularized, and purists scorn the old songs that have been given a newer and slicker beat. There are two major areas in Lisbon where the wailing cry of fado can be heard nightly: the **Alfama** and the **Bairro Alto** (upper quarter). Both of these are the old sections of the city, spared in part from the ravages of the 1755 earthquake.

You can spend an entire evening—till dawn if you wish—"fado hopping" in Lisbon. You can begin with a meal around 9:30 p.m. and continue throughout the night, sipping the heady Portuguese wine and sinking deeper and deeper into a sweet melancholia. To begin your hop in the Alfama, go to the **Largo do Chafariz,** a little plaza about a block from the harbor. Three of Lisbon's top-ranking clubs are within a one- to five-minute walk from this point. The Bairro Alto fado district is found just off the **Largo de San Roque.**

While fado is without question the major attraction of Lisbon nightlife, there are other divertissements as well: discos for agile bodies, hotels and nightclubs for conventional dancing, vaudeville and opera, theater and ballet. Motion pictures are shown in their original languages, with Portuguese subtitles. Local newspapers contain listings of what's on after dark. Or refer to a weekly copy of *What's On In Lisbon,* usually obtainable from your hotel concierge.

The Fado Cafés

Lisboa à Noite, 69 Rua das Gáveas (tel. 36-85-57), is a re-creation of a 17th-century tavern, complete with several open rooms separated by thick stone arches. Near the kitchen is a stone well, yielding fresh water since the 17th century. The decor consists of leather and brass-studded chairs, blue-tiled walls, and old engravings and prints. At one time the club was a stable, but now glamour prevails, a proper backdrop for some of the best fado in Lisbon.

In winter, eucalyptus logs burn in an open fireplace. *Típico* touches are added by the collection of pewter candlesticks on a mantel, the hanging hams and strings of garlic in the open kitchen, and the old leather bottles. Waitresses wear white lace on black, the waiters black on brown.

All of this forms a setting for the great *fadista*, Fernanda Maria, the owner of the café. When it comes time for Fernanda to perform, the air becomes charged with intensity.

Lisboa à Noite is not the cheapest place to drink or dine, but worth every escudo. You can order from an extensive à la carte menu in English, enjoying a "flambé evening" by selecting either dry codfish Fernanda Maria or steak Lisboa à Noite. Expect to spend from $25 (U.S.) up for an evening here.

O Faia, 8 Rua da Barroca (tel. 32-67-42), is a typical fado restaurant and café originally created for the famous Lycília do Carmo, a well-known *fadista. Fadistas* perform on a raised stage lodged between a series of connecting, air-conditioned rooms, partially separated by sweeping, thick arches. In between songs, dancers dressed in regional costumes present folk numbers. A whisky costs 500$ ($3.75). Typical Portuguese dinners are served for 2500$ ($18.75). It is closed Sunday.

Parreirinha da Alfama, 1 Beco do Espérito (tel. 86-82-09). Seemingly, every *fadista* worth her shawl has sung at this old-time café, just a one-minute walk from the docksite of the Alfama. It's fado and fado only that enthralls here, not folk dancing. You can order a good regional dinner beginning early, but it's suggested that you go toward the shank of the evening . . . and stay late. It's open for most of the night. In the first part of the program, the *fadistas* get all their popular songs out of the way, then settle in to their own more classic favorites.

Drinks average around 600$ ($4.50) for hard liquor. You can order a filling dinner for 2500$ ($18.75), and the menu often includes specialties from nearly every region of Portugal. The atmosphere is self-consciously taverna, with all sorts of Portuguese provincial oddments. The singers selected by management are first-rate.

A Severa, 49-61 Rua das Gáveas (tel. 36-40-06), is one of the oldest and most consistently successful fado houses in the Bairro Alto. Many *fadistas* who went on to greater fame got their start here. It's bistro-style, and you can have either drinks or order a complete Portuguese dinner with all the trimmings. The house specialty is chicken cooked and served in a clay pot. A typical dinner, including wine, costs about 2500$ ($15). Closed Thursday.

A Cesaria, 20 Rua Gilberto Rola (tel. 66-57-45), is not well-known by foreigners, but it's patronized by Portuguese who shun the touristic fado houses. In business for more than a quarter of a century, it is a typical tavern, its floors in mosaic stones as are the sidewalks of Lisbon. Some two miles from the center of Lisbon, it is decorated with bright flowered tablecloths, wrought iron, and 17th-century hanging wall lamps. The entertainment here is likely to be spontaneous, with professional singers and artists often performing with the regular clientele. Sometimes all of them, on the spur of the moment, improvise poems, finishing the night in a songfest. The chef will prepare braised codfish, a grilled pork filet, or beefsteak. A regular dinner costs 1800$ ($13.50), including wine.

The Casino in Estoril

The magnet for international society along the Costa do Sol, the Casino is a super-contemporary structure, with walls of glass opening onto a wide formal garden stretching to the shore road. The magnetic attraction, of course, is the gaming room of the casino, which is open from 3 p.m. to 3 a.m. You can clear the official barrier by presenting your passport and purchasing a tourist card for 400$ ($3), which is valid for two days. Once upstairs, you can play baccarat, chemin de fer, blackjack, craps, French Bank, slot machines, and lots more. And you're likely to rub elbows with deposed royalty. Men are required to wear jackets and ties in the gaming room.

In the **Grand Salon Restaurant,** you can sample a standard international dinner, a three-course meal costing from 3000$ ($22.50) up, not including wines or coffees. However, you can dine either in Estoril or Cascais, then drop in for drinks only, paying a minimum of 800$ ($6) from Sunday to Thursday, although the minimum tab goes up to 1000$ ($7.50) on Friday, Saturday, and the eves of national holidays. The first floor show, which starts at 11:30 p.m., is usually a lavish production in the tradition of Paris or Las Vegas. You can count on lots of show-girls in glittery gauze—most often crowned with billowing feather headgear—strutting and demonstrating their curves. Striptease has been added. The second show is at 1 a.m.

Movies from around the world—with their original sound tracks—are shown at the **Casino Cinema,** and you can attend matinees or nighttime showings for 150$ ($1.13).

The Valor of Port Wine

Solar do Vinho do Porto, 45 Rua São Pedro de Alcântara (tel. 32-33-07). Portuguese port wine is known in every country of the world. The English were the first foreigners to discover rich, blended port, which they've enjoyed since the 17th century. The wine comes from grapes grown in the mountainous Douro River Valley in the north of Portugal. After port is fortified with brandy, it is shipped out to the "ports" of the world from Porto, Portugal's second-largest city.

The soil and climate of the Douro are said to be unique in the world, hence the special taste of the wine. Vintage port is the best wine produced from an especially good year. Crusted port, another vintage-like wine, takes it name from the fact that its "crust" must be decanted before it can be drunk.

"Wood ports," matured in wooden casks, fall into three major types: ruby, white, and tawny, made from the blending of the grape yield over a period of many years, assuring a consistent quality. The ruby-colored port is the young wine, but as it ages becomes tawny.

Owned and sponsored by the Port Wine Institute, this establishment contains many relics related to the history of port wine. You can stop here at any time of the day, ordering from its *lista de vinhos.* If you want a glass *(cálice),* you can get it, or even a vintage bottle, should you prefer to make an afternoon of it. The place is open every day, except Sunday, from 10 a.m. to midnight.

The Discos of Lisbon

Stone's, 1 Rua do Olival (tel. 66-45-45), is the most expensive and exclusive disco in Portugal, and it's maintained that position for more than 15 years. A clubby atmosphere prevails; the patrons are attractive or a least attractively dressed, and the drinks are good. You pay the highest door charge in all of Lisbon—4000$ ($30), but you are allowed to use this up in ordering drinks. Go late. It's more fashionable.

Carrousel, 77 Rua Castilho (tel. 68-15-71), is one of the capital's leading and most festive discos, drawing an attractive crowd in their 20s and 30s. It's on the periphery of the Ritz Hotel compound, facing the Park of Edward VII. True to its name, it's decorated in the carousel theme, in red, white, and blue stripes, with walls of black infinity, a bas relief of Lisbon, and twinkling stars, as well as a man in the moon.

Guests sit on white chairs, jumping up occasionally to dance to records. There's a minimum 1000$ ($7.50), with most drinks priced at 500$ ($3.75). Closed Sunday and during the entire month of August, the club is open all other days from 10:30 p.m. till 4 a.m., depending on the crowd (or lack of one).

Ad Lib, 28 Rua Barata Salgueiro (tel. 56-17-17), is one of the chicest discos in Lisbon, created by a coterie of society lads who wanted to have an elegant and discreet place for young people to meet and dance. Just a few minutes from the Ritz Hotel compound, its on the seventh floor of an ultramodern apartment house. Downstairs there isn't a sign or a clue as to what is going on upstairs. A uniformed doorman screens guests, escorting them to the elevator. Readers are advised to telephone first.

Inside, the penthouse club offers a shimmering sky view—a world of black mirrors with two levels of tables opening onto a plant-filled terrace. The decor is sophisticated, with stone Buddhas from Macao and many mirrors and flickering candles. The latest records imported from America, England, Italy, and France are played. Most of the cocktails, including a "kiss in the dark," go for 600$ ($4.50). The minimum entrance fee is 1500$ ($11.25), which can be applied to drinks.

O Porão da Nau, 1-D Rua Pinheiro Chagas (tel. 57-15-01), is a central boîte/disco which is about the best place in the capital if you want to dance to a live combo. Popular with the under-25 set, it is a skillfully reproduced hold of a 15th-century Portuguese man-of-war. Upon entering, you feel at any moment that the gangplank will be lifted, and you'll be embarked upon a voyage of discovery. The decor consists of carved wooden figures, stained glass, an early map of Portuguese possessions, a rope railing, lanterns, and a gun collection. The minimum consumption is 600$ ($4.50). Whisky is from 500$ ($3.75) up. It is open nightly from 10 p.m., often staying open until 4 a.m.

Whispers, Edifício Aviz, 35 Avenida Fontes Pereira de Melo (next to the Sheraton Hotel; tel. 57-54-89), is a chic disco. The minimum is 2500$ ($18.75) including tax and service. Most whiskies begin at 500$ ($3.75). It is open nightly from 11 p.m. to 4 a.m.

Sampling Portuguese Specialties

In Sintra, **O Chico**, Rua do Arco do Teixeira, (tel. 293-19-42), in the old part of town, is just great if you want to sample local specialties. Large codfish hang from the ceiling, and occasionally a chicken will run in and out—and no one pays it any mind. At the horseshoe-shaped bar, an endless array of food items are turned out, including caldo verde, the green broth of the north. The fried sardines and the dry codfish pastries are really good. The atmosphere is relaxed and cordial and there's even a guitar provided for guests. Port wine, regular or vintage, ranges in price from 100$ (75¢) to 250$ ($1.88) a glass. It's the leading choice for those in pursuit of local color.

Bars In and Around Lisbon

Café Concerto Procópio, 21 Alto de S. Francisco (tel. 65-28-51). In Lisbon, Procópio could easily become your favorite bar. In a turn-of-the-century atmosphere, it leans heavily on nostalgia. The café is an ingratiating social center for Lisboans, enjoying a certain chic at the moment. Owner Luíz Coelho is an avid collector of art nouveau, as well as a film buff (a small projector shows early movie masterpieces on the wall). Guests sit on red tufted velvet, enjoying the atmosphere of stained and painted glass, ornate brass hardware—and a piano awaiting any amateur player. It's like being in an intimate living room, where all the guests know each other. Whisky or bourbon costs 500$ ($3.75). Occasionally you can get someone to put a small steak on the grill.

Metro e Meio, 174 Avenida 5 de Outubro (tel. 77-59-97), has as its façade a giant yellow ruler, with the entrance cut into it. The management rented a certain amount of space, but carpenters renovating the bar discovered many more rooms hidden for decades. The overall effect is grotto-like, with stone and brick arches, a maze of salons, and a central fireplace. The unusual decor is a mélange of artifacts—handloomed wool wall hangings, gilt mirrors, statues, hanging lamps, Victorian fringed shades, and contemporary painting. Recordings are piped in. Whiskies begin at 400$ ($3), although you may prefer onion soup at 250$ ($1.88), an omelet, or a club sandwich, 280$ ($2.10). Near the Gulbenkian Museum, the bar is a taxi ride from the center of town.

The Café of the Literati
A Brasileira, 102-A Rua Garrett (tel. 36-87-92), in the Chiado district, is the last old coffeehouse of Lisbon—basking in a nostalgic turn-of-the-century atmosphere. Its habitués would turn into potential demons if it were ever redecorated. Behind its art nouveau façade, life goes on at a slow pace. For decades, it has attracted artists, writers, showgirls, respectable matrons, university students—each in his or her own way enjoying a moment of peace and contemplation. You sit at minuscule tables on tooled leather chairs. The walls have big mirrors between marble pilasters. Along the top of the side walls hangs a large collection of paintings, impressionistic or cubistic. An overscale clock wearily ticks away the passing hours, and old men drag along the floor, polishing shoes. Coffee is only 60$ (45¢) per cup, and the price is about all that's changed over the years.

Ray's Cocktail Bar and Lounge, 25 Avenida Saboia, Monte Estoril (tel. 268-01-06), is a good place to gather for drinks and gossip in a sophisticated and eclectic atmosphere. Ray, a New Yorker, came to Portugal to get away from it all, first establishing an interesting antique shop. Cordial and outgoing, he kept asking friends in for drinks. Before long he was building a bar and then arranging the antiques around his cocktail lounge. No one leaves here a stranger. Sitting in the French provincial chairs —arranged as if in a living room—you can also look at the collection of paintings besides making friends. Ray's bar opens nightly at 6, closing at 2 a.m.

Trem Velho, Alameda Duquesa de Palmela (tel. 28-67-355), right on the rail tracks at Cascais, is a converted coach. Taking your seat on the train that never pulls out of the station, you can order a drink of the day at a special price. For example, Cuba libres are featured on Tuesday. Drinks cost around 180$ ($1.35) and up, and you can also order hamburgers for 250$ ($1.88).

Estalagem Muchaxo, Praia do Guincho, in Guincho (tel. 28-50-221), has stark drama, a unique and ideal place for a drink, with whiskies costing around 500$ ($3.75). Of course, you can come here for lobster (very expensive), even a room; but many prefer to drive out from Lisbon just to enjoy the jagged coastal rock, the Cabo da Roca, marking the westernmost point of Europe. The inn has a rustic atmosphere, with a rugged stone fireplace, Madeira wicker stools, and rows of waterside tables.

Chapter VII

SHOPPING IN LISBON

ALL THE MAJOR Portuguese handicrafts get their best showing in Lisbon. Shopkeepers or their agents scan the country, as well as Madeira and the Azores, ferreting out the best work from the most skillful artisans and crafts people. Owing to the versatility of the Portuguese and their ability to absort other styles, handicrafts often betray exotic influences.

Although frowned upon in prestigious shops, bargaining is still a respectable custom throughout Lisbon. You'll have to let your intuition be your guide. A good rule of thumb to follow is to determine if the shop is small enough to be owner managed. If it is, you might possibly work out a deal.

Shops are spread throughout the city, but the major area for browsing is the **Baixa,** the district forming downtown Lisbon. Its three principal streets are the Rua do Ouro (Street of Gold, with major jewelry shops), Rua da Prata (Street of Silver), and Rua Augusta. To the west is the more fashionable, **Chiado,** the second major shopping district, whose main street is the Rua Garrett.

You'll find especially good buys in Portugal in handmade embroideries (blouses, tablecloths, napkins, and handkerchiefs) from the Madeira Islands and the Azores; cork products in every size, shape, and description—everything from placemats to cigarette boxes—decorative *azulejos* (glazed tiles); porcelain and china from Vista Alegre; Nazaré fishermen's sweaters; gold and silver filigree jewelry; Arraiolos carpets; local pottery; and fado records, of course.

Most stores open at 9 a.m., closing at noon for lunch. They generally reopen at 2 p.m., shutting down at 7 p.m. However, many proprietors prefer to shut down for lunch from 1 to 3 p.m., so keep a watch out. Most stores in Lisbon and elsewhere in Portugal remain open a full day on Saturday.

MADEIRA EMBROIDERIES: Madeira Superbia, 75-A Avenida Duque de Loulé (tel. 53-79-68), is an outlet for one of the finest embroidery factories on the Madeira Islands. This showcase of the exquisite craft offers excellent—although not inexpensive—linens, tapestries, and women's apparel, such as embroidered blouses, and petit-point handbags. High-quality fabrics are often imported from Ireland and Switzerland, then embroidered in the islands. The collection of hand-embroidered bedspreads, sheets, pillowcases, tea cloths, napkins, and table centers is exceptional. Placemats often come in organdy with a linen appliqué (some double-edged with shadow work embroidery). Another popular item is monogrammed linen handkerchiefs. There are branches at the Hotel Ritz in Lisbon and the Hotel Estoril Sol in Cascais.

EMBROIDERIES FROM THE AZORES: Casa Regional da Ilha Verde, 4 Rua Paiva de Andrade (tel. 32-59-74), in the Chiado district, is the "Regional House of the Green Island." As such, it specializes in handmade items—especially embroideries—from the Azores. Every piece of merchandise is guaranteed to have been made by hand. Good buys are found in linen placemats with napkins. Some of the designs have been in use for centuries. Other gift items include products made of sperm whale teeth, such as cigarette holders, letter openers, and rings.

PORCELAIN AND CHINA: Vista Alegre, 18 Largo do Chiado (tel. 36-14-01), numbers diplomats and royalty, or whoever demands the very best, among its regular clientele. For china and glassware, it is unparalleled in Portugal. Of special interest to the casual shopper is the colorful porcelain from Ilhavo, with many of the figurines depicting regional costumes.

Decorators, both professionals and do-it-yourselfers, are fond of the porcelain birds and figures. Amazingly lifelike, they are also alarmingly priced. However, you'll do better ordering a set of dishes or porcelain fruit bowls.

FILIGREE JEWELRY: W. A. Sarmento, 251 Rua Aurea (tel. 32-67-74), is the most distinguished silver- and goldsmith in Portugal. The shop at the foot of the Santa Justa elevator provides Lisboans with treasured confirmation and graduation gifts, and is favored by diplomats, movie stars, and the Costa do Sol aristocracy. In 1970, Sarmento celebrated its 100th anniversary—it's remained in the hands of the same owners all the while.

Gold is considered a good buy in Portugal, as the government strictly regulates its sale, requiring jewelers to put a minimum of 19¼ karats in articles made of the precious metal. Sarmento specializes in lacy filigree jewelry in gold or silver. Just hold an earring or brooch up to the light and enjoy its intricacy and delicacy. Especially popular are small gold filigree caravels which come in many prices. Less expensive filigree jewelry is made of silver and plated with gold. In this category earrings and cufflinks predominate. For the charm collector, Sarmento is a Roman holiday. Literally dozens of choices are offered.

AZULEJOS: **Sant'Anna,** 95-97 Rua do Alecrim (tel. 32-25-37), founded in 1741, is Portugal's leading ceramic center. In the Chiado section, Sant'Anna is known for its *azulejos* (glazed tiles). The Rua do Alecrim location is the showroom outlet; however, you can also visit the factory at 96 Calçada da Boa Hora, but you must call ahead and make an appointment. The craftspeople who create and decorate the tiles are among the finest in Europe, many of them following designs in use since the Middle Ages. Items I recently purchased and considered bargains were a ceramic two-holder candelabrum, a group of framed scenic *azulejos,* a tiled hors d'oeuvres tray, and a three-foot-high ceramic umbrella stand.

A rival to Sant'Anna, **Fábrica Cerâmica Viúva Lamego,** 25 Largo do Intendente (tel. 57-59-29), sells contemporary pottery and tiles, including an interesting selection of planters and umbrella stands. When you reach the address, you'll know you're at the right place: its façade is decorated with these colorful *azulejos* with figures in their rich plumage and dress.

SUEDE: A "one-couple" show is **Caprice,** 67-B Rua Joaquim António de Aguiar (tel. 53-86-28), diagonally across from the Ritz Hotel. M. and Mme. Gaulier sell a fine line of washable suede items, including both jackets and pants suits. Philippe L. Gaulier's mother was a Lanvin stylist, and apparently he inherited a great deal of her taste. He and Mme. Gaulier (English-speaking) will present you with an assortment of aqua-suede garments, particularly dresses and coats, that are wrinkle free and machine washable. The suede comes in an interesting assortment of colors, including dark chocolate, pink, aqua, navy, and caramel. In addition, the Gauliers offer a selection of hand-crocheted suits and dresses, but, regrettably, the high cost of producing these items has made them suitable only for the carriage trade.

CORK PRODUCTS: **Casa das Cortiças,** 4 Rua Escola Politécnica (tel. 32-58-58). "Mr. Cork" became somewhat of a legend in Lisbon for offering "everything conceivable" that could be made of cork, of which Portugal controls a hefty part of the world market. Mr. Cork is gone now, but his widow carries on. In her shop you'll be surprised at the number of items that can be made from cork, including a chess set or a checkerboard. Perhaps a set of six placemats in a two-toned checkerboard style will interest you. For souvenirs, the cork "caravels" are immensely popular. Other items include a natural cutting board and ice bucket.

ROSSIO RAILWAY STATION SHOPPING MALL: There are some 150 boutiques, shops, and snackbars installed in four of the five floors of the Rossio Railway Station, in the heart of downtown Lisbon. The fifth floor is where the trains arrive and depart. Banks of escalators whisk you from floor to floor, and shopping in the maze of small shops is easier than walking on the congested streets. Conveniently, the shops are open every day of the year from 9 a.m. to midnight. The street floor is deceivingly shabby—ignore it and take the escalator to the boutiques. You'll find apparel for men, women, and children, shops specializing in jewelry, fado records, whatever. There's a pharmacy for "naturalists," beauty parlors, hairdressers, bookstores, leather goods, sweaters, and Portuguese handicrafts.

ANTIQUE ALLEY: Along both sides of the narrow street, Rua de S. José, are treasure troves—shops packed with antiques from all over the world. Antique dealers from America come here to pick up bargains. You'll find ornate carvings or time-seasoned woods, brass, plaques, copper pans, silver candelabra, crystal sconces, and chandeliers, plus a wide selection of old wooden figures, silver boxes, porcelain plates, and bowls.

Rua Dom Pedro V is another street of antique shops, of which my personal favorite is **Solar,** 68-70 Rua Dom Pedro (tel. 36-55-22). It is stocked with antique tiles salvaged from some of Portugal's historic buildings and manor houses. The condition of the tiles varies, of course. Many go back as far as the 16th century. The store also sells antique furniture and pewterware.

ARRAIOLOS CARPETS: In the little town of Arraiolos, the fine woolen rugs made here have earned the place an international reputation. Legend says these rugs were first made by Moorish craftsmen expelled from Lisbon in the early 16th century. Those designs were said to be in imitation of those from Persia. Some of these carpets eventually found their way into museums.

In Lisbon, the showcase for the Arraiolos carpet is **Casa Quintão,** 30-34 Rua Ivens (tel. 36-58-37). Rugs here are priced by the square foot, according to the density of the stic stitching. Casa Quintão can also reproduce intricate Oriental or medieval designs in rugs or tapestries, and create any custom pattern specified by a client. The shop also sells materials and gives instructions on how to make your own carpets and tapestry-covered pillows. The staff seems genuinely willing to help.

THE THIEVES' MARKET: This open-air street market—called the **Feira da Ladra**—is similar in character to the flea markets of Paris and Madrid. Almost every conceivable article is offered for sale in the street stalls. Vendors peddle their wares on Tuesday and Saturday (it's best to go in the morning when the pickings are riper).

In the Alfama district, about a five-minute walk from the waterfront, the market lies in back of the Military Museum, adjoining the Pantheon of S. Vicente. Begin your shopping expedition at the Campo de Santa Clara. The hilly street with its tree-lined center is lined with portable stalls with individual displays.

You may pick up a valuable object here, but you'll have to search through an abundance of cheap clothing and useless junk to find it. The following types of merchandise are displayed: old brass door knockers with clasped hands, brass scales, brass beds, oil lamps, portable bidets, cow bells, old coins, Macao china, Angola woodcarvings, antique watches, meat grinders, broken torchiers, ships' lanterns, and gas lamps.

Yes, you not only can bargain, you *should* bargain. After the stallkeeper quotes you the first price, assume a not-interested stance. Then the fun commences, the price (usually) sliding downhill like a toboggan ride.

Chapter VIII

THE ABC'S OF PORTUGAL

IT'S MADDENING to have your trip marred by an incident which could have been avoided if you'd been tipped off previously. Seeking medical care, getting your hair cut, or ferreting out the nearest toilet can at times become a paramount problem. Although I don't promise to answer all your questions, there are a variety of services in Lisbon that can ease your adjustment into the city.

The concierge in your hotel is a usually reliable dispenser of information, bullfight tickets, advice about whether you can "bring somebody back to the room" or assistance in pleading with your wife (or husband) to speak to you again after your too-friendly attention to a *fadista*. However, should your hotel not be staffed with an English-speaking person, or should you desire more detailed answers to your questions, the following brief summary of some of Lisbon's "facts of life" may prove helpful.

AIRPORT: Both foreign and domestic flights arrive at Lisbon's **Portela Airport,** which lies about four miles from the heart of the city. For all airport information, telephone 80-20-60. A green line bus, called *Ligne Verte,* carries passengers into the city. However, I'd recommend a taxi instead, as the cost is only about $5, which is certainly worth it considering the comfort and convenience.

AMERICAN EXPRESS: STAR in Lisbon is the representative of American Express and can accommodate most banking and mailing needs from its offices at 4-A Avenida Sidónio Pais (tel. 53-98-71). It's open daily from 9 a.m. until 12:30 p.m. and from 2 to 6 p.m. weekdays; closed on Saturday and Sunday. The offices are near the Pombal square and eaily reached by bus.

BABYSITTERS: Check with the staff of your hotel for arrangements. Most first-class hotels can provide competent women or girls for babysitting from lists which the concierge keeps. At smaller establishments, the girl is likely to be the daughter of the proprietor. Rates are low. Remember to request a babysitter no later than in the morning if you're going out that evening.

BANKS: Check with your home bank before your departure, as many banks in Canada and the United States have affiliates in Lisbon. The majority of the banks open at 8:30 a.m., closing at 11:45 a.m. Afternoon hours are from 1 to 2:45 p.m. A trio of major Portuguese banks include **Banco Português do Atlântico,** 112 Rua Aurea (tel. 36-64-15); the **Banco Espírito Santo e Commercial de Lisboa,** 195 Avenida da Liberdade (tel. 57-80-05); and at the airport a branch of **Banco Totta & Açores** (tel. 88-40-11), which is open at all hours of the day and night, including holidays.

CIGARETTES: The price of American-brand cigarettes (which varies) is always lethal. Bring in at least 200 cigarettes as allowed by Customs. If you're saving money, try as an adventure one of the Portuguese brands. Many smokers have found Portuguese tobacco excellent.

CLOTHING SIZES: See "The ABCs of Spain," Chapter XVI.

CUSTOMS: You may be asked how much tobacco you're bringing in: the limit is 200 cigarettes or 50 cigars. One still camera with five unexposed rolls of film is allowed duty free; also a small movie camera with two reels; a portable tape recorder; a portable record player with ten "used" records; a portable typewriter; a portable radio; a portable musical instrument; and a bicycle (not motor bikes). Campers and sporting types are allowed to bring in one tent and camping accessories (including a kayak not exceeding 18 feet), a pair of skis, two tennis rackets, a tackle set, and a small firearm (for hunting only) with 50 bullets. A normal-size bottle of wine and a half-pint of hard alcohol are permitted, as are a "small quantity" of perfume and a half-pint of toilet water.

Upon leaving Portugal, citizens of the United States who have been outside the U.S. for 48 hours are more are allowed to bring in $400 worth of merchandise duty free—that is, if they have claimed no similar exemption within the past 30 days. Beyond this free allowance, the next $600 worth of merchandise is assessed at a flat rate of 10% duty. If you make purchases in Portugal, it's important to keep your receipts. On gifts, the duty-free limit has been increased to $50.

DENTIST: Place a call to Centro de Medicina Dentaria (tel. 68-41-91).

DOCUMENTS FOR ENTRY: Canadians, Americans, and the British need only a valid passport to enter Portugal.

ELECTRIC CURRENT: Many North Americans find that their plugs will not fit into sockets in Portugal, where the voltage is 200 volts AC, 50 cycles. Adapters and transformers may be purchased once you're in Lisbon. It's always best to check at your hotel desk before plugging in any electrical equipment.

EMBASSIES: If you lose your passport, or have some other pressing problem, you'll need to get in touch with the **American Embassy**, on the Avenida das Forças Armadas (à Sete Rios) (tel. 72-56-00). Hours are 8:30 a.m. to 12:30 p.m. and 1:30 to 5 p.m. If you've lost a passport, a photographer will be recommended who can provide the proper size photos for American passports. The **Canadian Embassy** is at 2 Rua Rosa Araujo (tel. 56-38-21), and the **British Embassy** is at 37 Rua São Domingos à Lapa (tel. 66-11-91).

EMERGENCIES: For the police (or for an ambulance) in Lisbon, telephone 115. In case of fire, call 32-22-22. The Portuguese Red Cross is reached at 66-53-42.

FILM: This is so expensive that I suggest you bring in all that Customs will allow. It takes two weeks or so to process film in Lisbon (in some places even more time) so I recommend that you wait until you return home. There are no special restrictions on photographs, except in certain museums.

GAS: Lisbon is well provided with garages and gasoline pumps; some are open around the clock. If you're motoring in the provinces, best fill up, as in some parts of the country gasoline stations are few and far between.

HAIRDRESSERS: Men are advised to go to any of the big barbershops in the deluxe hotels, such as the Ritz Inter-Continental in Lisbon. For women, two hairdressers in Lisbon are particularly recommendable—**Cabeleireiro Martins,** 31-1° Dt. Avenida Defensores de Chaves (tel. 54-89-33), and **Cabeleireiro Isabel Queiroz do Vale,** 35-1° Avenida Fontes Pereira de Melo (tel. 54-82-38).

HITCHHIKING: There's no law against it, yet it isn't commonly practiced. If you decide to hitchhike, do so with discretion.

HOLIDAYS AND FESTIVALS: Watch those holidays and adjust your banking needs, or whatever, accordingly. Aside from the regular holidays such as Christmas, Portugal has a few all its own: Universal Brotherhood Day on January 1; a Memorial Day to the country's greatest poet, Camões, June 10; Assumption Day, August 15; the anniversary of the republic, October 5; All Saints' Day on November 1; Independence Day on December 1; and the Feast of the Immaculate Conception on December 8. Good Friday and the Feast of Corpus Christi are also holidays, but their dates differ every year.

LANGUAGES: One writer suggested that Portuguese has "the hiss and rush of surf crashing against the bleak rocks of Sagres." If you don't speak it, you'll find French, Spanish, and English commonly spoken in Lisbon, along the Costa do Sol, and in Porto, as well as many parts of the Algarve. In small villages and towns, hotel staffs and guides usually speak English. The native tongue is difficult, but the Portuguese people are helpful and patient. Gestures often suffice.

LAUNDRY: Most hotels in this guide provide laundry services, but if you want your garment returned on the same day, you'll often be charged from 20% to 40% more. Simply present your maid or valet with your laundry or dry cleaning (usually lists are provided). Note: Materials needing special treatment (such as

certain synthetics) should be called to the attention of the perso
handling your laundry. Some establishments I've dealt with i
the past treated every fabric as if it were cotton. Do-it-yourselfer:
in Lisbon may want to take their clothes to a self-service laundry,
Lavimpa, 105 Avenida Estados Unidos da America (tel. 76-65-
44). It's part of a chain.

LIBRARIES: The **Biblioteca Nacional de Lisboa**, 83 Campo
Grande (tel. 76-77-86), near University City, contains more than
a million volumes and is open Monday to Friday from 9:45 a.m.
to 9 p.m., in August and September from 9:45 a.m. to 5:30 p.m.
In addition, the **American Cultural Center**, 22-B Avenida Duque
de Loulé (tel. 55-51-41), opposite the American Embassy, has a
library of some 8000 volumes and 1500 records, and is open daily
from noon to 8 p.m. except on weekends.

LIQUOR LAWS: You have to be 18 years of age to drink liquor
in the bars of Portugal. Liquor is sold in most markets, as opposed to package stores in the United States. In Lisbon you can
drink till dawn. There's always some bar or some fado club open
serving alcoholic beverages. Portugal is a long way from England
about restrictions on pub hours.

MAIL DELIVERY: While in Portugal you may have your mail
directed to your hotel (or hotels), to the American Express representative, or to General Delivery in Lisbon. Your passport must
be presented for mail pickups. Open 24 hours a day, the general
post office in Lisbon is at Praça dos Restauradores (tel. 37-00-
51).

MEDICAL CARE: Portugal does not have free medical service.
The concierge at your hotel can usually put you in touch with
the house doctor, or summon him or her in case of emergencies.
You can also call the **American Embassy**, Avenida das Forças
Armadas (à Sete Rios) (tel. 72-56-00), and ask the consular
section there to give you a copy of its list of English-speaking
physicians; or the **British Hospital**, 49 Rua Savaiva de Carvalho
(tel. 60-20-20), where the telephone operator, staff, and doctors
all speak English.

RIC MEASURES: See "The ABCs of Spain," Chapter XVI.

SPAPERS: The *International Herald Tribune* is sold at most tands in Lisbon, either in major hotels or else along the The *Trib* is also sold in leading newsstands throughout the y, including Porto and the Algarve.

HOURS: Hours in general are from 9 a.m. to 5 or 5:30 ith a two-hour break for lunch between 1 and 3 p.m.

Pets brought into Portugal must have the okay of the local narian and a health certificate from their home country.

ARMACIES: The Portuguese government requires selected armacies (*farmácias*) to stay open at all times of the day and ght. This is effected by means of a rotation system. So check vith your concierge for locations and hours of the nearest drugstores, called *farmácias de serviço*. In general, chemists in Portugal are open from 9 a.m. to 1 p.m. and from 3 to 7 p.m. A popular one is the **Farmácia Azevedo,** 31 Rossio (tel. 32-74-78).

POLITICS: The dust of the revolution has long settled. Portugal is one of the safest countries to travel in in Western Europe. The Portugese Republic, after years of dictatorship, is a democratic state, and tourists can travel without restrictions into every province of the land.

RADIO AND TV: In Lisbon there are two major TV channels—Channel 1 (VHF) and Channel II (UHF). Many foreign films are shown, often in English with Portuguese subtitles. Visitors to Portugal may want to listen to the radio every day at 8:15 a.m. when a 45-minute program—called "Holidays in Portugal"—is broadcast on the Metropolitan wavelength in English. Much helpful advice is offered for touring the country.

RAILWAY INFORMATION: For information about rail travel in Portugal, telephone 32-62-26 in Lisbon.

If you're visiting the environs of Lisbon, such places as Cascais or Sintra, refer to the section on "Electric Trains" in Chapter II, "Getting Acquainted with Lisbon."

If you're going farther afield, know that Portugal doesn't have a vast railway network. It is possible, however, to travel by electrified train to Porto in the north, leaving from Sta. Apolonia Station in Lisbon. Reservations are absolutely necessary.

Daily express trains in summer depart Lisbon for the Algarve (except on Sunday). These leave from the Barreiro Station (across the Tagus—take one of the ferries departing frequently). Off-season service is reduced to four times weekly.

RELIGIOUS SERVICES: Portugal is a Catholic country, and there are places of worship in every city, town, and village—far too numerous to document here. If you're a Protestant, a Baptist evangelical church exists in Lisbon. It's the **Igreja Evangélica Baptista de Lisboa**, 36-B Rua Filipe Folque (tel. 53-53-62), with Sunday services at 10 and 11 a.m. and 7:30 p.m. (also at 7:30 p.m. on Wednesday). For Jewish readers, services are usually held twice daily at the **Sephardi Synagogue**, 59 Rua Alexandre Herculanto (tel. 68-15-92).

REST ROOMS: All major terminals (airports and railways) have such facilities, and Lisbon has several public ones. However, you can often use one at a café or tavern, as one of these establishments exists practically within every block. It is considered polite to purchase something, however—perhaps a small glass of wine or whatever.

SENIOR DISCOUNTS: Persons who are 65 years or more benefit from the 50% discount policy followed by the **Portuguese Railway Company.** These tickets are good all year.

TAXES: As of this writing, Portugal is not a member of the European Common Market. So there is no Value Added Tax. However, it may soon join. You pay no additional government departure tax at the airport, or car-rental tax, as in France.

TELEGRAMS: At most hotels the receptionist will help you send a cable or telegram. If not, there is a cable dispatch service, open 24 hours a day, at **Marconi** (the Portuguese Radio Communications Office), 131 Rua S. Julião (tel. 36-45-38). To send international telegrams, telephone 113.

TELEPHONES: If you're calling locally in Lisbon, you can place your call at any number of telephone booths. However, you'll need some 1$00 coins, and preferably some 5$00 coins if you plan to talk more than three minutes or telephone long distance in the country. For most long-distance telephoning, particularly transatlantic calls, go to the central post office in Lisbon at the Praça dos Restauradores (tel. 37–00–51). Give an assistant there the number you wish, and she'll make the call for you, billing you at the end.

TELEX: Ask your hotel for assistance.

LISBON: AVERAGE MONTHLY TEMPERATURES

	HIGH	LOW		HIGH	LOW
January	56	46	July	81	63
February	59	47	August	82	64
March	62	50	September	78	62
April	66	53	October	72	58
May	69	55	November	63	52
June	76	60	December	57	47

TIME: Portugal is six hours ahead of the United States (Eastern Standard Time). For the local time in Lisbon, phone 15.

TIPPING: The following tips on tipping are merely guidelines.

The **hotels** add a service charge (known as *serviço*) which is divided among the entire staff. But individual tipping is also the rule of the day: 50$ (38¢) to the bellhop for errands run, 50$ (38¢) to the doorman who calls you a cab, 50$ (38¢) to the porter for each piece of luggage carried, 150$ ($1.13) to the wine steward if you've dined often at your hotel, and 150$ ($1.13) to the chambermaid for stays of less than a week.

In first-class or deluxe hotels, the concierge will present you with a separate bill, outlining your little or big extras, such as charges for bullfight tickets, etc. A gratuity is expected in addition to the charge, the amount depending entirely on the number of requests you've put to him.

Hairdressers: For a normal haircut, you should leave 50$ (38¢) behind as a tip to the barber. But if your hair is cut at the

Ritz, don't dare leave less than 100$ (75¢). Beauticians get 150$ ($1.13); a manicurist, around 100$ (75¢).

Taxis: Figure on about 20% of the regular fare for short runs. For longer treks—for example, from the airport to Cascais—15% is adequate.

Porters: The porters at the airport or train stations generally charge you 50$ (38¢) per piece of luggage.

Restaurants: Restaurants and nightclubs include service charge and government taxes. As in the hotels, this service in distributed among the entire staff, including the waiter's mistress and the proprietor's grandfather—so extra tipping is customary. Add about 5% to the bill in a moderately priced restaurant, up to 10% in deluxe or first-class establishments.

Services: Hatcheck women in fado houses, restaurants, and nightclubs expect at least 50$ (38¢). The women who stand on sentinel duty in washrooms usually get no more than 25$ (19¢). The shoeshine boys of Portugal are the most undertipped creatures in Portuguese society. Here I recommend greater generosity, providing the shine was good.

TOURIST INFORMATION: The **Portuguese National Tourist Board** is at 86 Avenida António Augusto de Aguiar in Lisbon (tel. 57-59-81). The public information section is housed at the Palácio Foz at Praça dos Restauradores (tel. 36-36-24), and at the Lisbon airport (tel. 72-59-74). If you desire travel information or facts about Portugal before heading there, you can make contact with the **Portuguese National Tourist Office**, 548 Fifth Ave., New York, NY 10036 (tel. 212/354-4403); 919 N. Michigan Ave., Suite 3001, Chicago, IL 60611 (tel. 312/266-9898); and 3440 Wilshire Blvd., Suite 616, Los Angeles, CA 90010 (tel. 213/380-6459).

WEATHER INFORMATION: If you don't speak Portuguese, ask someone at your hotel desk to translate one of the weather reports which appear daily in the leading newspapers of Lisbon.

Chapter IX

PORTUGAL IN A NUTSHELL

FOR YEARS, GUIDES have told their clients: "If you want the sun, go to the Algarve. If you want history and monuments, head for the north of Portugal." With some exceptions, this is good advice.

Portugal is still a relatively undiscovered country. A travel agent in Lisbon—in the business for more than 30 years—said that only two of his clients had ever asked to see every province. Most visitors, assuming that Portugal is so small it can't offer *that* much, never allow enough time for adequate exploration.

Before winging out of the Portuguese capital, why not take the extra days and pleasurable effort at least to skim the surface of some of the most rewarding spots on the Iberian peninsula?

While still based in Lisbon, you can day-trip it to the **Costa do Sol** (Estoril and Cascais) for fun at the beach; or go to the medieval fortress city of **Óbidos**; or the 12th-century Cistercian monastery of **Alcobaça**; the "battle abbey" of **Batalha**; the famous fishing village of **Nazaré**; or the world-renowned pilgrimage site of **Fátima**.

On a second day, you can head south across the Tagus to the fishing village and resort of **Sesimbra**, or take in the spectacular scenery of **Portinho da Arrábida**, or the ancient city of **Setúbal**. On yet a third day, while still based in Lisbon, you can drive to **Evora**, the ancient Roman city of Alentejo.

Take your pick of the following: fun in the sun, or history, monuments, and a bit of culture.

THE COSTA DO SOL: The strip of beach on the north bank of the mouth of the Tagus is called the "Coast of Kings" because of all the exiled royalty who live in and around its shoreline. As mentioned in Chapter V (see Sintra), the Count of Paris, the pretender to the throne of France, lives here and is a dairyman-farmer.

Humbert II, the son of King Victor Emanuel III, was forced into exile in 1946 when the Italians voted out the monarchy. Charlotte Curtis of the *New York Times* wrote that "He spends his days cataloguing family medallions, art works and books, and playing with grandchildren."

Don Juan; the Count of Barcelona, was the son of the last king of Spain, Alfonso XIII, who went into exile in 1931. Ever since his father's death in 1941, he has claimed the throne of Spain. However, in the summer of 1969, Generalíssimo Franco named the pretender's son, Don Juan Carlos, a young man trained and educated in Spain, as his successor and king of Spain, a position he assumed following the death of the Spanish dictator.

The "Coast of Kings" is sometimes known as the Portuguese Riviera, as it does evoke the Mediterranean. Even if you arrive in January, you should take the electric train out from the Cais do Sodré station in Lisbon. The scenery is that intriguing. It's been called "a microcosm of Portugal."

You'll pass *azulejo*-fronted houses, red-tiled roofs, and, in summer, cabana after cabana of bronzed Portuguese bodies. Try to avoid the Sunday rush, however, as what appears to be every family in Lisbon heads out to the sun strip. While the folks fight it out for a place in the sun, the aristocrats are languishing in their *quintas* (farms) in the hills around Cascais and Sintra.

Already previewed in the hotel chapter, the fashionable resort of Estoril lies about 15 miles west of Lisbon and is your first stopover. However, you can continue along the coast to the following two most rewarding targets.

Cascais

Over the years, returning travelers have waxed rhapsodic about the "fashion and chicness" of Estoril, while praising the so-called fishing village of Cascais for its picturesque quality and quaintness. But Cascais today is no longer a fishing village (many are calling it a city), and it is now rivaling Estoril for supremacy along the Costa do Sol.

Once the monarchy of Portugal summered at Cascais, thus creating its reputation as a royal village. In time, its 17th-century citadel was occupied by Gen. António de Fragoso Carmona, the military dictator who named Dr. Salazar minister of finance in 1928.

Before the advent of a string of deluxe and first-class hotels, life in Cascais centered around its fish market, where auctions are still held. In the harbor, colorful fishing boats and nets bob up and down in the water alongside luxury yachts.

The fish market, overlooking the Hotel Baía, continues to delight those searching for local charm—and many of the denizens of Cascais like it, too. They're earning their livelihood, and not just putting on a show for foreign visitors. Nevertheless, they are photographed indiscriminately, as if they were tourist attractions and not a people of staunch pride and vigor. In fact, the fisherman claim that one of their own, Afonso Sanches, discovered America (quite by accident) in 1482, a decade before Columbus got all the attention.

On Sunday in summer, half of Lisbon seemingly drives out to attend the bullfights at the **Monumental de Cascais.** If you are among them—and especially if you're driving yourself—don't get caught in the impossible serpentine trek back to Lisbon after the *corrida* is over. Wait about two hours, idling away your time walking the cobbled streets of the resort, or else sipping port in a sidewalk café.

Better yet, take an excursion outside of town (on the road to Guincho) to the **Boca do Inferno.** The Mouth of Hell was so named because of its ferocious roar when the sea is rough. It's worth seeing.

Cascais, four miles west of Estoril, is easily reached by taxi, bus, or electric train from Lisbon. The train stops across the street from Cascais' most famous restaurant, **Fim do Mundo** ("The End of the World").

The reputation of Cascais as a place in the sun dates back for centuries. Writing in 1620, Father Nicolau de Oliveira called it "one of the most pleasant and healthy resorts within Portugal." It still is.

Guincho

The open Atlantic surges in against the shore. The undertow is dangerous, but the site is ruggedly inspiring. Four miles west of Cascais (reached by bus or car), Guincho is at a point the Portuguese call **Cabo da Roca,** the most westerly site on the continent of Europe. In the background, beyond the hearty pines beaten by the Atlantic wind, looms the Serra de Sintra, sometimes covered with a misty spray on wintery days.

In summer, the dunes of the **Praia do Guincho** draw beach devotees who like to flirt with danger. For those who defy the sea, Jennings Parrott wrote this advice: "If you are caught by the current, don't fight it. Don't panic. The wind forces it to circle, so you will be brought back to shore. A local fisherman, however, advises that you take a box lunch along. Sometimes it takes several days to make the circle."

After listening to the sea on a rough day, you'll know why the beach is called "Guincho," which means "screech, shriek, or scream" in Portuguese.

SESIMBRA: This village is "rich in fish"— or so wrote Luís Vaz de Camões, author of the 16th-century *The Lusiads,* the national epic of Portugal. That statement is still true in the 20th century. In addition to the action at the colorful fish market, anglers are also attracted to Sesimbra.

With the opening of a gem of a hotel scaling a hillside, the **Hotel do Mar,** 10 Rua Combatentes do Ultramar (tel. 223-33-26), many visitors are finding that they can not only enjoy the individual quality of the still unspoiled village, but they can do so in comparative luxury at a rate of 6500$ ($48.75) in a double room. Overlooking the town and sea is the **Castle of Sesimbra,** rebuilt after the earthquake of 1755, but now in ruins. Originally, it was a Moorish stronghold.

Sesimbra lies only 15 miles from Lisbon, across the Ponte 25 de Abril, the spectacular expansion bridge, the largest in Europe.

For another day trip, we strike out to the east for:

ÉVORA: Dubbed a "living museum," Évora was once an ancient Roman town known as *Liberalitas Julia.* Nowadays, it's the district capital of Alto Alentejo province, that region of cork trees, wheatfields, and olive branches. The city of whitewashed houses and ancient monuments lies 96 miles east of Lisbon, and can be reached by train.

The city is especially noted for its Corinthian-style **Temple of Diana,** dating from the second century A.D. Among its curiosities is the macabre **Chapel of Bones** in the Royal Church of St. Francis, built in the Gothic-Manueline style in the 15th century. The government-owned **Pousada dos Lóios,** Largo Conde de Vila Flor (tel. 24051), is acclaimed as the most spectacular inn in Portugal. Installed in what was a former convent, it makes for an ideal luncheon stopover, as it features regional specialties from Alentejo.

ÓBIDOS: This fortress town is almost too perfect a gem of the Middle Ages. No wonder King Denis once offered the town to his saintly wife as a wedding gift. The turreted towers and ramparts of what was a 12th-century castle dominate the hilltop.

The government has installed a honey of an inn, the **Pousada do Castelo** (tel. 95015), in a former wing. The *pousada* is in good taste, its bedroom windows opening onto views of Estremadura. If you're touring, you can visit for a lunch or dinner at a cost of 1200$ ($9).

The village is accurately considered one of the most unspoiled in Europe, and is cared for by the state as a national monument. Seek out the baroque **Church of Santa Maria,** where Afonso V, at the age of 10, is said to have married his 8-year-old cousin.

Óbidos lies 59 miles north of Lisbon. From Rossio Station, a Western Line train leaves at 7:45 a.m., arriving in Óbidos around 10 a.m. Tardy trekkers can take a 10 a.m. train out of Lisbon's Rossio.

ALCOBAÇA: People come here today to see Alcobaça's 12th-century Cistercian monastery. In it, the "Romeo and Juliet" of Portuguese history, Dom Pedro and his murdered mistress Inez de Castro, lie in tombs facing each other. Pedro wanted it that way—so that when he was "resurrected," the first person he'd face would be his beloved Inez. The tragedy: Pedro's father, the king, secretly had Inez murdered (by slitting her throat). After learning of the murder, Pedro kept his cool, but when he became king, he sought revenge—rounding up the killers of his fair Inez and ripping their hearts out. He then exhumed Inez's body, placed it by him on a throne, and forced his court to pay homage to her as his queen by kissing her hand.

Ahem. After that gloomy tale, you're best off slipping away from the tombs and walking down to the lower level to see the monastic kitchen, through which a brook was directed. The monastery dates from the 12th century, having been founded by Portugal's first king, Afonso Henriques. It lies about 67 miles north of Lisbon. If you're driving, you can stop here following a visit to Óbidos.

If you go by train, catch a 7:45 a.m. car from Lisbon, arriving at a station called Valado at 10:57 a.m. From the train station at Valado, buses connect to Alcobaça.

BATALHA: The "battle abbey" of Portugal rises from the plain, in stark contrast to the flat countryside. It's called the Monastery of Our Lady of Victory. King John I (João I) had a monastery and church built about a mile from the battlefield of Aljubarrota in 1385, in which the Portuguese defeated the Castilians. This battle had far-reaching consequences, not only for Portugal by preserving her independence, but also for the world in that it enabled the Portuguese to carry out their maritime discoveries.

In the shadow of the abbey, a village bearing the same name has sprung up. Begun at the end of the 14th century, and continued through the 15th and 16th centuries, the monastery is in the Gothic and Manueline style. The monastery shows much originality in its features. For example, it has a degree of austerity, in spite of the florid type of Gothic style adopted in its architecture. The color of stone used is especially interesting, a golden and pinkish limestone from the Serra de Aire. It gives off a warm, coral-like hue. Many English and French architectural influences are seen as well.

The visitor will want to explore the naves in their ethereal elegance. In an octagonal chapel are the tombs of the founder, King João I, and his wife, Philippa of Lancaster, daughter of John of Gaunt of England. Their tombs are surrounded by those of the princes, their sons. The bathroom in the royal cloister is also of interest.

The *Capalas Imperfeitas,* the so-called unfinished chapels, have a lushness of style, showing their potential decorative beauty. They make one regret that the artisans abandoned their work to join the task force building Jerónimos Monastery at Belém.

Batalha lies about 73 miles north of Lisbon. To reach it by train, you must go first to Valado where you can make bus connections bound for Batalha.

NAZARÉ: The fishermen of this village-turned-summer resort are unique. Seymour Pearlman once wrote about these sailors who "appear different from other Portuguese and who remain seemingly unchanged in a rapidly changing world."

Their colorful dress—the plaid trousers and shirts—evoke the Highlands. Legend has it that these plaid and tartan designs were copied from seafaring Scots shipwrecked centuries ago in

Nazaré. However, others attribute the origin to the troops of Wellington, who camped near Nazaré during the wars with Napoleon. The young girls of Nazaré are said to wear seven petticoats, but it's illegal to count them! Also, note the fishermen's distinctive high-prowed boats. The style is said to date from the time of Nazaré's Phoenician settlers.

The lower part of the village is known as the Praia, the upper part—a promontory towering over the bay—is called Sítio. At the latter, reached by a funicular, the view is spectacular.

A train (three hours) from Lisbon arrives at Valado, from where it's possible to make bus connections to Nazaré. Trains leave Lisbon at 7:45 and at 10 a.m.

FÁTIMA: On May 13, 1917, three shepherd children claimed that a vision of a young girl appeared before them and that she made a sacred vow to reappear every month on the same day until October. Word of the vision gradually spread across the world, stirring enthusiasm and bitter controversy.

The final vision on October 13 drew an estimated 70,000 who watched the phenomenon of "The Miracle of the Sun." Although no one except the three children claimed they saw the Virgin Mary that day, hundreds upon hundreds reported seeing the sun hurtling toward the earth. Many screamed and panicked, fearing the Last Judgment.

Eventually in 1930, the church finally accepted the story that the three children had indeed been "visited" by the Virgin Mary. By then, two of the children had died of fever. The third still lives as a nun in a convent at Coimbra. Even today Fátima draws thousands upon thousands of pilgrims on the 13th of every month from May through October.

Reached on the Northern Line, it lies about 36 miles east of Nazaré, some 88 miles north of Lisbon. You can take a train from Lisbon at 3:10 p.m. From the train station, you can take a bus or a taxi to the site.

Those who want to continue on the northward trip can visit the two following cities.

COIMBRA: This is the university city of Portugal, lying on the banks of the Mondego River, the capital of Beira Litoral province. Its university is reputed to be the second oldest in the world, dating from 1290. In its stunning baroque library, built in the 18th century, are about one million volumes, including a rare first edition of Camoes' *Os Lusíadas,* the Portuguese national epic.

From Lisbon, you can catch a 7:45 a.m. train, arriving at Coimbra at 10:20 a.m.

PORTO: Portugal's "second city" is the home of port, the world-famous Portuguese wine. Near the mouth of the Douro River, Porto is an industrial city, although it has many worthy attractions. Once a Roman encampment, it is one of the oldest cities in Europe. In particular, seek out its Romanesque Sé (cathedral); **Clérigos Church,** with its landmark tower; and the **Church of the Carmelites,** a fine example of Portuguese Baroque.

Opposite Porto is the thriving center of the port business, **Vila Nova da Gaia.** Visit one of its wine cellars. You'll not only learn something about port, you'll get to drink it.

From the city, you can travel through the **Douro Valley,** known as "port wine country." The best time to visit is when the grapes are harvested in September.

Porto lies about 175 miles north of Lisbon. You can take a train from Lisbon at 7:45 a.m. Reserve your seat ahead of time.

THE ALGARVE: For fun in the sun, the Portuguese, along with increasing hordes of bikini-clad foreigners, head south to the Algarve, where the scenery strikes many as similar to that of North Africa. It's a delight even in late January and early February, when the almond blossoms dot the landscape like snow.

Stretching along a hundred-mile coastline, the Algarve begins at **Cape St. Vincent** in the west (the most southerly point of Europe), running to **Vila Real de Santo António** near the Spanish frontier. For five centuries, the province was ruled by the Moors, and much of their influence remains.

To the east of Cape St. Vincent, is **Sagres.** It was from here that Prince Henry the Navigator directed his caravels on their world exploration.

Continuing east, you come across **Lagos,** overlooking a bay of the same name. Henry once lived here. To the east of it is **Praia da Rocha,** with its grottoes—and some of the finest beaches in the country. The capital of the province is **Faro,** a terminal point for trains from Lisbon. You can take the train from Lisbon at 7:45 a.m. In addition, the local jet airport reduces travel time from Lisbon to less than an hour.

Chapter X

GETTING ACQUAINTED WITH MADRID

MADRID IS THE MOTHER SUPERIOR of Spain, more to be venerated than loved.

In *The Sun Also Rises*, Hemingway described her as ". . . a white sky-line on the top of a little cliff away off across the sun-hardened country."

Papa would not know her today. The little pueblo that was Madrid continues to grow at a dramatic rate, expanding rapidly in land area and industrial development, sprouting suburbs of apartment houses for the burgeoning population.

On a plateau of the Sierra de Guadarrama, the capital of Spain is the highest in Europe, reaching a peak of 2373 feet above sea level at its loftiest point.

The sierra air is dry, almost crystal pure, the sky cerulean as painted by Velázquez.

As Spanish cities go, Madrid is still young. *Don Quixote* was known throughout the world when Philip II made Madrid the capital of Spain in 1606. The location was apt: geographically it was the heart of the Iberian peninsula.

On your way into Madrid from Barajas Airport, you're likely to see an aging *dueña* shrouded in black—perhaps mourning for her husband who died in the Spanish Civil War in the late '30s. Or your eyes will fall on a weather-hardened old man riding a heavily laden donkey, a scene undisturbed by the centuries in Spain. These are *tableaux vivants*, frozen in time and space.

As you near the center of the city, however, skyscrapers herald tomorrow's world. Flashy billboards implore everybody to "*bebe* Coca-Cola," or to wear Yankee-style Levis for greater sex appeal.

Spain is in metamorphosis. Now that the country is justifiably called "the playground of Europe," authorities are forced to grant concessions to the hordes of invaders pouring across its borders or winging in from the skies. For example, ever-increasing numbers of visitors now stroll the streets of Madrid in summer shorts. In the not-too-distant past, such apparel would have given a skimpily clad visitor firsthand experience for an autobiography, "My Life in a Spanish Jail."

It is impossible to separate Madrid or Castile from the saga of the nation as a whole. It was from the barren, undulating plains of the country's heartland that the proud, sometimes arrogant, Castilians emerged. They were destined not only to unify the country, but to dominate it. And to go even further, carving out an empire that was to embrace the Aztecs and Incas, even the faraway Philippines.

In Castile you'll meet a survival-sharpened people. One scholar put it this way: "The Spaniards are a fierce, idealistic, generous people, capable of great sacrifice and heroism when driven by their proud and burning passions, but they are also intolerant, dogmatic, and individualistic."

Regardless, know that the Spaniard—whatever his or her background—is generally friendly, especially to the well-behaved *gringo*. As hosts, they have great style and graciousness, and are today among the most hospitable nations in Europe.

A WORD ABOUT CLIMATE: In Madrid, climate is subject to rapid change. July and August are the most uncomfortable months. In fact, the government virtually shuts down in August except for a skeleton crew, going into "exile" at the northeast Atlantic resort of San Sebastián.

The temperature can *average* a high of 91 degrees Fahrenheit in July, 76 degrees in September. In winter, it can plunge to 34 degrees Fahrenheit, although it averages around 46 degrees.

In October (average temperature: 56 degrees Fahrenheit), Madrid enjoys its "season." Hotel space is at a premium. Every bullfighter, doll manufacturer, Galacian hotelier, Andalusian olive grower, or Santander vineyard keeper having business with the government descends on Madrid at this time. In the same month, wealthy Spanish aristocrats flock here from the secluded ducal palaces in Andalusia and Castile, to savor the sophistication of the capital, its opera, theater, and endless rounds of parties and dinners.

The air is clear, the sun kind; the restaurants and *tascas* (bars) overflow with Iberian joie de vivre.

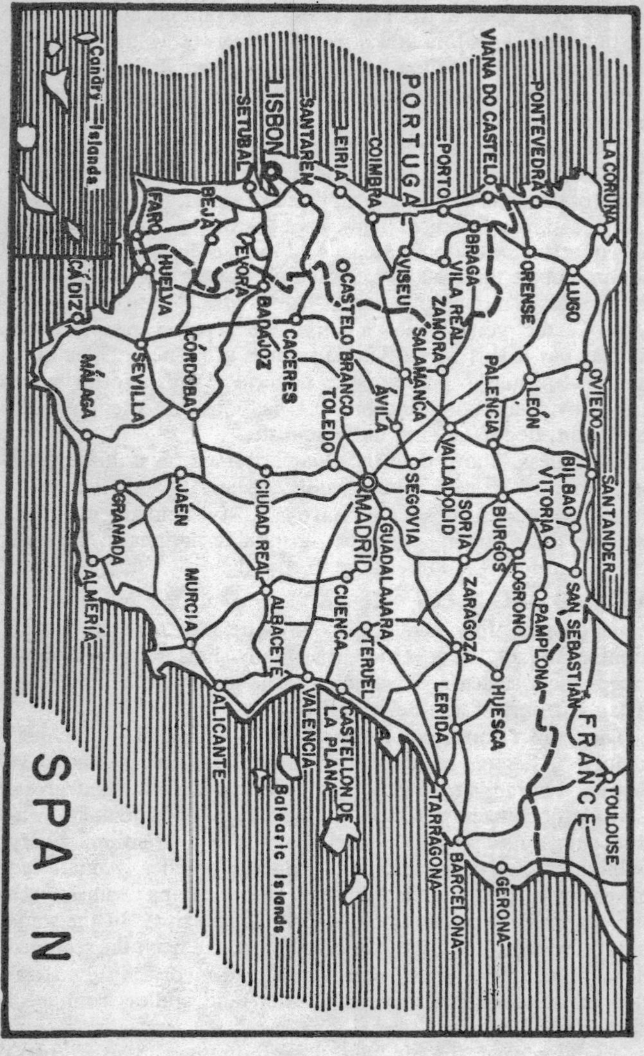

SPAIN
PORTUGAL
FRANCE
Canary Islands
Balearic Islands
LISBON
SETUBAL
SANTAREM
LEIRIA
COIMBRA
PORTO
VIANA DO CASTELO
PONTEVEDRA
LA CORUÑA
LUGO
ORENSE
BRAGA
VILA REAL
ZAMORA
SALAMANCA
VISEU
O CASTELO BRANCO
BEJA
FARO
HUELVA
EVORA
BADAJOZ
CACERES
TOLEDO
AVILA
PALENCIA
LEÓN
OVIEDO
BILBAO
VITORIA
SANTANDER
SEVILLA
CÓRDOBA
MÁLAGA
GRANADA
JAEN
CIUDAD REAL
MADRID
SEGOVIA
VALLADOLID
SORIA
BURGOS
LOGROÑO
ZARAGOZA
PAMPLONA
SAN SEBASTIAN
ALMERÍA
MURCIA
ALBACETE
CUENCA
GUADALAJARA
TERUEL
LERIDA
HUESCA
TOULOUSE
ALICANTE
VALENCIA
CASTELLON DE LA PLANA
TARRAGONA
BARCELONA
GERONA
CÁDIZ

In my view, however, the balmy month of May (average temperature: 61 degrees Fahrenheit) is the best date for making your own descent on the capital.

FLYING TO MADRID: If you wish to fly directly to Madrid from North America, as most visitors will, there are two major airlines which do so: **Iberia** (the Spanish international airline), and **Trans World Airlines.**

As part of my continuing policy to travel on many airlines and report on the services of dozens of national carriers, I recently chose Trans World Airlines for my flight from New York to Madrid, and was very pleased with the experience.

In summer, TWA has at least one flight every day (and sometimes more) which goes nonstop from New York's JFK airport to Madrid. Service is slightly reduced in wintertime. Easy connections can be made from most points throughout North America, often with a minimum of waiting at airports.

The least expensive fare is a midweek APEX (Advanced Purchase Excursion) ticket, which is available to passengers traveling in both directions on Monday through Thursday inclusive. TWA requires a reservations and prepayment at least 14 days in advance, with stopovers lasting from seven to 180 days.

There is also a regular APEX fare, requiring 21 days' advance purchase, with a stopover of between seven and 180 days. On both types of APEX fares, the departure date and the return date must be specified in advance, with penalties imposed for any changes in itinerary.

Yet another ticket, the excursion fare, differs from APEX fares in that no advance purchase or reservation is necessary. This fare is costlier, although it allows passengers to leave their return date "open" for specification at a later date, after travel plans are set. An excursion ticket allows a 30-day minimum stay or a maximum stay of one year.

Of course, if you don't qualify—or don't want the limitations —of either the APEX or excursion fares, you then must pay the regular coach fare. Business people generally gravitate to the more expensive Ambassador Class, where seats are wider, deeper, and more comfortable, and where food service is upgraded. Passengers savoring the most that luxurious travel can offer—at the greatest expense—book a first-class ticket. All flights are on 747s or L-1011s.

Charter Flights

Transatlantic air fares have continued to climb steadily, although charter flights, which many passengers criticize for their lack of convenience and rigidity of scheduling, can be arranged through **Nueva York Hispaño,** 261 West 70th Street, New York, NY 10023 (tel. 212/595-2400). This office uses both Iberia, the national airline, and Spantax, a private Spanish charter firm.

You can also investigate the charter flights offered by **Spanish Heritage Association,** 116-53 Queens Boulevard, Forest Hills, NY 11375 (tel. 212/520-1300). Sometimes their flights are a few dollars less than Nueva York Hispaño.

NAVIGATING YOUR WAY: No one ever claimed that knowing or getting around Madrid was easy. Surprisingly, many of the Madrileño taxi drivers are often unfamiliar with their own city, once they branch off the main boulevards.

Everything in the Spanish capital is spread out, and this may cause you initial difficulty until you get the feel of it. For example, on one typical night, you may want to sample the *tapas* (hors d'oeuvres) at a *tasca* on the Ventura de la Vega; dine at a restaurant opening onto the fairly far-off Plaza Mayor; witness an evening of flamenco near the Ritz Hotel; then head for your hotel, at—say, the gateway to Toledo. The easiest, most sensible and practical means of getting around to all the above mentioned, widely scattered places is by:

Taxi

Fortunately, the cabs are cheap—among the least expensive in Western Europe, in fact. At the start of a ride, the meter registers 60 pesetas (39¢), and that fare will surely have gone up by the time of your visit. An average ride costs about 400 pesetas ($2.60). There are extras as well. Trips to the railway station or to the bullring carry a supplement, plus an additional fee tacked on to the fare on Sunday and holidays. It's customary to tip at least 10% or more of the fare.

A ride is usually tantamount to an adventure, as Madrileño drivers go fast and furiously, occasionally (but not always!) stopping at a red light.

Although inexpensive, taxi-riding is fraught with some minor traps that a visitor will do well to avoid. There are two types of taxis: black with horizontal red bands and white with diagonal red bands. Their rates are usually the same.

Many *unmetered*, unbanded taxis also abound in Madrid, their drivers renting their services as guides for the day or half day. But when business is slow, these guides sometimes operate as "gypsy" cabs, picking up unsuspecting passengers, taking them to their destinations, and charging them whatever they think the market will bear.

Beyond that pitfall, you must be careful to require that your driver turns down the meter when you enter his cab. Otherwise, he may "assess" the cost of the ride to your disadvantage.

Another means of transportation in Madrid is the:

Subway (Metro)

The system, first installed in 1919, is quite easy to learn, and you can travel in the underground if not comfortably, at least without any congestion or crushing, as in former years.

Line No. 7 is completely different from the rest, and as modern as some of Europe's newest underground systems. The future lines under construction will be the same type as No. 7.

The central converging point of the metro is at the **Puerta del Sol.** The subways begin their runs at 6 a.m., shutting down at 1:30 a.m. It's best to try to avoid traveling on the subways during the rush hours, of course. The metro fare is 35 pesetas (23¢).

Bus

A network of buses also traverses the city, fanning out to the suburbs. The route of each bus is clearly marked at each stop on a schematic diagram. Buses are fast and efficient, traveling down special lanes made for them all over the city. The fare begins at 60 pesetas (39¢). For information on buses from the airport into Madrid, refer to the "Airports" section in Chapter XVI, The ABC'S of Spain.

Car Rentals

If you're planning to tour Spain, a car will ease the burdens considerably. Even if you're limited to extensive touring in the environs of Madrid, you'll find that a rented automobile will come in handy, allowing you to stop off at that *típico* roadside tavern for a sherry or to make that side detour to a medieval village. You'll be your own master, exploring at your leisure places not covered—or covered too hurriedly—on the organized tour.

On my most recent trip to Spain, I tried the services of **Budget**

Rent a Car, whose offices are scattered strategically throughout Spain. My report on their facilities should give you an idea of the prices and procedures of the other major firms, which include ATESA, Hertz, and Avis.

The smallest—and least expensive car—in Budget's inventory includes a Fiat Panda or its equivalent. Suitable for up to four passengers, including their luggage, the car is available for an unlimited mileage rate of $99 per week, with a $14 a day charge for each additional day. To qualify for this rate, clients must reserve through a Budget reservations office at least three business days in advance. An additional 5% VAT is added to these figures, and all gasoline, of course, is the responsibility of the renter. For short rentals, it's possible to hire a car on a per-day basis, with a fee for each kilometer driven, but most visitors usually prefer the longer period.

An attractive medium-size car available through Budget would be a Renault 14 or a Ford Escort. With manual transmission, it costs $139 per week, with another $20 charged for each additional day. A more expensive choice is a five-passenger Renault 18 or a Seat 131 Diplomat. It rents for about $360 a week, with unlimited mileage. If you are comfortable driving it, a car with manual transmission is much cheaper. Likewise, if you're cutting costs, don't request air conditioning.

More information about the discounted rates available through Budget can be obtained by calling their toll-free U.S. number: 800/527-0700.

Other rental companies include the government-owned **ATESA,** whose offices are at 59 Gran Vía in Madrid (tel. 247/730-001). **Avis** is also well represented in Spain, with about twenty depots and kiosks, including ones at all the major airports (call toll-free within the U.S. at 800/331-2112). Finally, **Hertz** will accept your reservation before you leave America. Their toll-free number is 800/654-3134.

THE DIFFERENT MADRIDS: The Spanish capital, as mentioned, is a fast-growing city, its development somewhat sporadic and largely haphazard. It can be described in many ways and from many points of view.

If you're interested in "Royal Madrid," you'll think of the **Palacio Real,** fronting the handsome **Plaza de Oriente,** with its Valázquez-inspired equestrian statue of Philip IV. The gardens and parks, the wide avenues appropriate for state receptions and parades take on new significance with the restoration of the Spanish monarchy.

If you're a romanticist nostalgic for the 19th century, you'll watch in sadness as the mansions along the **Paseo de la Castallana** and its satellite streets are torn down to make way for modern offices and shops, deluxe hotels, apartment buildings. Thankfully, a few are still preserved and used today by foreign embassies.

If you're an artist or devotee of art, you'll spend most of your time at the great old Prado, treasure house of Spanish masterpieces, sheltering a once-royal collection of European art. If you're on a shopping spree, you'll gravitate to the **Gran Vía,** called the Avenida José Antonio during the long dictatorship of Franco, the main street of Madrid, with its stores, cinemas, and hotels, the latter both luxury and budget. The wide avenue—flanked with sidewalk cafés—ends at the **Plaza de España** with its Edificio España, one of the tallest skyscrapers in Europe. Or you'll wander past the multitude of shops, boutiques, coffee-houses, and couturiers' salons of the more prestigious **Calle de Serrano.**

If medieval Madrid intrigues you, you'll seek out the Moorish towers of the old quarter, looking for the *mudéjar* style of architecture. You'll photograph (in your mind, if not in your Instamatic) the **Plaza de la Villa,** and focus especially on the **Torre de los Lujanes.** According to tradition, Francis I of France was held captive at the tower after he was taken prisoner in Pavia, Italy.

The colonnaded and rectangular **Plaza Mayor,** one of the most harmoniously designed squares in Europe, recalls the Madrid of the 17th century. The scene of many an *auto-da-fé,* bullfight, or execution of a traitor, it is today one of the best spots in the city for a *paseo,* especially if you take time out from your walking to explore the adjoining shops, some of which sell sombreros. Later you can select a restaurant, perhaps one with a table opening right on the square.

If you walk through one of the vaulted porticoes of the Plaza Mayor to the south, down the street of *típico* restaurants and taverns—the **Calle de Cuchilleros**—you'll reach the **Calle de Toledo.** Then you'll be entering a special world of Old Madrid, still preserved. Known as the *barrios bajos,* it is home to the Madrileño lowest on the economic scale. In some cities it would be called a ghetto or slum. But in Madrid the area abounds with such style—screaming gypsy *niños,* arcaded markets stuffed with

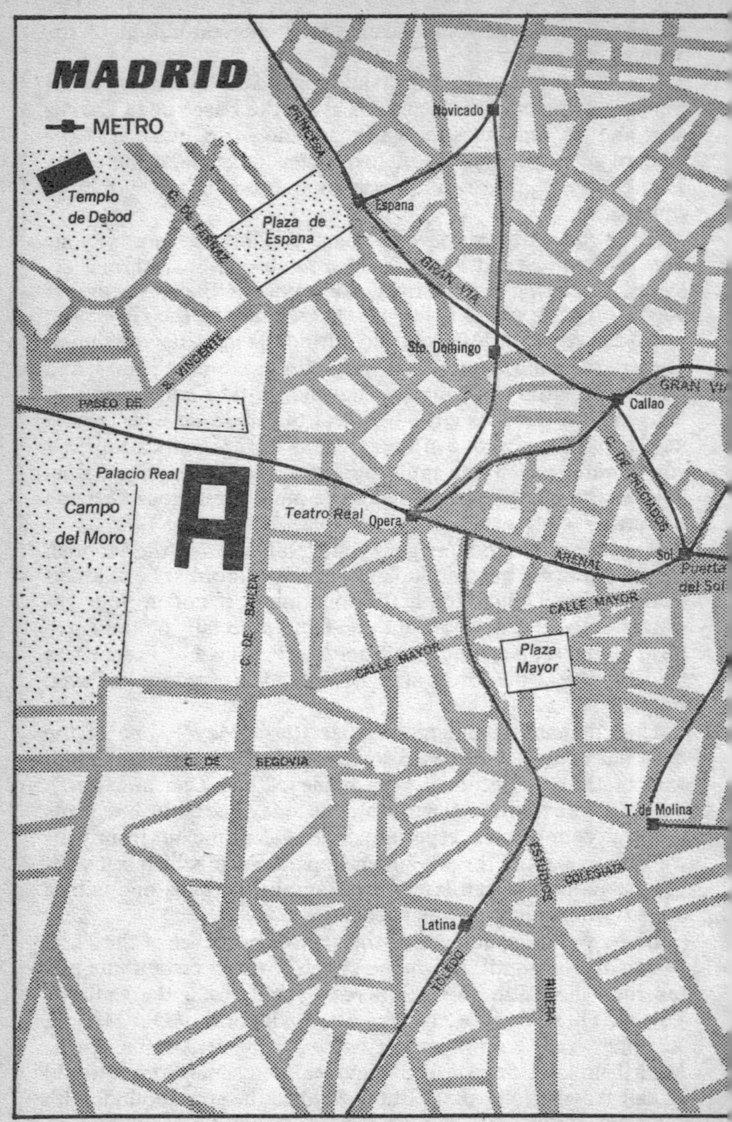
MADRID
METRO
Templo
de Debod
Plaza de
España
España
Novicado
GRAN VIA
Sto. Domingo
GRAN VIA
Callao
PASEO DE
S. VINCENTE
C. DE FERAZ
Palacio Real
Campo
del Moro
A
Teatro Real
Opera
C. DE PRECIADOS
ARENAL
Sol
Puerta
del Sol
CALLE MAYOR
Plaza
Mayor
C. DE BAILEN
CALLE MAYOR
C. DE SEGOVIA
COLEGIATA
ESTUDIOS
RIBERA
T. de Molina
Latina
TOLEDO

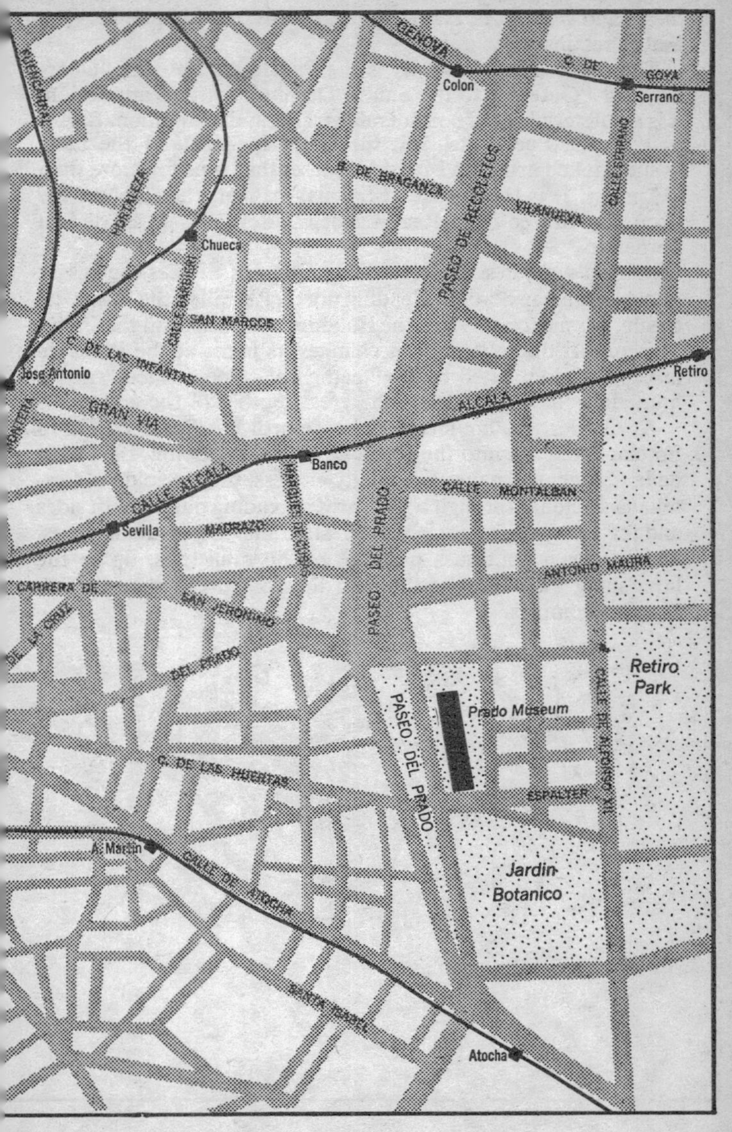
FUENCARRAL
GENOVA
C. DE
GOYA
Colon
Serrano
HORTALEZA
P. DE BRAGANZA
PASEO DE RECOLETOS
VILANUEVA
CALLE SERRANO
Chueca
CALLE BARBIERI
SAN MARCOS
C. DE LAS INFANTAS
Jose Antonio
ALCALA
Retiro
GRAN VIA
CALLE ALCALA
Banco
CALLE MONTALBAN
Sevilla
MADRAZO
MARQUES DE CUBAS
ANTONIO MAURA
CARRERA DE
DE LA CRUZ
SAN JERONIMO
PASEO DEL PRADO
DEL PRADO
Retiro
Park
C. DE LAS HUERTAS
PASEO DEL PRADO
Prado Museum
CALLE DE ALFONSO XII
ESPALTER
A. Martin
CALLE DE ATOCHA
Jardin
Botanico
SANTA ISABEL
Atocha

meats and vegetables, shops, *tascas, cuevas* (see Chapter XIV)—that it retains great punch.

The real center of the city is the **Puerta del Sol** (the "Doorway" or "Gateway to the Sun"). Despite its grand appelation, it is a dull terminus of considerable traffic and congestion. Beginning at the Puerta del Sol, the **Calle de Alcalá** is the most traffic-choked artery in Madrid, a street that runs for more than 2½ miles. It is the avenue of Spanish bankers, and houses the Escuela y Museo de la Real Academia de Bellas Artes de San Fernando.

Madrid's greatest boulevard, its Champs-Élysées, begins at Atocha Railway Station. Heading north, it's called the **Paseo del Prado,** passing on its right the Botanical Gardens and the Prado Museum. It doesn't end, but changes its name at the **Plaza de la Cibeles,** dominated by the "cathedral of post offices" and a fountain honoring Cybele, "the great mother of the gods."

At Cibeles, the boulevard is henceforth the **Paseo de Carvo Sotelo,** and leads into the **Plaza de Colón.** At Colón, the **Paseo de la Castellana** begins. Seemingly endless, the Paseo de la Castellana stretches through a posh area spreading out on both sides and featuring apartment houses, restaurants, department stores, and hotels; it continues past the public ministries, up to the flourishing **Plaza de Castilla,** and then on to the huge La Paz hospital complex.

Elderly bench-warmers, Madrid

Chapter XI

THE HOTELS OF MADRID

THE HOTEL BOOM in Madrid has been spectacular: three-quarters of my recommendations have opened their doors since 1964.

What about the relics of yesteryear? Except for those grand old ladies, the Ritz and the Palace (circa 1910–1912), most other older hostelries in Madrid haven't really kept abreast of the times. A handful haven't added improvements or overhauled bedrooms substantially since the 1890s.

Traditionally, hotels in Madrid were clustered around the Atocha Railway Station and the Gran Vía. In my search for the most outstanding hotels in all price brackets, I've almost ignored these two popular, but noisy, districts. The new hotels are being erected away from the center, especially on residential streets jutting off from the Paseo de la Castellana.

A CEILING ON PRICES: The government controls and sets the tariffs that a hotelier may charge in Spain. These rates are posted (or should be) at the reception counter in the lobby as well as in your bedroom (usually on the back of a closet door). A minimum and maximum rate are listed, but in Madrid you'll always pay the maximum rate. The minimum tab is most often charged in winter at beach resort hotels seeking to lure off-season vacationers. The rates set by the government include all surcharges for service and taxes. Deluxe hotels, however, are exempt.

THE STAR SYSTEM: Spain officially rates its hotels by star designation. Riding the crest of the Milky Way are hotels granted a constellation of five stars. That is the highest rating in Spain, signaling a deluxe establishment, complete with all the amenities and high tariffs associated with such accommodations.

Most of the establishments recommended in this guide are three- and four-star hotels falling into that vague "middle bracket" category. Hotels granted one and two stars, as well as pensions (guest houses), are far less comfortable, although they may be perfectly clean and decent places, but with limited plumbing and other physical facilities. The latter category is strictly for dedicated budgeteers.

Some Deluxe Hotels

Villa Magna, 22 Paseo de la Castellana (tel. 275-12-27), on the city's most fashionable boulevard, is one of the finest hotels in all of Spain. And for good reason: a small group of the elite teamed up to create a setting in which their special friends, along with an increasing array of discriminating international visitors, would be pleased to live and dine. They hired an architect, imported a French decorator, and the result is elegant and appropriately expensive.

Separated from the busy boulevard by a parklike garden, its façade has severe contemporary lines. In contrast, its opulent interior recaptures the style of Carlos IV, with its richly paneled walls and marble floors. Through the stunning lobby and elaborate drawing room passes almost every film star shooting on location in Spain. In the Mayfair cocktail lounge, sedate and leathery à la London, the bartender can mix any drink you conjure up.

This luxury palace offers 200 stylized bedrooms—perhaps Louis XVI, Regency, Italian provincial—each, along with its sumptuous marble and tiled bath, designed to give you that pampered feeling. And even if you're not one of those "special friends," a bowl of fragrant fresh flowers inevitably awaits you. Single rooms are 18,000 pesetas ($117); a twin-bedded room costs 24,000 pesetas ($156).

The big news here is the splendid restaurant, the Rue Royale (see my restaurant recommendations in the next chapter).

The most famous hotel in Madrid is the **Ritz,** 5 Plaza Lealtad (tel. 221-28-57). If offers all the luxuries and special attentions that world travelers have come to expect of the Ritz. The director suggests that guests book very, very early, as rooms are hard to come by at this veritable citadel of gracious and somewhat snobbish living.

Wealthy Spanish families of the aristocracy and foreign diplomats have favored it for years, and its guest book is a who's who of heads of government, kings and personalities such as Barbara Hutton. An international rendezvous point, it has been considerably updated and modernized, although efforts have been made to retain its *belle époque* character, unique in Europe. Recently acquired by Trusthouses Forte, the Ritz has undergone millions of dollars of "refreshening" to maintain its position as one of the leading hotels in the world.

The Ritz stands next to its neighbor, the Palace, another legendary landmark Madrid hotel which will be recommended later. One of Les Grand Hôtels Européens, founded by Georges Marquet in 1910, the Ritz looks out onto a big circular plaza near the 300-acre Retiro Park and facing the Prado Museum and the Stock Exchange. The new hotels going up in Madrid simply can't match its grand-manner elegance. The Ritz was constructed when costs were relatively inexpensive, and when spaciousness, luxury, and comfort were the styles of the day. To be coddled in plush comfort, in a setting of beautiful but restrained furnishings, will cost from 18,000 pesetas ($117) to 21,000 pesetas ($136.50) in a single room and from 23,000 pesetas ($149.50) to 25,000 pesetas ($162.50) in a double. Some of the marble bathrooms of the Ritz are the finest I've seen in some two decades of inspecting hotels of Europe. For those who can afford it, staying here can be one of the highlights of a trip to Europe.

Like the cognoscenti of old, who have long had a liking for the Ritz, today's guest likes its grandeur, comfort, impeccable service, and gracious living, including 24-hour room service. It's not only elegant in the thick-carpeted sense, but it's also quiet. In these days of casual dress, it's important to know that guests at the Ritz dress up, even for breakfast. This is not a "resort" hotel.

The five-star Ritz Restaurant is one of the most attractive in Europe, and a Spanish magazine called it "the top restaurant of the year." It is decorated in cream, blue, and gold, with paneled mirrors and 16th-century Flemish tapestries. Its chefs present an international menu, and its paella is said to be the best in Madrid.

Except for champagne, the wine list is staunchly Spanish.

Guests are treated to lavish bouquets of fresh flowers in their rooms. The façade of the hotel is classed as a historical monument, or at least it should be. No other hotel, except perhaps for the Palace, has a more varied history.

Next on the deluxe list is the **Eurobuilding** 23 Calle Padre Damián (tel. 457-17-00). Even while it was on the drawing boards, the rumor was that this new five-star sensation of white marble would provide in the architect's words, "a new concept in deluxe hotels." The Eurobuilding has lived up to its advance billing, reflecting a high level in taste and design. It is two hotels

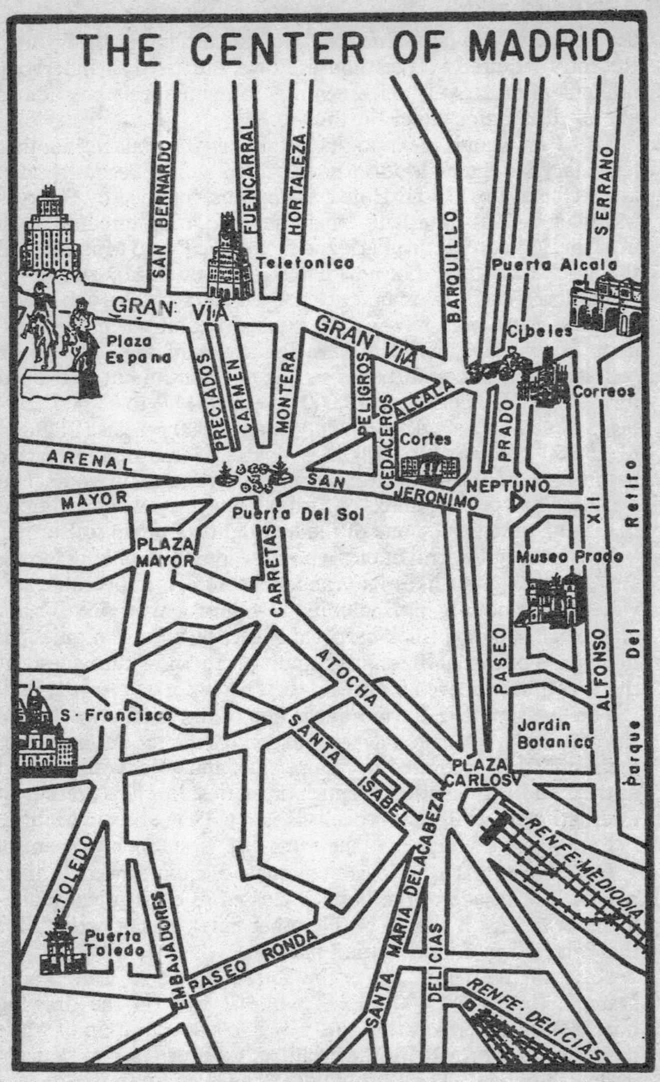
THE CENTER OF MADRID
SAN BERNARDO
FUENCARRAL
HORTALEZA
Teletonica
BARQUILLO
SERRANO
Puerta Alcala
Cibeles
GRAN VIA
GRAN VIA
Plaza Espana
PRECIADOS
CARMEN
MONTERA
PELIGROS
CEDACEROS
ALCALA
Cortes
PRADO
Correos
ARENAL
SAN
Neptuno
JERONIMO
MAYOR
Puerta Del Sol
XII
Retiro
PLAZA MAYOR
CARRETAS
Museo Prado
ATOCHA
PASEO
ALFONSO
Parque Del
S. Francisco
SANTA ISABEL
Jardin Botanica
PLAZA CARLOS V
TOLEDO
EMBAJADORES
PASEO RONDA
SANTA MARIA DELACABEZA
DELICIAS
RENFE-MEDIODIA
Puerta Toledo
RENFE. DELICIAS

linked by a courtyard, the complex away from the city center, but right in the midst of apartment houses, boutiques, night-clubs, first-class restaurants, and tree-shaded squares.

The more glamorous of the twin buildings is the main one, with 150 suites furnished in a stylized Iberian manner. Drinks await you in the refrigerator. Gold and white ornately carved beds, simple colors, background music, TV, a room-wide terrace for breakfast and cocktail entertaining—all is tastefully coordinated. The rate for a single (actually a double room) is 12,000 pesetas ($78); for a double, 15,000 pesetas ($97.50).

Across the courtyard, the sister Eurobuilding contains 480 single and double rooms, all compactly designed, and each with a view from its private terrace of the formal garden and swimming pool below.

Shared by both buildings is the luxury restaurant, Balthasar, on the lower level behind a Turkish spindle screen. La Taberna, also on the premises, offers more rapid dining. Perhaps the ideal way to dine here is alfresco by the pool, enjoying a buffet luncheon.

Meliá Madrid, 27 Princesa (tel. 241-82-00), is one of the most up-to-date, sumptuously modern, yet uniquely Spanish hotels in the country, which comes as something of a surprise to the thousands of tourists Señor Meliá hauls around in his tour buses. España and the beginning of the Gran Vía, and its 23-floors' worth of wide picture windows have taken a permanent position in the capital's skyline. It would be difficult to call any of the 250 bedrooms "standard," but all are good-sized, many offer spectacular views of the city, all are air-conditioned, and all have chalk-white walls to dramatize the flamboyant use of color accents. The baths are done in snow-white marble; TV sets are common, and so too are refrigerators filled with cold drinks. With service and taxes, singles go for from 10,000 pesetas ($65); doubles for 15,000 pesetas ($97.50). The Restaurant Princesa here is a subdued and restful spot. Equally popular is the Don Pepe Grill (the nickname of the proprietor), which offers similarly stimulating meals. The cuisine throughout is international, including Japanese and Indian dishes. On the ground floor is a disco.

Miguel Angel, 31 Miguel Angel (tel. 442-00-22), just off the Paseo de la Castellana, is sleekly modern and has quickly built a reputation for providing some of the finest accommodations in the Spanish capital. It has much going for it—location, contemporary styling, imaginative furnishings and art objects, an efficient staff, and plenty of comfort. Behind its façade, there is an expansive sun terrace on several levels, with clusters of garden furniture, surrounded by lush semitropical planting. The Farnesio bar is decorated in a Spanish Victorian style, and piano music is played from 8 in the evening. All the deluxe facilities are provided—an indoor heated swimming pool, sauna baths, hairdressers, and also a drugstore. Best of all, the hotel has style with its luxurious accoutrements. Art exhibitions are sponsored in the arcade of boutiques (on one recent occasion, children's art was featured).

In the large bedrooms, fabrics and carpets are color coordinated, and many of the furnishings are reproductions of classic Spanish styles. The 307 rooms are soundproofed and air-conditioned, containing TVs, radios, and minibars. Singles rent for 12,000 pesetas ($78); regular doubles go for 16,000 pesetas ($104). A set luncheon or dinner goes for around 3000 pesetas ($19.50) in either the Florencia or Renacimento restaurants, and the Zacarias restaurant/disco, also on the premises, serves dinner until 3 a.m.

Wellington, 8 Velázquez (tel. 275-44-00), with its impressive antique-tapestried entrance, is one of Madrid's more sedate of Spain's leading matadors. In a lovely residential area near Retiro Park, the Wellington offers redecorated rooms furnished in English mahogany; the doubles with private terraces at no extra charge are the choice accommodations. The bathrooms are immaculate and up-to-date; the marble sparkles and new fixtures are added yearly. The single rate is 10,000 pesetas ($65); the standard double charge is 15,000 pesetas ($97.50).

In addition to an outdoor swimming pool, the Wellington offers a garage, beauty parlor, cocktail bar and lounge, air conditioning, and same-day dry cleaning and laundry. An added bonus here is the El Fogón grill room, styled like a 19th-century tavern, where many of the provisions for the typically Spanish dishes are shipped in from the hotel's own ranch.

Other Top Choices

The **Palace,** 7 Plaza de las Cortes (tel. 429-75-51), is the grand *dueña* of Spanish hotels. The establishment had an auspicious beginning, inaugurated by the late King Alfonso XIII in 1912. Covering a city block, it is superbly located, facing the Prado Museum and Neptune Fountain, in the historical and artistic area, in walking distance of the main shopping center and the best antique shops. Some of the city's most intriguing *tascas* and restaurants are only a short stroll away.

Architecturally, it captures the elegant pre-World War I "grand Hotel" style, with an emphasis on space and comfort. Even though it is one of the largest hotels in Europe—1000 beds in all—it retains a personal atmosphere.

All the rooms are conservatively decorated, with plenty of space for leisurely living, color TV, and direct-dial telephones. The bathrooms are large enough to have separate showers and toilets. Single rooms cost from 12,000 pesetas ($78), doubles from 16,000 pesetas ($104).

The hotel is entirely air-conditioned, with a splendid and attractive lobby, restaurant, grill room, and bar.

Princesa Plaza, 40 Calle Princesa (tel. 242-35-00), is a sprawling deluxe hotel designed like a series of massive rectangular solids set together. The concrete and glass façade looks over a busy series of boulevards in the center of Madrid. The interior contains 406 attractively modern rooms, freshly decorated in springtime colors, as well as a large collection of conference rooms, an underground garage, hairdressers, a restaurant, a bar, and a musical salon. Singles rent for 12,000 pesetas ($78) nightly, with doubles going for 16,000 pesetas ($104).

Castellana Hotel, 49 Paseo de la Castellana (tel. 410-02-00). Now that the Inter-Continental hotel chain is in full charge here, the Castellana has risen fast, until today it is one of the finest hotels in the Spanish capital. From the moment you enter, you detect an alert staff, one of the friendliest and most helpful of all the major hotels. Checking in is easy, and soon you're whisked to one of the 322 handsomely furnished and completely air-conditioned bedrooms. The rate in a double is 15,000 pesetas ($97.50), dropping to just 11,000 pesetas ($71.50) in a single.

The location is ideal, in the center of Madrid on a fashionable and famous tree-lined "paseo." It is convenient to both business offices and banks. The Inter-Continental is always sensitive to the needs of the business traveler, and the Castellana is no exception, as it can arrange secretarial and translation services. But the tourist isn't neglected either. At the concierge's desk, information is willingly dispensed from sightseeing to golf or skiing (yes, even skiing). Car rentals can also be easily arranged.

A quick call brings an efficient room service, carrying either a breakfast tray or else summoning someone to pick up your laundry or dry cleaning. Thoughtful facilities include color TV with in-house movies, a mini-bar, and, in many cases, balconies.

Many of your needs can be taken care of right at the hotel, as the premises contain an airlines reservation office, a travel agent, and theater ticket desks. You can also go on a shopping expedition in the arcade of the hotel. There are also telex and cable facilities.

At night, the hotel becomes quite romantic, as guests gather to listen to Spanish guitar music in the garden patio. You can also enjoy pre-dinner drinks at La Ronda Bar, before having dinner at the hotel's informal restaurant. There is also a coffee-shop for those who want their meals in served in a hurry. A host of other facilities include a garage, a health club with a gymnasium, and a massage and sauna room. The Inter-Continental has telephone reservations offices around the world.

Hotel Apartamento Escultor, 3 Miguel Angel (tel. 410-42-03), offers the luxuries of apartment living for the price of a room. Apartments are rented to couples for 12,000 pesetas ($78). The location is supreme, just off the Paseo de la Castellana, in a district of leading hotels and restaurants. The apartments have their own charm and contemporary styling. Lots of white leather and chrome are used. Each room has an electronic mini-bar, video films system, and color TV. Down a long mirrored corridor with a wash basin and wardrobe area (the bath and toilet are separate), you enter the small bedrooms which open into a terrace. Everything is compact, with "bullet" reading lights. The hotel has a small, comfortable lounge and a bar where a nighttime disco operates. In addition, the hotel offers a sophisticated modern restaurant, Vanity, seating 40 to 45 persons. The hotel is fully air-conditioned and contains a garage.

Plaza Hotel, 8 Plaza de España (tel. 247-12-00), could be called the Waldorf-Astoria of Spain. A massive rose and white structure, it soars upward to a central tower 26 stories high. It is a landmark visible for miles around and one of the tallest skyscrapers in Europe, crowned by a panoramic disco, swimming pool, and sun terrace.

The accommodations are varied, ranging from conventional singles and doubles to luxurious suites, 82 of these with sitting rooms. A standard single rents for 8500 pesetas ($55.25), a double for 11,000 pesetas ($71.50). All the rooms are air-conditioned. The furniture in the regular bedrooms is standard modern, with harmonious colors (such as gray and mulberry), space for lounging, and expansive marble bathrooms.

You can order a quick meal and drinks in the coffeeshop in the basement.

More from Señor Meliá—the **Meliá Castilla,** 43 Calle Capitán Haya (tel. 270-80-00), and this is a blockbuster: a mammoth hotel with 1000 rooms, it qualifies along with the already-mentioned Palace, as one of the largest hotels in Europe. Built primarily for the convention trade, it caters with grace to the needs of the individual traveler. Everything is larger than life here: indeed, you need a floor plan to direct yourself around its precincts. The lounges and corridors of pristine marble are vast, seemingly endless. As you wander around, you'll find a swimming pool, a shopping arcade, a coffeeshop, a seafood restaurant, a restaurant specializing in paella and other rice dishes, cocktail lounges, a landscaped garden, saunas, a gymnasium, a parking garage, the Trinidad nightclub, even a showroom full of the latest model cars. In addition to these features, there's the restaurant/show, Scala Meliá Castilla. You'll be charmed by the elegant decor, as well as by the scenery changes and the varying musical numbers.

As for the accommodations, each of the twin-bedded rooms comes complete with private bath, refrigerator, radio, and color TV. The specific furnishings, all in the modern Spanish idiom, vary from room to room, everything tasteful and luxurious. Double rooms range in price from 12,000 pesetas ($78) to 18,000 peseta ($117), the higher tab for "superior" accommodations. A standard single room costs 10,000 pesetas ($65). The Meliá Castilla is in a rapidly developing section in the north of Madrid.

Moderately Priced Hotels

Hotel Victoria, 7 Plaza del Angel (tel. 231-45-00), is about as important to the legends of Madrid as Manolete himself. The famous bullfighter used to stay here, giving lavish parties in one of the reception rooms, and attracting mobs in the square below when he went out on his balcony for morning coffee. Other clients have traditionally included historians, writers, and lesser bullfighters, all of whom enjoy the dozens of tapas bars in the neighborhood and the old-world charm of the ornate stone and metal façade.

The hotel was built in 1925, and named after the grandmother of the present King of Spain, Juan Carlos. Although the hotel is in a congested area in the center of Madrid, is opens onto its own little plaza, rich in tradition as a meeting place of intellectuals during the 17th century. Today the area is usually filled with flower vendors and older persons catching rays of midafternoon sun. The rooms are quite comfortable, although not lavishly furnished, and a staid but polite atmosphere prevails. The hotel often rents out its banqueting room to middle-class Spanish families for wedding receptions. Doubles here rent for 5200 pesetas ($33.80), with singles going for 3500 pesetas ($22.75).

Emperatriz, 4 López de Hoyos (tel. 413-65-11), just off the wide Paseo de la Castellana, is only a minute of so from two of Madrid's leading deluxe hotels. And although the prices have risen due to a complete overhaul, they are still considerably less than the deluxe hotels. It charges 5000 pesetas ($32.50) for a single room, 8500 pesetas ($55.25) for a double- or twin-bedded room. Each room has a private bath and air conditioning. On the premises are many facilities, including a beauty salon, barbershop, and well-upholstered lounges in which you're likely to meet fellow globe-trotting Americans. If possible, ask for a room on the eighth floor, where you'll get a private terrace. The decor in the bedrooms is a safe mixture of traditional and modern, with the primary emphasis on comfort and cleanliness. In the downstairs dining room, a set luncheon or dinner is offered for 1500 pesetas ($9.75).

Hotel Chamartín, at the Chamartín railway station (tel. 450-90-50), is a 378-room hotel rising nine stories, part of the major transportation and shopping complex in this modern train station. The owner of the hotel is Renfe, the government's railroad system, and it's operated by Entursa Hotels, which is an organization best known for deluxe "museum" hotels. Chamartín is the first of the company's budget properties.

The hotel lies a 15-minute ride from the airport and a five-minute jaunt from the city's major business and sightseeing areas.

All guest rooms are air-conditioned, featuring TV, radio, a refrigerator/bar, a private safe, and specially insulated windows for maximum quiet and privacy. Eighteen one-bedroom suites, some with balconies, are also available. Rates in the standard rooms are 5200 pesetas ($33.80) in a single, from 6800 pesetas ($44.20) in a double.

Especially oriented to the business traveler, the Chamartín offers a currency exchange, travel agency, bank, car rental, and complete communication services. A screen in the lobby posting the arrival and departure of all trains affords special convenience to the traveler.

A coffee bar serves a continental breakfast daily, and room service is also available. A choice of drinks is featured at the hotel's bar off the main lobby. Guests can dine at a variety of restaurants and snackbars in the Chamartín complex.

Among the extensive facilities and services available to hotel guests are 13 shops, four movie theaters, a roller-skating rink, a disco, and ample parking.

For more information and reservations, write Marketing Ahead, Inc., 512 Madison Ave., New York, NY 10022, or call 212/759-5170.

Gran Hotel Colón, 117-119 Avenida Doctor Esquerdo (tel. 273-59-00), provides resort-level living, but in a not terribly central sector of Madrid, west of Retiro Park. Still, it's only a few minutes by subway from the center, and it does offer comfortable yet moderately priced accommodations in one of the city's most modern hotel structures. More than half of its excellently designed bedrooms have individual balconies. To literally top everything off, there is a swimming pool on the roof, 11 stories up, where you can sunbathe with the skyline of Madrid before you. Other assets of the hotel include two dining rooms, a covered garage, and bingo.

One of the Colón's proprietors is an accomplished designer, which accounts for the unusual stained-glass windows and murals in the public rooms and the paintings by Spanish artists in the lounge. The furnishings in the rooms are all built-in; each comes with private bath and sitting area. They rent for 5500 pesetas ($35.75) for a double, 4000 pesetas ($26) for a single.

A Hotel That's an Art Gallery

El Prado, 11 Calle del Prado (tel. 429-65-31), doesn't compete with its more famous namesake, the museum, but all its art decorations are for sale. The lobby is decorated with copies of old masters and antiques, some from the antique shops for which the Calle del Prado is known. Conveniently near the Teatro Español and the American Express office, this modern, four-star hotel has 45 pleasantly furnished accommodations, many in the old style. Single rooms range in price from 5000 pesetas ($32.50); doubles, 9000 pesetas ($58.50). Downstairs is a small sitting room, also decorated with antiques, and a simple cafeteria. Incidentally, the hotel is air-conditioned and has its own parking lot, the latter a rarity in Madrid.

Residencia Bretón, 29 Bretón de los Herreros (tel. 442-83-00), is an ingratiating little modern 60-room hotel on a side street several blocks from the Paseo de la Castellana. It is well furnished with excellent reproductions of Iberian pieces. As a *residencia,* it doesn't offer a major dining room, but it does possess a little bar and breakfast room adjoining the reception lounge. Single rooms, all with bath, go for 4000 pesetas ($26). All doubles have twin beds, a complete bath, and toilet, and rent for 6500 pesetas ($42.25). All rooms have bar-refrigerators and four channels of music. Highlighting the living areas are attractive wooden beds, black wrought-iron electric fixtures, ornately designed tiled floors and baths, wall-to-wall curtains, and sitting areas. The Bretón is air-conditioned and steam-heated.

Mayorazgo, 3 Flor Baja (tel. 247-26-00), offers a warm Spanish experience. It's almost my preferred choice in the Gran Vía area, a mere fandango step away from the main boulevard. The hotel and its restaurant are owned by a Mexican family. Together they have cast their know-how, skill, and outgoing charm into the running of this hotel—a case of the New World returning to the Old, for a switch. The bedrooms are pleasant; more than half are spacious enough to offer sitting areas. Most of them have high-posted headboards, with fringed bedspreads, set on islands of Oriental rugs. Reproductions of Iberian chests and armchairs have been placed throughout. All of the rooms have private baths. The single rate is 4500 pesetas ($29.25), increasing to 6500 pesetas ($42.25) for a twin-bedded room.

Cuzco, 55 Avenida Generalísimo Franco (tel. 456-06-00), popular with businesspeople and American tour groups, lies in a new Madrid business area of big buildings, government ministries, spacious avenues, and the main Congress Hall, only 500 yards away. The Station Madrid-Paris is 1000 yards away from the Cuzco, so it's a popular, convenient address.

Now more so than ever. It has been redecorated and modernized, and it was completed in 1967, a 15-floor structure set back from Madrid's longest boulevard. The architect of the Cuzco allowed for spacious bedrooms, big enough to have a sitting area.

The decorator provided simple, but appropriately modern furnishings, patterned rugs, and left the feeling of spaciousness intact. The management supplies direct-dial phones, air conditioning, color TV, and an electronic wake-up call. A twin-bedded room with bath rents for 12,000 pesetas ($78), going for 10,000 pesetas ($65).

Classified as a *residencia,* the hotel doesn't contain a full-fledged dining room, but there is a bi-level snackbar and cafeteria. The lounge is a forest of marble pillars and leather armchairs, the ambience enhanced by contemporary oil paintings and sedate tapestries. Facilities include a free parking lot, covered garage, and a low arcade with shops, a beauty parlor, sauna, massage, gymnasium, barbershop, and haridresser plus a cocktail bar with a warm atmosphere and a cafeteria.

Hotel Claridge, 6 Plaza Conde de Casal (tel. 251-94-00), is a contemporary building beyond the Retiro Park, about five minutes from the Prado by taxi. The air-conditioned bedrooms are well organized and styled: small, compact, and coordinated furnishings and colors. The bathrooms are bright, and the tile setter was given carte blanche to make them lavish. All 150 rooms have private baths. A single rents for 3500 pesetas ($22.75), a double for 6500 pesetas ($42.25). You can take your meals in the cafeteria or just relax in the modern lounge.

Residencia Alcalá, 66 Alcalá (tel. 435-16-50), is the inspired product of four canny and artistic entrepreneurs who in 1968 created this establishment for choosy travelers. Just off Retiro Park, it offers 153 rooms with private baths and air conditioning. Good news for the lone vacationist: about half the rooms are singles, priced from 4000 pesetas ($26) to 5000 pesetas ($32.50). The rate for a double is 6000 pesetas ($39).

The room decor is especially tasteful, with bold colors. Wall-to-wall draperies, wide-striped bedcovers, tile and wood headboards, are all harmoniously coordinated. The two-level public lounge has a circular fireplace, black hood, hearth, and surrounding black leather armchairs. Other facilities include the ornate Restaurant Basque, a lower-level coffeeshop, a bright Toledo-red American bar opening off the lounge, an underground garage, plus the Mini-Club 66.

Residencia Liabeny, 3 Salud (tel. 232-53-06), is yet another demonstration of Spain's almost instinctive talent for creating comfortable 20th-century hotels that please fastidious travelers. It's in a prime location between the Gran Vía and the Puerta del Sol. Distributed among seven floors are well-maintained, air-conditioned bedrooms. In a single, the rate is 5000 pesetas ($32.50) nightly, 8500 pesetas ($55.25) in a double, including a continental breakfast. The bedrooms have an English touch, with mahogany furniture, wall-to-wall draperies, lounge chairs, and desks, as well as private entryways.

The Budget Range

Anaco, 3 Tres Cruces (tel. 222-46-04), is a modestly modern 37-bedroom hotel, just off the shopping thoroughfare, Gran Vía. Opening onto a tree-shaded plaza, it attracts those seeking a resting place featuring contemporary appurtenances and cleanliness. The bedrooms are charmingly compact, with built-in headboards, reading lamps, and lounge chairs. Each room is individually air-conditioned and contains a private bath (some with showers). The maximum rate for a single with bath is 4000 pesetas ($26). In a double room, the rate is 6500 pesetas ($42.25). Useful tip: Ask for one of the five terraced double rooms on the top floor renting at no extra charge. English is spoken. Nearby is a municipally operated garage.

Aristos, 34 Avenida Pío XII (tel. 457-04-50), is a 25-room, three-star hotel in an upcoming residential area of Madrid, not far from the Eurobuilding. Its main advantage is a pleasant garden in front, where you can lounge, have a drink, or order a complete meal. In addition, there's a small swimming pool in back for those torrid days. The rooms come with terraces and are decorated with modern decor. Singles cost 4500 pesetas ($29.25); doubles, 6500 pesetas ($42.25).

Tirol, 4 Marqués de Urquijo (tel. 248-19-00), a short walk from the Plaza de España and the swank Meliá Madrid, is a good choice. A three-star hotel, it offers singles for 3000 pesetas ($19.50), doubles for 4500 pesetas ($29.95). Eight of the 100 rooms contain terraces. Furnishings are simple and functional, somewhat characterless and old-fashioned, but adequate. In the cafeteria downstairs you can order a snack or light meal. There's also a garage in the building.

Hostal Embajada, 5 Calle Santa Engracía (tel. 447-33-00), is a clean, pleasant three-star hotel about one block from the Plaza Alonso Martínez, a rather distinguished residential area. Still standing across the street is a great 19th-century palace. The Embajada has 84 rooms, and doubles with bath cost 4500 pesetas ($29.25). Singles go for 3500 pesetas ($22.75). You'll find the bedrooms tastefully decorated and the bathrooms modern. There's a modest lounge but no bar.

Hotel Mercátor, 123 Atocha (tel. 429-05-00), only about a three-minute stroll from the Prado draws a clientele seeking a good, modern hotel—orderly, well run, and clean, with enough comforts and conveniences to please the weary traveler. Some of the rooms are more inviting than others, especially those with desks and armchairs. Color is often utilized effectively. The best

> ### Nostalgia Along Old Gran Vía
>
> **Lope de Vega,** 59 Gran Vía (tel. 247-70-00). Despite its commercial location between shops on the main street of Madrid, this is a charmer of enduring appeal to traditionalists in pursuit of fast-fading, old-world atmosphere in the city. A small elevator lifts you to this three-star hotel managed by English-speaking Enrique Luís Indeguy Olivar and named after the great Spanish dramatist. Wood paneling, red velvet, and antiques evoke the ambience of a city clubroom. The bedrooms, each one different, are well maintained and comfortable, although slightly dated. Each has a private bath. The most expensive single costs 2200 pesetas ($14.30), peaking at 3500 pesetas ($22.75) in a double. You can sit in the lobby of the hotel, looking out onto a view of the royal palace. Only breakfast is served.

twin-bedded rooms with private bath rent for 5000 pesetas ($32.50). Singles peak at 3600 pesetas ($23.40). The Mercátor is a *residencia*—that is, it offers breakfast only. However, it has a bar and cafeteria serving light meals such as *platos combinados* (combination plates). Happily, the hotel has a garage, and is within walking distance of the Iberia air terminal and American Express.

Hotel Francisco I, 15 Arenal (tel. 248-43-14), offers 57 modern, clean rooms. Doubles with a shower-bath (sit-down tub) range from 4500 pesetas ($29.25). Singles—only four in this category—with similar baths go for 2800 pesetas ($18.20). There's a pleasant if aseptic, lounge, a bar, Muzak, and on the sixth floor you'll find a comfortable, rustic-style restaurant where a set meal costs 1200 pesetas ($7.80). Unfortunately, there's no view, but the spacious dining room is pleasantly decorated, nonetheless.

Hotel Nuria, 52 Fuencarral (tel. 231-92-08), just three blocks from the Gran Vía, has some bedrooms with especially interesting views of the capital. Completely renovated in the late '60s, the 58-room pension offers double rooms with private bath or shower for 3500 pesetas ($22.75), breakfast included. The most expensive singles, with breakfast, rent for 2000 pesetas ($13). The food is highly praised by those who have sampled it. The price of a complete luncheon or dinner is 1000 pesetas ($6.50).

Chapter XII

LATE DINING IN MADRID

AT BEST, THE CUISINE of Spain is controversial. It inspires some to unqualified praise, others to fulmination.

The kitchen, or kitchens, of Spain turn out a pungent, varied, and imaginative fare, ranging from squid cooked in its own ink to Valencian paella to Andalusian gazpacho to grilled pink prawns to garlic soup (said to have powers of longevity) to the tail of a bull.

For the versatile, adventurous diner, there is no problem. If you fall into that category, you're in luck, with loads of temptation—such as *anguilas* (baby eels)—waiting to lure you. Still, if you grow faint at the mention of creatures from the deep, never fear. The chefs of Spain, now more so than ever, are prepared to accommodate you with what has come to be known as an "international" cuisine.

Whether you're an epicurean of the caliber of Lucullus or the possessor of a milquetoast palate, you should not rush too rapidly into the Spanish cuisine. If you overindulge in the dishes cooked in olive oil and the wines called "noble" but strong, chances are you'll come down with that traditional tourist malady euphemistically known as "Toledo tummy."

If you don't like garlic, instruct your waiter *(camarero)*. If he or she doesn't speak English, say: "No *ajo* " (pronounced ah-ho). The word for butter is *mantequilla*. Of course, many dishes of combined ingredients such as paella or gazpacho depend on garlic for their basic flavor.

LIQUID SALAD AND AROMATIC PAELLA: All the major Spanish cuisines, ranging from Galician and Asturian to Basque (the Basques are said to be the best cooks) to Andalusian and Levantine, are represented in Madrid, along with the traditional Castilian cuisine, which predominates.

Two of the best known specialties, the *paella* of Valencia and the "liquid salad" or *gazpacho* of Andalusia, need little introduction, as they are served in North America and throughout continental Europe. Both items vary greatly, depending on the skill of the chef and the quality of ingredients used.

At its worst, paella—the Spanish rice dish—is made with whatever leftovers the chef has salvaged from the night before. At its finest, it is cooked with such well-chosen items as tender chicken, artichoke hearts, prawns, clams, bits of sausage, peas, garlic, pimientos—all aromatically seasoned and served on saffron rice. Traditionally, the paella is then presented to you in a piping-hot black iron skillet.

Gazpacho is especially good in summer. Ideally, it should be chilled thoroughly, in the tradition of vichyssoise. Basically, it is a soup of olive oil, vinegar, garlic, fresh tomatoes, with cucumber, peppers, croutons, and raw onions. Another soup in which the Spaniards excel is *sopa de pescado,* literally "soup of fish," again made in infinite varieties from province to province, but usually a taste treat worthy of featuring on any menu.

SUCKLING PIG AND A ZARZUELA: One of the most exciting taste treats of Spain originates in the province of Segovia. It is the roast suckling pig, so beloved by Hemingway at his Casa Botín in Madrid. Called *cochinillo asado,* it is a rich-tasting banquet—and so is the price. At its finest, the suckling pig is tender enough to be carved with china. Roast lamb *(cordero asado)* also draws many admirers. Otherwise, meat dishes, especially beef, sometimes disappoint North Americans used to finer cuts.

In their fish dishes, the Spaniards are quite remarkable and most inventive. Thanks to speedy transportation facilities, inland cities such as Madrid receive daily supplies of fresh fish. Mountain river trout *(trucha)* is superb, as is the paralyzingly priced lobster *(langosta).* A great fish dish is *zarzuela de mariscos,* with hunks of prawn, lobster, and other shellfish.

MEET THE "MENÚ DEL DÍA": The fixed-price *menú turistico* is no longer enforced. However, most restaurants feature a *menú del día.* The principle behind this set meal is to give a tourist (or a Spaniard, if he or she so desires) a complete meal, including soup or hors d'oeuvres, a meat or fish dish, plus dessert, a small carafe of the house wine, service, and taxes—all for one standard charge.

Now for my specific restaurant recommendations:

The Leading Restaurants

Jockey, 6 Amador de los Ríos (tel. 419-24-35), is considered by many to be the finest restaurant in Spain. At any rate, it is the favorite of international celebrities, diplomats, and heads of state, and some of the more faithful patrons look upon it as their own private club.

The restaurant, with tables on two levels, isn't overly large. Wood-paneled walls and colored linen provide autumnal warmth. Against the paneling are a dozen prints of horses mounted by jockeys—hence the name of the place. Reservations are necessary. If you go early—1:30 p.m. or 9:30 p.m.—you'll stand a better chance of getting a table. You'll also have the dining room virtually to yourself.

If you'd like your decisions made for you, two or more persons can order a "Special Menu," which is changed monthly. My most recent sampling of this menu began with sweetbreads in a puff pastry (perfumed with truffles) and went on to partridge and ended with a cold mandarin soufflé, among other courses.

The chef is always coming up with new dishes, including smoked Asturias salmon, sea bass in papillote, smoked eel mousse with sardines, Aranjuez pheasant in grape sauce, and deboned duck with figs in wine. The cost of a meal here will begin at 6000 pesetas ($39), going up. The restaurant is open daily, except Sunday, although it closes during the entire month of August.

Horcher, 6 Alfonso XII (tel. 222-07-31). A so-called global gourmet once wrote of this restaurant, "Dishes that enchanted the Kronprinzes of another period, now captivate the cosmopolitan bons vivants of the Jet Age." Herr Horcher created the restaurant in Berlin in 1904, winning the Grand Prix in Paris in 1937. In a sudden move, Horcher went to Madrid in 1943, and has continued in the same grand tadition. Many Germans make the pilgrimage to Madrid just to sample some of the classic dishes.

A jacket and a tie are imperative—as is a reservation. Your best chance of getting a seat is to go early. The restaurant is open daily from noon to 4 p.m. and from 8 p.m. till midnight (closed Sunday). The service is excellent indeed.

Where to start? If you're flush, try the seafood mousse. Wild duck salad also attains distinction. Both the venison stew in green pepper with orange peel and the crayfish with parsley and cucumber are excellent. Other main courses include veal scalloppine in tarragon. For dessert, the house specialty is crêpes Sir Holden, prepared at your table, with fresh raspberries, cream, and nuts, or you may prefer a Sachertorte. Expect to spend from 5000 pesetas ($32.50), plus wine.

Rue Royale, Villa Magna Hotel, 22 Paseo de la Castellana (tel. 261-49-00). This glamorous restaurant is joined to the most deluxe hotel in Madrid. A talented French decorator created an atmosphere appropriate to the excellently prepared viands. The appointments are rich and sumptuous: red velvet, gilt, loads of crystal. Beginning with the Limoges plate placed before you, the table appointments are faultless.

Recommended to first-time visitors for an opener is the onion-soup gratinée. Among the house specialties is a plate of the filets of sole Rue Royale or pepper steak. After the richness, you can retreat to the Tulipe Villa Magna. Meals cost 5000 pesetas ($32.50) and up.

Zalacaín, 4 Álvarez de Baena (tel. 261-48-40), is outstanding both in food and decor. It's reached by an illuminated walk from the Paseo de la Castellana, housed at the garden end of a modern apartment complex. In fact, it's within an easy walk of such deluxe hotels as the Luz Palacio, the Castellana, and the Miguel Angel. It's small, exclusive, and expensive. In an atmosphere of quiet refinement, you can peruse the menu, perhaps at the rust-toned bar. Walls are covered with textiles, and some are decorated with Audubon-type paintings. The menu is interesting and varied, often with nouvelle cuisine touches, along with many Basque and French specialties. It might offer sole in a green sauce, a superb dish, but it also knows the glory of grilled pigs' feet. Among the most recommendable main dishes are steak with a béarnaise sauce, veal escalopes in orange sauce, and guinea fowl. Appetizers are tempting as well—oxtail soup, chef's pâté, and smoked fish crêpes. For desserts, I'd suggest a sorbet or crêpes Zalacaín style. Depending on what you order, many tabs climb as high as 5000 pesetas ($32.50). The management runs the restaurant with a velvet hand. The Zalacaín is closed on Saturday afternoon, on Sunday, and during the entire month of August.

Other Top Restaurants

El Bodegón, 15 Calle Pinar (tel. 262-31-37), is imbued with the atmosphere of a gentleman's club for hunting enthusiasts—in the country-inn style. Many of its discriminating clientele number it among the top four or five restaurants in Madrid. International globe-trotters are attracted here, especially in the evening, as the restaurant is near three deluxe hotels, the Castellana, the Miguel Angel, and the Luz Palacio. At lunch, you're likely to find men only. King Juan Carlos and Queen Sofia have dined here.

Waiters in black and white, with gold braid and buttons, bring dignity to the food service. Even bottled water is served champagne style, chilled in a silver floor stand. There are two main dining rooms—conservative, oak-beamed.

The following à la carte suggestions are recommended to launch your meal: cream of crayfish bisque or a cold, velvety vichyssoise. Main-course selections include grilled filet mignon with classic béarnaise sauce or venison à la bourguignonne. Other main-course selections include shellfish au gratin Escoffier, quails Fernand-Point, and salmon smoked by the chef. For dessert, try homemade apple pie. A complete meal here is likely to cost from 3500 pesetas ($22.75) to 5000 pesetas ($32.50).

Los Porches, 1 Paseo Pintor Rosales (tel. 247-70-53), is open all year in a garden setting next to an Egyptian temple, the Templo de Debod, which once stood in the Nile Valley. Because of the Aswan Dam project, it was dismantled and shipped stone by stone as a gift to Madrid, where it was reassembled. The menu at Los Porches is typically and elaborately gourmet, in the tradition of many of Madrid's finest restaurants, including such savory viands as roast quail with grapes, or duck with pears and prunes. The roast baby lamb is also recommendable. The lobster soup is the best; the lemon tart, the perfect finish. Expect to pay from 3500 pesetas ($22.75) to 4000 pesetas ($26) for a complete meal.

La Bola, 5 Bola (tel. 247-69-30), just north of the Te Teatro Real. If you'd like to savor the Madrid of the 19th century, then this *taberna* is an inspired choice. It's one of the few restaurants (if not the only one) left in Madrid that's painted with a blood-red façade. Once, nearly all fasshionable restaurants were so coated. La Bola hangs on to tradition like a tenacious bull. Time has galloped forward, but not inside this restaurant, where the soft, traditional atmosphere, the gentle and polite waiters, and the Venetian crystal, the Carmen-red draperies, and the aging

> ### A "Clockwork Orange" Decor
> **Ruperto do Nola,** 2 Corazón de María (tel. 416-45-67), is named
> after Philip II's chef. The most spectacular thing about it is that it's
> perched on the 21st floor of the Torres Blancas apartment house, a
> controversial building whose apartments are among the costliest in
> the city. It's a weird, updated, Gaudí-like structure, reminding some
> critics of Kubrick's *Clockword Orange* decor. The view is spectacular.
> You sit under sagging *Yellow Submarine* ceilings in roomy and circular
> chambers (there isn't a straight line in the whole building). The food
> is standard international cuisine, although well done. You may select
> baked turbot, grilled sea bass, or tournedos, among other main
> dishes. Desserts include bananas flambés and soufflés. An average
> meal will run from 2000 pesetas ($13) to 3000 pesetas ($19.50). The
> restaurant is closed on Sunday and from July 24 until September 4.
> You can see the Torres Blancas on the way from the airport.

velvet preserve the 1870 ambience of the place. Ava Gardner, with her entourage of bullfighters, used to patronize this establishment, but that was long ago before La Bola became so well known to tourists.

A specialty is the sopa Wamba, which is soothing to those who have had too much rich fare, made as it is with ham and rice in a broth over which chopped hard-boiled eggs are sprinkled. The roast chicken *(pollo asado)* is always reliable as is the sole *(lenguado)* menuière. Depending on your selections, the cost of a complete meal ranges in price from 1200 pesetas ($7.80) to 2000 pesetas ($13.)

El Mesón de San Jávier, 3 Calle del Conde (tel. 248-09-25), has a long history going back to the 16th century, during which period it was owned by a secretary to Philip II. Bandits, musicians, and composers of famous zarzuelas met here under the tavern's various ownerships. Clients of yore have included Ava Gardner and Frank Sinatra, but today you are more likely to see the present king and queen of Spain.

The walls are dotted with various food awards, unusual artifacts, hand-painted pottery, and an antique rifle. The restaurant's owner, Denis, used to direct glamorous dining rooms in such places as Paris, Biarritz, and Argentina. His specialties include tender duckling served with chestnuts and applesauce, roast suckling pig, and lamb and beef dishes. For an appetizer, try one of his shrimp-stuffed avocados, and, for dessert, one of various tempting concoctions, including raspberry crêpes.

The service is first rate, and your meal is likely to be accompanied by music from a group of strolling minstrels known as "La Tuna." Expect to pay around 2500 pestas ($16.25) if you order the more expensive à la carte items; however, it's possible to dine here for around 1200 pesetas ($7.80) by sticking to the menu of the day.

The well-concealed restaurant may be difficult to find, as it's down a flight of steps off the Calle Sacramento, near the Puerta Cerrado.

El Pescador, 75 José Ortega y Gasset (tel. 401-30-26), is a simple fish restaurant which has become a favorite of the Madrileños who appreciate the more than 30 kinds of fish which are prominently displayed in a glass case. Many of these are unknown in North America, and many originate from off the coast of Galicia. Management air-freights them in, and prefers to serve them grilled (*à la plancha*).

You might precede your main course with a spicy fish soup, and accompany it with one of the many good wines served from Northeast Spain. If you're not sure of what to order (even the English translations might sound unfamiliar), try one of the many varieties and sizes of shrimp. These go under the name of *langostinos, cigalas, santiaguinos,* and *carabineros.* Many of them are expensive and priced by the gram, so be careful when you order. Expect to spend around 3000 pesetas ($19.50) per person. Closed Sunday and during all of August.

Lhardy, 8 Carrera de San Jerónimo (tel. 221-33-85), opened its doors in 1839. I'm told the food served today isn't as good as back then, but there's really no one around to verify that claim. This is a place with a great tradition as a gathering place of Madrid's literati, its political leaders, and the better-heeled members of the city's business community. Your consommé is likely to be presented in cups from a large silver samovar, if you drink it in the ground-floor tea room. This adjoins a deli shop, where you can buy some of the delicacies you tasted at the bar or in the restaurant upstairs. There, the decor, known as "Isabella Segundo," gives off a definite aura of another era. Specialties of the house include an excellent roast beef and a *cocido,* the celebrated stew of Madrid. This might be served with a selection from the extensive wine cellar. Meals range from around 3000 pesetas ($19.50). It is open daily except Sunday with dinner served until 11 p.m. (closed from the last week in July until around mid-September).

Basque Specialties
(Moderate)

Alkalde, 10 Jorge Juan (tel. 276-33-59), has been known for decades for serving top-quality Spanish food in an old tavern setting. It's decorated like a Basque inn, with beamed ceilings and hams hanging from the rafters. The gambas à la plancha (grilled shrimp) is excellent, but you may prefer the cigalas (crayfish). Another fish dish is mero salsa verde (that is, brill in a green sauce). Two other well-recommended main dishes include trout Alkalde and chicken steak Alkalde. The dessert specialty is a copa Cardinal. For around 3500 pesetas ($22.75) and up, you can enjoy a very satisfying meal.

Upstairs is a large, *típico* tavern. Downstairs is a maze of caves, pleasantly cool in the summer, although the whole place is air-conditioned anyway. The service is fast, efficient, and friendly. It's closed Saturday night and Sunday.

Best for Seafood

O'Pazo, 20 Reina Mercedes (tel. 254-90-72), is a super-deluxe Galician restaurant, considered by the local cognoscenti as one of the top seafood places in the country. The fish is flown in daily from Galicia. It is decorated in a chic, tasteful style for the distinguished clientele it caters to. In front is a cocktail lounge and bar, all in polished brass, with low sofas and paintings—in all, the feel of a private seignorial living room. The restaurant has carpeted floors, cushioned Castilian furniture, soft lighting, and colored-glass windows.

Most diners begin with assorted smoked fish or fresh oysters. The house specialty is hake Galician style, but you may prefer the sea bass, baked in the oven, and served with a mustard sauce. O'Pazo sole is also recommended. Your tab for a full meal is likely to be about 4000 pesetas ($26). It is closed on Sunday and in August.

Bajamar, 78 Gran Vía (tel. 248-59-03), is one of the best fish houses in Spain, and it's right in the heart of the city, near the Plaza de España. The fish is shipped in fresh daily, although it carries very expensive tabs, especially if you order lobster, king crab, prawns, and soft-shell crabs, all priced according to weight. However, there is a large array of reasonably priced dishes as well. The setting is contemporary and attractive, and the service is smooth and professional. The menu is in English. For an appetizer, I'd recommend half a dozen giant oysters or half a dozen rover crayfish. The special seafood soup is a most satisfying selection, a meal in itself. Try also the lobster bisque. Some of the more recommendable main courses include turbot Gallego style, the special seafood paella, even baby squid cooked in its ink. Desserts are simple, including the chef's custard. Seafood dinners begin at 4500 pesetas ($29.25).

For Valencian Paella
(Moderate)

La Barraca, 29-31 Reina (tel. 232-71-54). Like a country inn —right off the Gran Vía—this Valencian-style restaurant is a four-fork establishment recommendable for its tasty provincial cooking. There are eight dining rooms, all on different levels, and they're colorfully cluttered with ceramics, paintings, photographs, Spanish lanterns, flowers, and local artifacts. The house specialty is paella à la Valenciana, made with fresh shellfish. The portions are enormous—only the most ravenous will clean out the skillet. Other recommendable main dishes include roast suckling pig and the roast leg of lamb. The sorbet makes a good finish. A complete meal will cost about 2500 pesetas ($16.25).

Dining in Old Madrid
(Budget to Moderate)

Right on or near a corner of the historic and immense square, the **Plaza Mayor,** are clustered fine typical restaurants and taverns, as well as *tascas,* all of which quickly capture the spirit of Madrid's colorful past. No matter which restaurant you favor with your patronage, you're likely to be entertained by the strolling bands of *tuna,* students dressed in Castilian capes with ribbons fluttering, guitars by their sides and tambourines for after-the-songfest collections.

The **Mesón del Corregidor,** 8 Plaza Mayor (tel. 266-30-24), shares the best vantage point on the Hapsburg plaza. Tables are set out in fair weather, providing an unobstructed view of the entire square. Flowers are placed on the tables, the lighting is soft—an ideal background for an operetta scene. In winter, you enter first a *típico tasca,* with hanging smoked hams, wagon-wheel chandeliers, vintage wine bottles, wrought iron, and ceramics. It's a well-tended slice of the past, with stone and

Hemingway's Roast Suckling Pig

Sobrino de Botín, 17 Calle de Cuchilleros (tel. 266-42-17). ". . .I would rather dine on suckling pig at Botín's than sit and think of casualties my friends have suffered," Ernest Hemingway told his mythical "Old Lady" in *Death in the Afternoon.* For countless thousands of Americans, Papa made Botín famous. In the final two pages of his novel *The Sun Also Rises,* he had Jake invite Brett there for the Segovian specialty, washed down with Rioja Alta.

By merely entering its portals, you step back to 1725, the year the restaurant was founded. You'll see an open kitchen, with a charcoal hearth, hanging copper pots, an 18th-century tiled oven for roasting the suckling pig, and a big pot of regional soup, the aroma wafting across the tables. The dining tables sit under time-aged beams—the wall literally covered with a mishmash collection of photographs, engravings, paintings, and bullfight memorabilia. Your host, Don António, never loses his cool—even when he has 18 guests standing in line waiting for tables.

The *menú de la casa* is priced in autumn and winter at 2500 pesetas ($16.25). The two house specialties are roast suckling pig and roast Segovian lamb. From the à la carte menu, costing from 3500 pesetas ($22.75), you might try the "quarter-of-an-hour" soup, made with fish. Good main dishes include the baked Cantabrian hake and filet mignon with potatoes. The dessert list features strawberries (in season) with whipped cream. For only 200 pesetas ($1.30), you can wash down your meal with Valdepeñas or Aragón wine, although most guests order sangría, 350 pesetas ($2.28).

cobbled floors, stained glass, and a fireplace. The honeycombed *cuevas* are downstairs. The specialty of the house is a shellfish paella for two persons. The chef also prepares a succulent, spicy roast suckling pig. Other typical dishes include baby eels, hake wrapped in ham, and tripe Madrid style. For 2500 pesetas ($16.25) to 3000 pesetas ($19.50), you can enjoy a complete meal.

Right down the steps is the even better known **Las Cuevas de Luís Candelas,** 1 Cuchilleros (tel. 266-54-28). It is entered through a doorway under an arcade on the steps leading down to the Calle de Cuchilleros, the nighttime street of Madrid, teeming with restaurants, flamenco clubs, and rustic taverns. The restaurant is named after the legendary Luís Candelas, a bandit of the 18th-century—sometimes known as "the Spanish

Robin Hood." He is said to have hidden out in this maze of *cuevas*. Although the menu is in English (the restaurant is very "touristy"), the cuisine is authentically Spanish. Specialties include the chef's own style hake. To begin your meal, another house dish—for garlic lovers only—is sopa de ajo Candelas, a garlic soup. Roast suckling pig and roast lamb, as in the other restaurants on the Plaza Mayor, are the featured specialties. This one can be expensive, with meals averaging from 2500 pesetas ($16.25) to 4000 pesetas ($26).

Typically Spanish Fare
(Budget)

El Callejón, 6 Ternera (tel. 231-91-95), off the Calle Preciados, was Hemingway's "other favorite." In fact, when a close friend was leaving Madrid, Papa recommended that he look at some canvases at the Prado, then take his "last supper" at Callejón. The restaurant honors its former patron with a picture of the author in the front dining room, along with excerpts from his writings. El Callejón is popular, crowded, animated—and it manages to serve some of the tastiest dishes in Madrid. It's on a narrow street in the midst of houses with grilled windows.

A three-course *menú de día*, complete with service and a ceramic pitcher of the regional wine, costs 1500 pesetas ($9.75). House specialties include (in season) eels Bilbao style, and you can order shrimp, also in the Bilbao style, as an appetizer. Among the main courses recommended is a veal stew served on Tuesday and Saturday. Many go here for the red beans with rice, real Spanish soul food. It's served only on Thursday. Recommendable main dishes include the special steak and calf's sweetbreads. For dessert, try either the cherries with fresh cream or two fried bananas. You'll pay from 1800 pesetas ($11.70) to 2500 pesetas ($16.25) for a full à la carte meal.

Mesón das Meigas, 6 Barbieri (tel. 221-07-57), is like a Galician country tavern, perched on a crowded noisy street of lively *tascas*, restaurants, and flamenco clubs. Out front is a *tasca*, decorated with hanging smoked hams, garlic "pigtails," and other goodies. In the beamed dining room in the back is a fireplace.

You sit on handmade chairs, against a decorative motif of Spanish farming implements: ox yokes, hay rakes, hunting guns. The cooking is hearty and provincial, without overtures to city sophistication. On the à la carte menu, the favored opener is

> ### The Cheapest Restaurant in the World
>
> The least expensive meal in Madrid is offered at **El Criollo,** 21 Barbiei, which is probably the cheapest restaurant in the world. For 300 pesetas ($1.95)—repeat, 300 pesetas—you are served paella, beefsteak, or veal (potatoes with everything), plus fruitcake or rice pudding. Three-quarters of a liter of country wine goes for an extra 75 pesetas (49¢). Although the tables evoke the cafeteria atmosphere of a dormitory, El Criollo is not at all institutional. It is run by a remarkable man of private enterprise, Alejandro Yubero. An avid fisherman, the good señor also owns a farm, which supplies a great deal of the produce for his now famous little restaurant. Hours are from 1 to 4 p.m., and 8 p.m. to midnight.

caldo gallego, a soup of greens and potatoes. The house specialty —rugged fare—is lacón con grelos, leg of pork with turnip greens. And, with your meal, you can order the sangría, served in a ceramic jug. One reader recommends the mariscada special, which can be served for two, four, or six persons. It is a huge plate of shellfish, containing not only the familiar shrimp but also, in the words of the reader, some "ye-gods!-what-in-the-world-is-this?" If you order à la carte, a dinner will cost from 2000 pesetas ($13).

The Foreign Colony

Once upon a time, a foreign restaurant was hard to find in Madrid. It seemed the Spanish were perfectly content with their own cuisine. However, in recent decades a noticeable change has occurred. For change-of-pace dining, today's restaurant shopper will find a fair selection of German, Italian, Chinese, French, Mexican, even Argentine and Japanese establishments. You'll even find American food, for a change of pace.

Edelweiss, 7 Jovellanos, is a German standby that has provided good-quality food and service at moderate prices since the war. You are served hearty portions of food, mugs of draft beer, and fluffy pastries. That's why there's always a wait at lunch and dinner. Tip: To beat the crowds, go for dinner at un-Spanish hours, say around 8 or 9 when tables are not at a premium. But even when it's jammed, service is almost always friendly and courteous. You can start with Bismarck herring, then dive into goulash with spätzle, or eisbein with sauerkraut and mashed

The Best Steaks in Madrid

Casa Paco, 11 Puerto Cerrada (tel. 266-31-66). Madrileños defiantly name Casa Paco when someone has the "nerve" to put down Spanish steaks. They know that here you can get the thickest, juiciest, most flavorsome steaks in Spain—and at half the price you'd pay in Chicago. Señor Paco reigns at the chopping block. His face breaks into a multitude of smiles when guests display their pleasure at his thick steaks, charcoal grilled for that home-on-the-range flavor. The tourist menu is 1000 pesetas ($6.50), but the reason most people come here is to order one of the deliciously thick steaks, priced according to weight, and served sizzling hot on a wooden board.

In the Old Town, the two-story restaurant offers three dining rooms, and reservations are imperative. Otherwise, you face a long wait, which you can while away sampling the *tapas* (hors d' oeuvres) in the *tasca* in front. Around the walls are autographed photographs of such notables as Frank Sinatra. You could order the roast lamb or a simple roast chicken, but steaks are really the thing here. A typical meal will run about 2500 pesetas ($16.25).

potatoes, the most popular dish at the restaurant. Finish with the homemade apple tart. A complete meal is likely to cost from 1800 pesetas ($11.70) to 3000 pesetas ($19.50). The decor is vaguely German, with travel posters and wood-paneled walls. It's air-conditioned in summer, but closes in August and always on Sunday.

A popular hangout for locals and visiting Yanks is **Hollywood,** 1 Calle Magallanes (tel. 448-91-65). It's a California-style hamburger extravaganza, a fashionable place to eat and be seen, serving, according to many travelers, "the best American food in Europe." It is owned and operated by an American couple from Detroit. Outside, you can sit in a director's chair on the terrace, with the name of a movie star on the back. You will find this one of the most comfortable and best people-watching sites in Madrid, while you enjoy sangría or your back-home favorite beverage. Inside, it's nostalgia time, with bentwood chairs and many framed photographs and posters. Some Spaniards have encountered problems in eating the hamburgers, as indeed would anyone not familiar with devouring food five inches high. Hamburgers weigh in at one-half pound, and they vary from simple and unadorned to one with cheese, bacon strips, and Russian dressing. They are served with french fries and salad. Other Stateside treats are chili con carne, homemade apple pie, cheesecake, and, as once reported in the *New York Times,* "probably the best onion rings in the world." Tabs begin at 1200 pesetas ($7.80).

The same food is also available at Hollywood's other locations at 3 Apolonia Morales (tel. 457-79-11) in the Castellana area near the Eurobuilding and Meliá Castilla hotels, and at 1 Tamayo y Baus (tel. 231-51-15) close to Plaza de Cibeles and the Prado.

Casablanca, 29 Calle del Barquillo (tel. 231-12-47), named after the famous movie whose principal role was rejected by Ronald Reagan, is a multi-level restaurant within walking distance of the Gran Vía and the Prado. A reader, Donald C. Hegebarth, discovered it for me. The walls of the restaurant are decorated with cinematic blowups of Bogart and Bergman emoting with one another in scenes from the cult film. An international cuisine served at the umbrella-covered tables is a combination of northern Spanish, continental, and Japanese. The personable owner is Dick Angstadt, an American. The restaurant is open every day from 1:30 to 4 p.m and from 8:30 p.m. to 12:30 a.m. (till 1 a.m. on weekends), charging around 2000 pesetas ($13) and up for an average meal.

Hostería Piamontesa, 18 Costanilla de Los Angeles (tel. 248-34-14), is my recommendation for those seeking good, rib-sticking Italian cooking.

Although there is a menu of the day for 1200 pesetas ($7.80), you'd be better advised to order à la carte, paying about 1800 pesetas ($11.70) for a meal. For an appetizer, try the stracciatella or perhaps a shrimp cocktail. Main-course specialties include lasagne and saltimbocca à la Romana. The pasta is homemade. With main platters, the waitresses bring an accompaniment of five vegetables. For dessert, I'd suggest the zuppa inglese. The restaurant, regrettably, is closed in August and on Monday.

Kuopin Restaurante Chino, 6 Valverde (tel. 232-34-65), is an interesting Chinese restaurant, only 100 long strides from the busy Gran Vía. It's approached through a long hallway in an old Madrid building. Inside you'll find the the usual Chinese decor with large lanterns. Many of your fellow diners will be Chinese, a fairly good gauge of authenticity and value. The chef offers a special budget dinner for 550 pesetas ($3.58), including, for example, egg drop soup, sweet-and-sour pork, and ice cream with walnuts. Bread and a beverage are included. À la carte temptations are sweet corn, egg, and chicken soup, Cantonese shrimp, and roast pork, Cantonese style. You can expect to pay about 1200 pesetas ($7.80) for a complete à la carte dinner. Kuopin is open from noon to 4 p.m. and from 8 p.m. to midnight.

Chez Lou, 6 Pedro Maguruza (tel. 250-34-16), near the Euro-building Hotel in the northern sector of Madrid, stands near the huge mural by Joan Miró, which alone would be worth the trek up here.

In this intimate setting, you get well-prepared and reasonably priced French food. The restaurant serves pâté as an appetizer, then a large range of crêpes with many different fillings. Folded envelope style, the crêpes are not tea-room size, and they're perfectly adequate as a main course. I've sampled several variations on the crêpe theme, finding the ingredients nicely blended yet distinct enough to retain their identity. A favorite is the large crêpe stuffed with minced onions, cream, and smoked salmon. The ham and cheese is also tasty. Crêpes cost from 750 pesetas ($4.58) up, and the price of your dessert and drink is extra.

Come here if you're seeking a light supper when it's too hot for one of those table-groaning Spanish meals. Chez Lou opens at 7 p.m. for dinner, which is wildly early for Madrid, and it also serves lunch except on Saturday. It closes up completely on Monday.

Light Fare

Ríofrío, Centro Colón, 1 Plaza Colón (tel. 419-29-77), where you can pause to refresh, is an ideal, central place for on-the-run snacks and drinks. Its terrace, overlooking the Columbus Circle of Madrid, is favored on sunny days. Otherwise, there is a more formal interior restaurant where you can get more substantial meals, as well as a self-service section. For snacks count on spending from 1000 pesetas ($6.50) up.

Cafeteria California, 49 Gran Vía (tel. 247-27-30), is a base for visitors as well as for the smart young Madrileño seeking "exotic" tastes. The California, a chain of cafeterias, caters to the ever-growing need to satisfy a taste for derivative dishes from the United States—milkshakes, cheeseburgers, club sandwiches. You can also order pancakes with caramel syrup and whipped cream. Other California Cafeterias are at 39 Gran Vía (tel. 232-35-72) and at 21 Salud (tel. 222-61-60). A meal costs from 1800 pesetas ($11.70) to 2500 pesetas ($16.25) here. Most chain members are open from 8 a.m. to 1:30 a.m.

Chapter XIII

THE ATTRACTIONS OF MADRID

TOURIST OFFICIALS in Madrid often confide, "We spend so much fuss to get people to visit Madrid. But when we get them here, and they've seen the Prado, and a bullfight, we send them off to El Escorial or Toledo."

Too true—and regrettably so, as Madrid is filled with many nuggets for the digger willing to pan for them.

As European capitals go, Madrid is hard to know. Her mainstream attractions—tree-shaded parks, wide *paseos,* bubbling fountains, the art treasures of the Prado—are obvious. And, of course, it is this Madrid that the routine visitor sees quickly before striking out on his next adventure, usually to one of the satellites such as Segovia.

But for the more determined traveler, willing to invest the time and stamina, the Spanish capital tucks away many hidden treasures behind her fan, discreetly revealing them to the courtier of her choice.

This grande dame of Spain is well worth the pursuit.

I don't believe in saving the best for last, so I'll lead off with:

SPAIN'S GREATEST MUSEUM—THE PRADO: A. E. Hotchner wrote of "Papa Hemingway": "Ernest loved the Prado. He entered it as he entered cathedrals." More than any other, one picture held him transfixed, "the girl whom he had loved longer than any other woman in his life," Hotchner relates—Andrea del Sarto's *Portrait of a Woman.*

The late American author wasn't alone in his passionate devotion to the Prado. Numerous citizens of Madrid go once or twice a month every month of their lives just to gaze upon their particular favorites (the reproductions at home are never adequate).

But the first-time visitor, with less than a lifetime to spend, will have to limit his viewing. That task is difficult, as the Prado owns more than 3000 paintings and is ranked among the top three art museums of the world.

In an 18th-century neoclassic palace designed by Juan de Villanueva, the Prado has been considerably improved in the past few years, especially in its lighting. Yet despite the addition of new wings, it is still forced to display a number of great works in dimly lit corridors.

The most hurried trekker may want to focus his attention on the output of three major artists: the court painters, Velázquez and Goya, plus El Greco, who was, in fact, a Greek (born in Crete in 1541 or 1542).

But don't overlook the exceptional visions of Hieronymus Bosch, the 15th-century Flemish artist who peopled his canvases with fiends and ghouls and conjured up tortures that far surpassed Dante's Inferno. In particular, seek out his triptychs, *The Hay Wagon* and *The Garden of Earthly Delights.*

Most of the products of these artists are on the second floor. However, on the ground floor, you'll find Goya's "black paintings," one or two of his most important paintings *(The Second of May),* and his remarkable sketches.

The Prado's single most famous work is *Las Meninas*—the maids in waiting—the masterpeice of Velázquez, in Room XV. Opposite is a mirror through which you look for perspective. Velázquez was court painter for Philip IV.

In the Goya room is displayed his *Naked Maja,* certainly one of the most recognizable paintings in the West—said to have been posed by the woman the artist loved, the Duchess of Alba. As a court painter to Charles IV and his adulterous queen, María Luisa, Goya portrayed all their vulgarity of person and mind— and got them to pay for the results.

Currently, the painting stirring up the most excitement is Picasso's *Guernica.* Long banned in Spain, the painting rested for years in the Museum of Modern Art in New York before it was returned to Spain. The Prado houses it in the Casón del Buen Retiro. Picasso's work reflected his sadness at Generalissimo Franco's bombing of Guernica, a little Basque town. Picasso requested that *Guernica* not be returned to Spain until the death of Franco and the "reestablishment of public liberties." Behind a glass barrier, the painting covers almost a whole wall—some

12 feet high and about 25 feet long. Visitors are kept about 25 feet from the world masterpiece.

Other paintings, by Raphael, Botticelli, Correggio, Titian, (Titzano), Pieter Brueghel, Murillo, Ribera, and Fra Angelico, will make the morning fade quickly into dusk. The museum (tel. 239-80-23), on the Paseo del Prado, is open from 10 a.m. to 6 p.m. all year. On Sunday and holidays, except Christmas and New Year's, it is open from 10 a.m. to 2 p.m. The entrance fee is about 300 pesetas ($1.95). Buses going to the museum are numbered 10, 14, 27, 34, 37, and 45.

The second major attraction in the capital is:

THE BULLFIGHT, A SPECTACLE OF DEATH: In art, literature, and life, the Spaniard is urgently concerned with the subject of death. The ritual killing of the bull, as reenacted in countless seasons of *corridas* from early spring till late October, sustains the Spanish soul. Perhaps it is in the back of the mind of some aficionados that the bull may not be the only one killed, that the matador may meet his "death in the afternoon."

Despite the fanfare and the fiesta mood enveloping the Plaza de Toros, bullfighting is a deadly serious business. Like a major industry, it supports a goodly number of the Spanish population —from the promoters, the *apoderados* biting down on their Havana cigars, to the poor soul who cleans up the horse dung and sells it as fertilizer.

In the way Americans growing up in the '40s and '50s dreamed of becoming movie stars, the Spanish boy often fantisizes about the acclaim, the shouts, and the cheers ringing in his ears in the bullring. For many a peasant boy born in poverty, bullfighting is his way to break out of the role life cast him in. A case in point is former matador El Cordobés, a poor boy who rose to become a symbol of wealth and glamor throughout Spain.

An aficionado, Ernest Hemingway, wrote: "The bullfight is not a sport in the Anglo-Saxon sense of the word, that is, it is not an equal contest or an attempt at an equal contest between a bull and a man. Rather, it is a tragedy; the death of the bull, which is played, more or less well, by the bull and the man involved and in which there is danger for the man but certain death for the bull."

Fortified by that definition, you may be ready to attend your first bullfight.

The day of the corrida is Sunday afternoon, although Madrid

may also hold fights on Thursday. It's becoming an increasing practice to stage an 11 p.m. Saturday *novillada,* in which amateur or inexperienced bullfighters test their skill against often "defective" bulls.

The spectacle of the bullfights opens with a parade—an exciting, dramatic experience, as the bullfighters stroll in in their "suits of light." This is followed by a matador's preliminary capework, often a *verónica,* in which he faces the bull for the first time. This act appears almost to be choreographed, and has been compared to a ballet.

The fight begins as *picadores* on horseback charge the bull to "pic" him with lances. The *banderilleros* are next, jabbing the beast with brightly ornamented *banderillas,* preparing the animal for the kill. A fight is considered much more enthralling if the bullfighter himself sticks in the darts.

After this ceremony, the matador faces the bull armed with a sword and a *muleta,* a scarlet cloth. The challenging of the bull—most hazardous—is a *natural.* After a series of such passes, the matador is ready for the kill, the so-called moment of truth.

Hopefully, he will kill the bull in one quick thrust, although many a leading matador has been forced to make repeated thrusts like a *novillero.* The more thrusts, the more hostile grows the reaction of the crowd toward the bullfighter. If he shows skill, the "lucky" matador will be rewarded with an ear *(òreja)* of the bull. The amateurish performer is likely to get a rotten tomato tossed at his kisser.

Madrid attracts the most skilled matadors in Spain to its 26,000-seat **Plaza de Toros,** 237 Calle de Alcalá. The height of the corrida season is the week of festivities on May 10, honoring San Isidore, patron of the city.

Although major hotels sell bullfighting tickets, you can go to the "official" agency at **3 Victoria,** reached by heading east from the Puerta del Sol, then walking two blocks down the Carrera de San Jerónimo, turning south onto Victoria. In a district of *tascas* and cheap restaurants—especially popular with aspiring matadors and their promoters, or would-be promoters—the agency saves you about 20% of the price of the ticket. But make absolutely sure it's the "official" agency, and not one of the other offices lining the street.

You can save an additional 25%, approximately, if you request *sombra y sol* (shade and sun) seats—meaning that for part of the fight you'll be in the sun. Prices vary from fight to fight.

The tariffs to follow are only a general guideline—and may not apply to the actual fight you attend.

Front-row seats are called *barreras*. *Delanteras* or third-row seats are available in both the *alta* (high) and the *baja* (low) sections. You can also request quite passable *filas,* which are adequate seats (but not special). The cheapest seats, not really recommended, are of the *sol* variety, in which you're exposed to the hot sun during the entire fight.

When a top-flight matador is performing, tickets disappear quickly—only to be resold at scalper's prices. Tickets cannot be obtained weeks in advance. As for ticket prices, they vary. Count on spending at least 750 pesetas ($4.88) for a just passable seat all the way up to 3000 pesetas ($19.50) or more for the more desirable seats in the shade.

If you're attending a fight on Sunday, it's best to go to 3 Victoria between 10 a.m. and 1 p.m. or from 5 to 9 p.m. on the Saturday before the corrida. The office is also open on Sunday from 10 a.m. to 5 p.m.

You can take the Metro tube to Ventas to reach the Plaza de Toros. To avoid a stampede, try to arrive at the ring early, and while you're at it, visit the Bullfight Museum (see below). After the fight, it's virtually impossible to get a taxi back into the city. Why not wait, having a coffee at a nearby sidewalk table?

Five Top Sights

After wandering through the Prado and watching the blood and gore of the Plaza de Toros, you may be in a mood for more relaxed browsing through Madrid. What follows is a subjective listing of five additional attractions.

In order of importance, I'd rate them as follows: (1) the Royal Palace, (2) the Royal Factory of Tapestries, (3) the Lázaro Galdiano Museum, (4) the Convent of Las Descalzas Reales, and (5) the Goya Pantheon.

THE ROYAL PALACE: Alfonso XIII, grandfather of King Juan Carlos, and his queen, Victoria Eugénie, were the last to use the Palacio Real as a royal abode, in 1931, before they fled into exile.

The private apartments of the royal family suffered damage during the Civil War; but Franco ordered that they be restored as they were in the 1920s. Franco then used the Royal Palace (also known as the Palacio de Oriente) for state functions and elaborate banquets for foreign dignitaries. But guides like to point out that he never sat on the king's chair in the Throne Room.

King Juan Carlos and Queen Sofia are more modest in their requirements. They have turned the Royal Palace over to history, choosing not to live there but in their much smaller suburban palace, the Zarzuela, named after the Spanish operetta or musical comedy.

On the landmark site of the former Alcázar of Madrid (destroyed by fire on the Christmas of 1734), the Royal Palace was launched in 1737. Its first tenant was Charles III, the "enlightened despot" of the House of Bourbon. In all, the number of rooms—many added at a later date—total around 1800. Not all are open to the public, of course. Nor need they be, as it would then take a week to tour the entire enclave.

Visitors are conducted on a guided tour of the State Apartments, the Tapestry Room, the Reception Salons, the Royal Armory, the Royal Pharmacy, and the Royal Library. If you're rushed—and want just a quick glimpse of the grandeur of the palace—then you'll want to confine your sightseeing to the state apartments and the reception rooms. Metro stop: Opéra.

After your tour, you can skip across the courtyard to the **Royal Armory,** considered one of the most impressive in Europe. Recalling the days of jousting and equestrian warfare, many of the exhibits date from the reign of Charles V (Charles I of Spain) of the Hapsburg Empire. Roughly, the collection spans about 200 years of the Spanish Empire.

Afterward, you can visit the **Royal Library,** with its leatherbound volumes—at least 190,000 different editions, many belonging to Spain's most famous kings and queens, such as Isabella I. Although seemingly ignored, the **Royal Pharmacy** merits a visit. It was, in its heyday, the "cure-all" source for any ailment that plagued the royal family.

If you wish to visit the Gallery of Tapestries *(tapices),* the State Apartments, Reception Salons, Armory, and Library, you'll pay a total admission fee of 400 pesetas ($2.60). If you don't want to see everything, you can visit only what you wish. For example, a single ticket to the Armory costs 70 pesetas (46¢).

The Palacio Real (tel. 248-74-04) on the Plaza de Oriente is only a short walk from the Plaza de España. Hours to visit are from 10 a.m. to 1:30 p.m. and from 3:30 to 6:30 p.m. (on Sunday, from 10 a.m. to 1:30 p.m.).

Worth a detour, the **Carriage Museum** on the grounds charges an entrance fee of 85 pesetas (55¢). It's not as impressive as its more famous counterpart in Lisbon, but you can view the *carrozas* that Spanish royalty and aristocrats used in the days when a person was judged solely on appearance.

After your whirlwind tour, you can wind down by strolling through the **Campo del Moro,** the gardens of the palace.

LÁZARO GALDIANO MUSEUM: Deserving of far more visitors than it receives, this remarkable, compact, and art-stuffed museum at 122 Serrano (tel. 261-60-84) spans the centuries of artistic development with seeming ease.

An elevator takes you to the top floor of what was once one of the great mansions of Madrid; then you weave your way from room to room (30 in all), descending the stairs as you go.

The collection begins with vestments, some dating back to the 15th century. Along the way, you can stop and stare at an assemblage of weapons, daggers, and swords, some with elaborate handles dating from the 15th century. Seals, such as one belonging to Napoleon, are displayed; and there is a rare exhibition of Spanish fans, one possessed by Isabella II.

In Room XX are two Flemish paintings by the incomparable Bosch—rats crawling through the eyes of humans, and so on. In the following room (XXI) is Rembrandt's *Firmado,* dating from 1634. In other salons, several of the major artists of Spain are represented: Velázquez, Zurbarán, El Greco, Valdés Leal, Murillo, and Ribera. Room XXV is the salon of English-speaking portraitists: Gainsborough, Sir Joshua Reynolds, Gilbert Stuart, and Constable. Many well-known works by Goya are in his salon (XXX), including some of the "black paintings" and portraits of Charles IV and his errant spouse.

Other intriguing showcases are filled with 16th-century Limoges crystal, French and Italian ivory carving from the 14th and 15th centuries, and a 15th-century Maltese cross. In Room VI hangs a small portrait of a woman encased in green velvet. Although the museum attributes this painting to Leonardo da Vinci, many art historians dispute this claim. The painting is more generally attributed to Ambrogio de Predis of Milan, with whom da Vinci lived his first years in that Lombard city. Calling it a da Vinci was denounced by one critic as "unwarranted and disturbing sensationalism."

You can come calling any time from 10 a.m. to 2 p.m. for an admission fee of 50 pesetas (33¢). On Sunday, the charge is

The Royal Factory of Tapestries

The making of tapestries—based on original designs by Goya, Francisco Bayeu (Goya's brother-in-law), and others—is still flourishing in Madrid. You can actually visit the factory where the *tapices* are turned out, and chat with the workers. Some of the hand looms on which they work date back to the days of Goya.

The great Spanish artist sketched numerous cartoons which were converted into tapestries to adorn the walls of the Royal Palace not only in Madrid, but in Aranjuez and La Granja. One of the most famous, reproduced hundreds of times, is *El Cacharrero* (The Pottery Salesman).

Some crafts people have copied the same design all of their lives, so that now they can work on it casually—perhaps with a cigarette dangling out of the corner of their mouths. Others, less cavalier, prefer to watch the design carefully through a mirror.

The factory—called **Real Fábrica de Tapices**— is at 2 Fuenterrabia (tel. 251-34-00). It may be visited daily, except Saturday and Sunday, from 9:30 a.m. to 12:30 p.m. Admission is 50 pesetas (33¢) per person. Closed August 1 to September 1. Metro stop: Atocha or Pelayo.

lowered to 25 pesetas (17¢). It is closed in August and on Monday. Metro stop: Maranon.

THE PANTHEON OF GOYA: Emulating Tiepolo, Goya frescoed the **Church of San António de la Florida** in 1798. Although he depicted in part the miracles of St. Anthony of Padua, his work was nearly secular in its execution. Mirrors are placed to allow you to capture the beauty of the ceiling better. The figure of a woman draped in a cape is one of the most celebrated subjects in Goya's work.

Beyond the North Station, the hermitage is at Glorieta de San António de la Florida (tel. 247-79-21). Goya died in exile in Bordeaux, France, in 1828, but his bones were later removed from there and interred here in the memorial that he unknowingly created for himself.

Some church officials once considered Goya's frescoes irreverent—hence, the hermitage not a fit place of worship. A twin of the 18th-century church was erected alongside it, and services are conducted there now. Facing both of them, go into the one on the right to pay your respects to Goya.

The pantheon is open from 11 a.m. to 1:30 p.m. and from 3 to 6 p.m. from October to June. From July to September, the hours are from 10 a.m. to 1 p.m., and from 4 to 7 p.m. Closed on Wednesday. On Sunday, it is open only from 11 to 1:30. The admission charge is 50 pesetas (33¢) on weekdays.

Convent of Las Descalzas Reales

What would you do if you were a starving nun surrounded by a vast treasure house of paintings, gold, jewelry, and tapestries? Sell them? Not possible. The order of the Franciscan Clarissas threw themselves upon the mercy of the government, which in turn opened the doors of the convent to the general public as a museum (with the pope's permission, of course). It's still an operational convent of approximately 30 sisters.

The collection includes tapestries based on Rubens's "cartoons," 16th- and 17th-century vestments, a silver forearm said to contain bones of St. Sebastian, and a statue of the Virgin wearing earrings, as is the custom in Andalusia. The most interesting chapel is dedicated to "Our Lady of Guadalupe" (the statue of the Virgin is made of lead).

One of the best paintings here is a *Virgin and Child* by Bernardino Luini of northern Italy; but the most valuable oil is Titian's *Caesar's Money,* worth millions of pesetas. The Flemish Hall contains other superb canvases—for example, one of a processional by Hans Baker.

The Convent of Las Descalzas Reales is open daily from 10:30 a.m. to 1:30 p.m. and charges 100 pesetas (65¢) for admission. Monday through Thursday, the convent is also open from 4 to 5:30 p.m. From the Plaza de Callao, a satellite square of the Gran Vía, walk down a narrow street, Postigo de San Martín, to the Plaza de las Descalzas Reales, one of the most charming squares in Madrid, and you'll find the convent (tel. 222-06-87) on your left. You must wait for a guided tour. Metro stop: Plaza del Sol.

Other Sights

For the visitor who'd like to know Madrid more intimately, I've compiled the following list of museums, a park, and even a flea market.

FINE ARTS MUSEUM: Right on Madrid's busy boulevard, an easy stroll from the Puerta del Sol, the **Museo de la Real Academia de Bellas Artes de San Fernando**, 13 Calle de Alcalá, is popular primarily because of its Goya salon. Works by that artist include a self-portrait, much reproduced, and a study of Manuel de Godoy, the confidant of the House of Bourbon and lover to Queen María Luisa at the time of the Napoleonic invasion of Spain. The two prized canvases by Goya here are his *The Crazy House* and a *Scene from the Inquisition,* brilliantly portraying his own brand of horror.

Displayed also are works by other famous Spanish artists: Murillo, Ribera, Sorolla, and Zurbarán (his robed monks). In particular, search out Rubens's *Susanna and the Elders,* the latter lecherous indeed. The museum is open daily, except Sunday, from 10 a.m. to 2 p.m., and charges 75 pesetas (49¢) for admission. Closed in August.

THE MUSEUM OF BULLFIGHTING: At the Plaza de Toros de las Ventas, in the Patio de Caba llos, this **Museo Taurino** (tel. 255-18-57) ideally should be visited before you see your first Spanish bullfight, as it serves as a good introduction to "the tragedy" in the arena. The complete history of the *torero* is traced in pictures, historic bullfight posters, and scale models.

Works of art include a Goya painting of a matador, plus an exquisite bust, sculptured in bronze, of Manolete. The museum may be visited daily, except Sunday, from 10 a.m. to 1 p.m. and from 3:30 to 6 p.m for an admission fee of 70 pesetas (46¢). You can take the subway to the Ventas stop.

THE HOUSE OF LOPE DE VEGA: Ironically, the Casa de Lope de Vega (tel. 429-92-16) stands on a street named after Cervantes (no. 11), his competitor for the title of the greatest writer of the Golden Age of Spain and a bitter enemy. The house is considered a *perfecta* reconstruction of the casa in which Lope de Vega lived, and it is furnished with pieces indigenous to his time (1562–1635). The Spanish writer, the major dramatist of Hapsburg Spain, wrote more than 1000 plays, many of which have been lost to history.

You'll be shown through the house, with its volumes upon volumes of manuscript reproductions, and then allowed to roam at random in the garden in back. The museum and memorial to Lope de Vega is open from 11 a.m. to 2 p.m. except Monday, and the price of admission is 100 pesetas (65¢). From mid-July to mid-September, the house is closed to the public.

THE WAX MUSEUM: The Museo Colón, Plaza Colón (tel. 419-26-49), in the Centro Colón, charges a steep 450 pesetas ($2.93) for adults, and 200 pesetas ($1.30) for children. The museum is a bit like London's Madame Tussaud's or the Musée Grevin in Paris; there are scenes depicting events in Spanish history, such as Columbus calling on Ferdinand and Isabella. Contemporary international figures aren't neglected either. Thus, we see Jacqueline Onassis having champagne at a supper club and Garbo all alone. The heroes and villains of World War II—everybody from Eisenhower to Hitler—are enlivened by the presence of the "Blue Angel," Marlene Dietrich, singing "Lili Marlene." Out-of-work filmmakers created the 400 figures in 38 tableaux, succeeding best with backdrops, falling shortest in the depiction of contemporary celebrities. Hours are from 10:30 a.m. to 2 p.m., and from 4 to 9 p.m.

THE CHURCH OF SAN FRANCISCO EL GRANDE: In lieu of a great cathedral, Madrid possesses this church, with a dome larger than that of St. Paul's in London. Constructed on the site of a much earlier church, San Francisco dates from the latter 18th century, owing much of its appearance to Sabatini, a celebrated architect of his day.

Its interior of Doric columns and Corinthian capitals is cold and foreboding, although 19th-century artists labored hard to adorn its series of chapels flanking the nave. The best painting—that of St. Bernard preaching—is by Goya.

You are conducted through the church by a guide, who notes the most outstanding artwork, especially the choir stalls dating from the 16th century. The church dominates its own square, the Plaza de San Francisco El Grande (1 San Buenaventura), and it may be visited from 11 a.m. to 1 p.m. and from 4 to 7 p.m. daily, except Sunday and Monday. Admission is 25 pesetas (16¢). In summer, the afternoon hours are from 5 to 8 p.m. Metro: La Latina. You can also take bus 3 from the Plaza de España, which goes right to the church.

THE RETIRO: This was formerly a much larger royal park through which the Hapsburg Philips romped. But after 1868, it was largely reforested and turned over to the people of Madrid.

Sprawling over more than 350 acres, it opens onto the eastern side of the Calle de Alfonso II. Near the center is a lake, **Estanque,** with a poorly designed monument to King Alfonso XII. All is tranquil in summer. You can rent rowboats, slowly traversing the waters.

Across the Calle de Alfonso XII in the southwestern part are the **Botanical Gardens.** The fountains of the Retiro, one honoring an artichoke, are handsomely sculptured and displayed. It is pleasant to stroll from one to another.

THE RASTRO (FLEA MARKET): This sprawling hillside market will warm the heart of anyone attracted to a mishmash of fascinating junk interspersed with bric-à-brac and paintings (don't expect to find a Goya). It's open every day of the week, but most popular late Sunday morning (go before 2 p.m.) when seemingly half of the Madrileños and many people from the nearby countryside jostle each other through the narrow streets, searching for bargains, real and imagined. Roughly, the flea market occupies a triangular district of streets a few minutes' walk south of the Plaza Mayor. The main center of the permanent antique shops—open daily—is on the **Plaza Cascarro** and the **Ribera de Curtidores.**

Much of the merchandise is displayed in open stalls, although many vendors simply spread their wares on patches of canvas on the street. The incongruity of merchandise and nonmerchandise offered may astonish and amuse: bits of ecclasiastical wooden statuary, such as armless madonnas and saints with missing halos, rusty keys large enough to fit that "castle in Spain," World War II motorcycle parts, brass scales, ornate antique watches, Victorian bureaus, umbrella stands, and second- (or third-) hand clothing. You name it! The nearest Metro station is La Latina, less than two blocks away. You can also take bus 3 or 17.

A Walking Tour

New Madrid is strictly for motorists, as it sprawls for miles in all directions. But in the center of Madrid cars get in the way. Old Madrid is strictly for walking, the only way to savor its unique charm.

The tour begins on the **Gran Vía,** a street whose position as *the* boulevard of Madrid is being fast overtaken by the Paseo de la Castellana. Still the busiest street in Madrid, the shop-flanked Gran Vía was opened at the end of World War I. Until recently it was called Avenida de José António. Long before deluxe hotels started to sprout up on the Castellana, the hotels of the Gran Vía were the most expensive and elegant in the Spanish capital. The street ends at the **Plaza de España,** a vast square overshadowed by one of the tallest skyscrapers in Europe.

From the square, you can walk up the Calle de la Princesa, turning to your left down the Ventura Rodríguez. At 17 Ventura Rodríguez is the **Cerralbo Museum,** which gives you a rare glimpse into the life of one of the most prestigious Spanish families. The museum is open daily except Monday from 10 a.m. to 2 p.m. and 4 to 7 p.m., charging an admission of 200 pesetas ($1.30). Closed Sunday afternoon and in August. Metro stop: Plaza de España or Ventura Rodríquez.

Returning to the Plaza de España, strike out down the Calle de Bailen until you reach the semicircular **Plaza de Oriente,** created in 1840. From that vantage point, you can explore the **Palacio Nacional,** or Royal Palace, described above.

After your tour, if you take a tiny side street to the northeast, the Calle Pavia, you'll arrive at the **Plaza de la Encarnación,** one of the most charming squares in Madrid. Sitting on this plaza is the **Convent de la Encarnación,** finished in 1616, in the reign of Philip III and his queen Margaret (sister of Emperor Ferdinand II). This convent and adjoining church can be visited daily from 10:30 a.m. to 1:30 p.m. and from 4 to 6 p.m. (on Sunday from 10:30 a.m. to 1:30 p.m.), for 150 pesetas (98¢).

From the square, walk down the Calle de Arrieta to the Plaza de Isabel II. There you can connect with the Calle del Arenal, leading to the **Puerta del Sol,** the "gateway to the sun," the historic heart of Madrid.

Organized Tours

A large number of agencies in Madrid offer organized tours and excursions—among them are **Marsan's International Travel, Inc.,** with offices at 15 San Nicolás (tel. 242-55-00). The most popular full-day excursion is to the imperial city of Toledo, the complete jaunt costing $22.50. Other heavily booked full-day treks encompass El Escorial and the Valley of the Fallen for $22.50, or Ávila, Segovia, and the summer palace of the Bourbons at La Granja, for $29, which includes, as do the others, lunch at a restaurant along the way. Half-day tours of Madrid, either artistic or panoramic, cost around $10.50.

Chapter XIV

MADRID AFTER DARK

THE MADRILEÑOS are called *gatos* (cats) because of their excessive fondness for prowling around at night. If you're going to see a show, the later you go, the better. Unaware of this, two American tourists once arrived at a restaurant at 10 p.m. for dinner, hoping to hear a young French singer. After their last brandy, they sat through a long, dreary revue, followed by routine dancing to orchestra music, then another drawn-out revue. Finally, the management announced the appearance of the headliner. The hour was 1:30 a.m., and this was his first show of the evening.

In spite of the late hours, the people of Madrid begin their evening as early as 8 p.m. by *tasca* hopping (see below). For the younger crowd, many discos open around 6 p.m., remaining open till 9 p.m., when they usually shut down for dinner. Later, at about 11 p.m., they reopen and stay that way until early in the morning.

Tasca Hopping

As mentioned earlier, dinner is fashionably served in Madrid at 10:30 p.m. But this late hour requires no iron will on the part of the Madrileño. From 8 p.m. on, you'll find him or her in the *tascas* (taverns), drinking a chato (small glass of vino) and eating *tapas,* literally "covers." *Tapas* are Spanish hors d'oeuvres, usually displayed on the counter of the bar. Most often they are crunchy fried fish, cold tortillas (omelets), squid, *gambas* (shrimp), olives, sausage, salads, mushrooms, even the tail of a bull. Each of the major *tascas* is noted for one or two specialties, which you'll usually find prominently displayed or advertised. Most of these taverns have waiter service at the tables, although the least expensive way to visit them is to order your tapas and drinks at the bar. Some of my favorite taverns—scattered about in interesting and colorful parts of Madrid—are the following:

La Casona, 3 Calle Echegaray, is a top-rated *tasca* on this colorful street of budget restaurants and bars off the Carrera de San Jerónimo, about a four-minute walk from the Puerta del Sol. It's in the typical *taberna* style, truly rustic, with hanging hams and whirling overhead fans, posters of *fútbol* teams, wrought-iron lanterns, and pastoral paintings. In the Iberian tradition, shrimp shells go on the floor for the porter to worry about. The house specialties are patatas Casona, crunchy and heavily salted fried potatoes in a hot red sauce, and champiñones (grilled mushrooms). But the favored entrée is gambas à la plancha (shrimp grilled in their shells). Food specialties range from 125 pesetas (81¢) to 400 pesetas ($2.60) with a glass of wine costing 50 pesetas (33¢). The *tasca* is open from 9 a.m. to midnight.

The **Taberna Toscana** (Tuscan Tavern), 22 Ventura de la Vega (tel. 222-70-22), doesn't look like much on the outside. But inside its theme is that of a country inn, with terrazzo floors, regional stools and tables, plus handhewn beams from which hang hams, sheaves of wheat, and garlic pigtails. Nearly two dozen *tapas* are set out at the bar. Tasty and recommended are the clams in a marinade at 300 pesetas ($1.95). A glass of wine is only 35 pesetas (23¢). The bar waiter keeps tabs on your plate by chalking up the damages on a carving board.

La Torre del Oro, 26 Plaza Mayor (tel. 266-30-16), is small in size but large in atmosphere. In summer, tables are placed right in the historic plaza. Inside, the walls decoratively adorned with Sevillian tiles, the massive black beams, and the hanging hams make for an alluring interlude. *Tapas* specialties include pinchos morunos (small shish-kebab on a skewer, a North African specialty), costing 200 pesetas ($1.30).

The Bars

Some visitors can't quite get into the hustle-bustle of the *típica tasca,* preferring the more sedate elegance of a bar. What follows is a random sampling of some of the most interesting bars—each one attracting a widely diverse clientele, many quite fashionable. The Palace, the Pickwick, and the Oliver are all suitable for two women traveling together. . .but if a woman drops in at Chicote alone, or on the arm of a girlfriend, only one assumption will be made.

The **Palace Bar,** 7 Plaza de las Cortes (tel. 221-11-10), basks in its tradition as *the* place in the capital for upper-crust Madrileños and international travelers from around the globe. In his book, A. E. Hotchner called it "the nerve center of Madrid social intrigue, where every woman looks like a successful spy." In the final chapter of *The Sun Also Rises*, Jake told Brett: "It's funny what a wonderful gentility you get in the bar of a big hotel." The panels of grained marble, the soft lounge chairs, the alert and polite waiters, are appropriate for the turn-of-the-century glamor of the Palace. Many a govermental policy has been made here; and many a female film star has preened her feathers in front of an admiring audience. The atmosphere is deliberately relaxed and cordial. The bar is open until 11 p.m. A brand-name scotch costs 600 pesetas ($3.90).

A Grand Old Literary Café

Gran Café de Gijón, 21 Paseo de Calvo Sotelo (tel. 231-91-21). Most old European capitals have a coffeehouse that traditionally attracts the literati. In Madrid, the counterpart of Les Deux Magots in Paris or the Antico Caffè in Rome is the Gijón. Artists and writers, as well as an international crowd of young people, patronize this café on Madrid's major boulevard. Many of them spend hours over one cup of espresso. In days of yore, you might have run into Tyrone Power, Ava Gardner, Manolete, or Luis Miguel Dominguín. The coffeehouse has open windows looking out onto the wide *paseo*. Watercolors, paintings, and etchings adorn the walls. In summer, you can sit in the garden enjoying, say, a blanco y negro (that's black coffee with ice cream), a popular drink. If you order outside, a coffee goes for 200 pesetas ($1.30). However, if you order your coffee at one of the black and white marble-topped tables inside, it is only 90 pesetas (59¢).

Oliver's, 3 Calle del Conde Xiquena, (tel. 221-01-47), only a minute from Calvo Sotelo, attracts a youthful, sophisticated crowd to its drawing-room atmosphere, like that of a private club. The street-floor room evokes a stage setting by one of London's gifted designers, what with its paneled scenic setting on the ceiling, the formal fireplace, recessed alcoves containing shelves of art and theater books, and record album covers. On the walls are old paintings and engravings, the color theme Mediterranean: faded red, sienna, bronze, and gold. You sit on upholstered chairs and sofas. Reached by a winding stairway, the lower level is more intimate, decorated with shades of Toledo red and sienna and furnished with sofas arranged for intimate get-togethers. Often someone plays the piano softly in the background. You pay 500 pesetas ($3.25) for an average drink. *Tapas,* or hors d'oeuvres, are available. The bar is open from 8 p.m. till 3 a.m.

Pickwick Pub, 48 Paseo Pintor Rosales (tel. 248-51-85), is a re-creation of the world of Dickens: timbered ceilings, high-backed settles, framed prints of the author's most famous characters, hunting horns, tiny nooks with a china collection, pewter mugs, an English fireplace, even a brass horse collection. Smartly attired in a Sherwood Forest green uniform, a doorman greets you and ushers you in.

It's a pleasant place at which to have a mug of beer—either at the tiny bar, or, preferably, on one of the soft leather sofas. Most drinks, accompanied by olives and peanuts, are 200 pesetas ($1.30). The Pickwick is open from 6 p.m. till 1:30 a.m. It's in a corner building where its *paseo* meets the Calle del Marqués de Urquijo.

The Bar of the Bottles

The **Chicote,** 12 Gran Vía, (tel. 232-15-12), belongs to Señor Chicote, one of the best known citizens of Madrid. Upstairs, the setting of olive banquettes and Scottish-plaid carpeting, with uniformed shoeshine boys making the rounds, has the aura of a gentleman's club. Most drinks such as a Cuba libre, are in the 300 pesatas ($1.95) range. In the cellar, Señor Chicote has collected beer, liquor, and wine bottles from all over the world. Many of the bottles were presented by celebrities, including Doña Fabiola de Mora y Aragón, who married the Belgian king, Baudouin; Cantiflas of Mexico; Onassis; Haile Selassie; as well as Tyrone Power and Ava Gardner, the stars of *The Sun Also Rises.* In all, there are more than 23,000 bottles, including one of the shape of a light blub, the gift of the Philips Corporation. Bottles come in odd shapes and sizes: one like a Rolls-Royce tank, another in the form of Charlie Chaplin. Many contain vintage whiskies, such as an 1820 Johnnie Walker. One bottle alone is worth more than $2500.

Cuevas del Duque, 16 Calle Princesa (tel. 248-50-37), is right in front of the Duke of Alba's palace, a few blocks along the Calle Princesa from the Plaza de España. It's a small restaurant, cum underground bar and mesón. A few tables have been placed outside, beside a small triangular garden, while other tables line the Calle Princesa side and are pleasant for an apéritif or an afternoon drink. Prices begin at 600 pesetas ($3.90). Within the ten-table restaurant, you can enjoy the standard Spanish dishes such as gazpacho, fabada (an Asturian pork-and-beans dish), and roast veal, with meals averaging 2500 pesetas ($16.25) and up.

Flamenco Clubs

By now, Americans are somewhat familiar with flamenco. Carmen Amaya toured with U.S.A. during most of World War II; Carmelita Maracci made her unique comment; through endless TV appearances, José Greco popularized the art form even more. The only catch is, Mr. Greco isn't from Spain. As one dance critic put it, he was "born in Italy, raised in Brooklyn, and is a great Spanish dancer."

Flamenco personifies the blood and guts of Andalusia, where it originated. Nowadays, the gypsies have virtually taken over the art form, making flamenco part of their own folklore. Their basic fire and flair do add another dimension.

The performers sit in a half circle around the stage, with the lead or head dancer on the end. At the left and right rear, the male singers and dancers await their turn. To the accompaniment of guitars, castanets, and rhythmic clapping, each performer does a solo, occasionally uniting with another partner—strutting, tapping, clapping, and stamping their feet with inner tension and pride. The songs are chanted in a passionate, tense tone, almost Arabic in origin. Age doesn't keep an artist off the center stage. Flamenco singers *(cantores)* seem to perform forever, until the lid on their coffin is lifted for a farewell olé.

Before you leave Madrid, you may want to attend at least one show, at one of the many *tablaos* throughout the city. Usually, you pay no cover charge, but the price is stiff for your first drink. The tabs are lowered for subsequent libations. My specific recommendations follow.

Café de Chinitas, 7 Torija (tel. 248-51-35), is one of the swankiest and most expensive flamenco spots in town. In the old part of Madrid, between the Opera and the Gran Vía, it features dancer La Chunga, as well as the guitarist Serranito. They join with 37 others to make up the *cuadro.* The show starts at 11 p.m., running until 3:30 a.m. The minimum, which entitles you to a drink at a table is 2200 pesetas ($14.30). You can also go for dinner at about 9:30 p.m., and then stay on for the flamenco. À la carte main dishes run about 1500 pesetas ($9.75) to 2500 pesetas ($16.25). The café is open daily except Sunday all year. You sit in an elongated room at tables with fair visibility. The stage is at the far end of the room. The decor is amorphously elegant, sometimes in questionable taste, and doesn't quite live up to the promise of the street exterior. You enter through a staircase lined with old bullfighting engravings, posters, and pictures, which takes you to two glass doors with bronze hands on them for handles.

Corral de lo Morería, 17 Morería (tel. 265-84-46). In the Old Town, the Morería—meaning a quarter where Moors reside—sizzles more in its flamenco than in its skillet. Strolling performers, colorfully costumed, get the proceedings under way around 11 p.m., but they are there only to warm the audience. A flamenco showcase follows, with at least ten dancers—the women have Gloria Vanderbilt waistlines. The star always appears late. The management has devised ways of putting tables in the most unlikely places; reserve near the front and go early if you really want a ringside table. You can order an à la carte dinner for around 2500 pesetas ($16.25) to 3000 pesetas ($19.50). The cost of your first drink is 1800 pesetas ($11.70).

Torres Bermajas, 11 Mesonero Romanos (tel. 232-33-22), is a cellar flamenco rendezvous, just a minute from the Gran Vía. You descend winding stairs to a tiny arena and stage—the rooms decorated with Andalusian tiles, creating a Moorish effect. You can order a complete dinner, but for the price of your first drink, 2000 pesetas ($13), you're allowed to see the entire show. You'll pay a supplement for name-brand whiskies. A complete set meal goes for 3000 pesetas ($19.50), including both wine and the supplements charged for the flamenco show.

If you're still on the flamenco trail, then you might try **Arco de Cuchilleros,** 7 Cuchilleros (tel. 266-58-67), near the Botín Restaurant. Lots of single men and women come here. A flamenco show with a girlie twist is often presented. All in all, it's fun to be here if you don't take the proceedings too seriously. The one-drink minimum will cost you 1800 pesetas ($11.70).

Spectacles

Madrid's nightlife is no longer steeped in conservatism, as it was in the Franco era. You can now see glossy cabarets and super-sexy shows, with lots of nudity.

For your big night out in the Spanish capital, I'd suggest the **Lido,** 20 Alcalá (tel. 232-21-01), which borrows its concept from its more celebrated namesake in Paris. It is nowhere near as successful, of course, but it's the best of its kind in Spain. The costumes are extravagant, and you get a lot of naked flesh, particularly if you wait around for the last show (at the hour of 3:15), when there are mostly men in the audience. Your first drink costs 2500 pesetas ($16.25) and up. Two other shows are offered at 10:45 p.m. and 1:15 a.m.

For another look at Madrid *erótico,* strike out for **Music Hall Pirandello,** 7 Ventura Rodríguez (tel. 247-63-12), where for the price of a drink—2000 pesetas ($13) and up—you're treated to a loud and racy show. Professional dancers swing it, strut it, and do the strip. The club is open from 11:30 p.m. till 4 a.m. The show goes on at 1:15 a.m.

Royal Cabaret, 43 Gran Vía (tel. 241-91-20), on the lower level of the Rex Hotel, right in mainstream Madrid, offers a combination disco/cabaret format. Beginning at 7 p.m., it offers recently released disco music. But at 12:30 a.m., it presents a flamenco show, and at 2 a.m. an international "girlie" show. Those who stuck around to 3:30 a.m. are treated to an erotica presentation. The cabaret part is open from 11 p.m. to 5 a.m., and you should count on spending 4000 pesetas ($26) and up.

CULTURAL: For an authentic Spanish experience, you can attend a *zarzuela,* a Spanish musical variety show with turn-of-the-century music enlivened by bright costumes. Often these vaudevillian presentations sandwich flamenco numbers and musical revues between their regular acts.

One of the best places to view this musical theater is the **Monumental Theater,** 60 Calle de Atocha (tel. 227-12-14). Even non-Spanish speaking visitors seem to enjoy performances here scheduled daily except Monday at 7 and 10:30 p.m. Tickets begin at 450 pesetas ($2.93).

Along with opera and ballet, zarzuelas are also presented at the **Teatro de la Zarzuela,** 4 Jovellanos (tel. 429-82-25).

Ballet, Spanish style, is presented at the **Centro Cultural de la Villa,** Plaza de Colón (tel. 275-60-80).

Parque de Atracciones

The "Park of Attractions" is a combination of a Coney Island and Copenhagen's Tivoli Gardens. Madrileños speak of it as *"Disneylandia."* Created almost overnight in 1969 to amuse the young at heart, it lies in the former royal hunting grounds of the Casa de Campo. The park is open all year, summer hours from 6:30 p.m. to 1 a.m. (Sunday, noon to 1 a.m.), charging 75 pesetas (49¢) for admission. Children aged 3 to 10 pay half-price.

At the core of the park is an illuminated tower; you can take the elevator up to its observation platform. The tower is surrounded by a large reflection pool. From the tower, water drops into a *cascadas* of pools and falls, all brilliantly lit at night.

Numerous attractions interest young and old: a toboggan slide, a carousel, pony rides, an adventure into "outer space," a walk through a maze of glass, a super-dash in a racing car, a jaunt in an antique automobile, a visit to "jungleland," a sound-and-light spectacle, a leisurely trip in a motorboat on a circuitous canal, a motor-propelled series of cars disguised as a tail-wagging dachshund puppy, and a gyrating whirl clutched in the tentacles of an octopus, "El Pulpo." The most popular rides are the roller coasters, "7 Picos" and "Jet Star."

You may also want to attend a performance at the open-air Greek-style *teatro,* where a one-hour show is presented nightly at 8 from May till the end of September, weather permitting. No admission is charged. The theater is a well-designed structure, with cast-cement seats facing a bowl-like shell and stage. The apron has a reflecting pool and fountains for a colored water display. The popular entertainment is strictly potluck—everything from Spanish ballet to a flamenco singer.

How to get to the park: A cable car leaves for the park from the intersection of the Paseo del Pintor Rosales and the Calle Marqués de Urquijo. At the terminus of the *teleférico,* a line of micro-buses awaits to complete the journey to the entrance to the park. An alternate approach is via a suburban train from the Plaza de España, which stops near an entrance to the park (the Entrada del Batán). Of course, the easiest way to get there is in an inexpensive taxi.

The Discos

Some discos are spectacular, complete with the latest gimmicks and live combos. Others are little cellar dives where the owner plays records to special but fickle claques who desert him the next day for a newer club. As earlier mentioned, the disco evening is broken into two cycles: one a predinner session, another a postdinner frolic. Before dinner, prices and admission tabs are usually cheaper. Of general interest are the following recommendations:

Bocaccio, 16 Marqués de la Enseñada, off the Plaza Colón (tel. 419-10-08), created a sensation when it opened in Barcelona, and an offshoot has survived a successful transplant to Madrid. It is now the most elegant disco in the Spanish capital. Everything is free form and stylized, a triumph of art nouveau. Tufted red velvet, crescent-shaped banquettes seat the most attractive young people in Madrid today. Serving them are catfooted, regally attired bartenders who become part of the show. They pour your drinks—and powerful ones at that—with one hand elaborately positioned behind their back. Your first drink of a name-brand whisky will cost 1000 pesetas ($6.50).

J.J. ("Hota Hota"), 4 Plaza del Callao (tel. 232-04-29), is a psychedelic madhouse right on the Gran Vía. The favorite of many a young Madrileña (who always seem to arrive in trios, never alone), it is hidden in the entrance to a building housing one of the city's largest movie palaces. Young men whose pesetas are low have learned to arrive alone, asking a girl to dance once she's paid her own entrance fee. To enter, a single person pays from 1000 pesetas ($6.50). Inside, J.J. is designed arena style, with a stage where live groups on weekends perform late at night. Graduated tier by tier, tables form a half moon around the stage and dance floor. A hard-working, glassed-in disc jockey is a show in himself, changing the discs and punching the electric keyboard which sets off a complex lighting system. Blinking spots and flashes of colored lights combine with four-screen projections to create an impression that one astounded viewer called "mad-mad-mad."

A JAZZ CLUB: **Whisky Jazz**, 7 Diego de León (tel. 261-11-65), is a hideaway for jazz enthusiasts just a block away from the American Embassy. Once inside, if you've appeared at the right moment, you'll be presented with one of the best showcases of jazz in all of Spain. The interior is a two-story brick building, with a stairway leading to an open mezzanine which projects out over a downstairs bar. The walls and especially a glass case contain intriguing jazz memorabilia, including autographs and photos of its heyday in Chicago and New Orleans. Featured nightly is Pedro Iturralde, who had many devoted followers in the Spanish capital. For the first show, arrive by 11:30 p.m. (other shows at 1 a.m. and 2:15 a.m.). In the early evening, the door charge is 500 pesetas ($3.25), that fee going up to 1000 pesetas ($6.50) in the early morning when live groups usually appear. On Saturday and holidays, the price goes up even higher —1500 pesetas ($9.75).

The Art of Cider Drinking

Casa Mingo, 2 Paseo de la Florida (tel. 247-50-31), is a sprawling old tavern, just a short way from the Goya pantheon, that for decades has been known for its Asturian cider, both the still and the bubbly kind. Cider is served at Casa Mingo in the old manner. The waiter or bartender holds the glass as low as he can in the left hand, and the bottle of still cider as high as he can in the right, and then pours the cider *(echa la sidra).* A few drops may fall on the ground but it's all part of the rite. The perfect accompanying tidbit is a piece of the local Asturian **cabrales** (goat cheese). The price of a snack such as chicken and cider is 1000 pesetas ($6.50). In summer, the staff places some tables and wooden chairs outdoors on the sidewalk. Or if you prefer, you can stand at the bar, under the huge casks of wine lining the walls.

"Cuevas" Hopping

Throughout Old Madrid—and especially south of the Plaza Mayor (head down the Calle de Cuchilleros)—are gypsy-like *cuevas* (caves) where for a *chato* of wine you can join in spontaneous songfests. One of the most famous establishments (recommended just to get you started) is the following:

Sesamo, 7 Príncipe (tel. 232-91-91), is a *cueva* both *cosmopolita y bohemio.* It has hosted Truman Capote and many other celebrated persons. Styles and cultural heroes change, but Sesamo goes on forever. Its two cellar rooms—beneath a snackbar—are reached via a long flight of steps. Downstairs you'll find seats gathered around tiny tables. The action warms up to a high level around 11 p.m. Guests often bring their guitars or banjos, spontaneously singing folk songs, laments of love, and protest. And there's always a piano player. It's customary to order a pitcher of sangría for four at 1000 pesetas ($6.50).

Chapter XV

SHOPPING IN MADRID

RIVALED BUT NOT SURPASSED by Barcelona, Madrid offers the best buys for the bargain hunter of any city in Spain. Thousands of tourists pass through the Spanish capital yearly; and, frankly, many shops are designed chiefly for what the proprietors think the well-heeled foreigner will like.

On the other hand, Madrid is chiefly an industrial and commercial capital, in which the majority of the stores and shops exist primarily for the patronage of Spaniards. As the average income of a Spanish family is far below that of an American, Canadian, English, or Scandinavian, managers or shopkeepers must keep prices in line with what they think the local traffic will bear. Consequently, the city offers some of the most moderately priced merchandise of any European capital.

HANDICRAFT EXHIBITIONS: Artespaña (Empresa Nacional de Artesanía), 32 Gran Vía, 14 Hermosilla, 3 Plaza de las Cortes, and 33 D. Ramón de la Cruz, are the government-sponsored exhibition and sales centers for Spanish handicrafts, some of the best establishments at which to purchase handmade furniture and decorative items from all the regions of Spain. The buyers know their country well, bringing to their showrooms excellently made items. You'll find furniture reproductions, Toledo damascene work, wrought-iron works, ceramics and glassware, carved wood, jewelry, plus hundreds of other accessories.

Much of the jewelry is made of sterling silver. Córdoban filigree boxes are a good buy. Other displays include tin lanterns (with inserts of ruby red, amber, or midnight-blue glass), pewter ashtrays, handmade regional dolls, ecclesiastical woodcarvings, fringed pillow covers and bedspreads, handmade Catalán chairs, and Córdoban leather goods.

The showrooms are supervised by English-speaking attendants, who can arrange for packing and shipping. The hours are from 9:30 a.m. to 1:30 p.m. and from 4:30 p.m. to 8 p.m.

For information, telephone 411-13-62 or 261-64-00.

Kreisler, 19 Serrano (tel. 276-53-38), is owned and operated by the seemingly tireless American midwesterner, Edward Kreisler, from Akron, Ohio, an entrepreneur of Spanish decorative handicrafts. Through his grapevine, he keeps in touch with artisans in obscure villages and towns, presenting their wares in his jam-packed galleries in the Serrano shopping district. Encased within are most of the Spanish items that the North American markets want, including olive-wood articles, "El Greco chairs," handmade mantillas, Toledo damascene work, woodcarvings, wrought iron, Spanish fans, purses in grained leather, and a line of Spanish soaps and dolls. Kreisler is also an official agency for Majorcan pearls and Lladro porcelain. Prices are competitive because Kreisler doesn't add on any percentage for commissions to guides. Purchases can be packed and shipped anywhere in the world. At the **Galería Kreisler,** in a separate section, some of the fine painters and sculptors in the country have found an important showcase for their talents. Here you'll find both the old master and the avant-garde artist. The Art Gallery features Spain's most reputable artists whose works generally are in the permanent collection of the National Museum of Contemporary Art.

Galería Kreisler Dos, 8 Hermosilla (tel. 431-42-64), another Kreisler enterprise, presents contemporary paintings, sculpture, and prints. It is open from 10 a.m. to 2 p.m. and from 5 to 9 p.m. It's about 75 yards around the corner from 19 Serrano.

WOMEN'S CLOTHING: One of the most popular retail outlets for women's clothing is **Herrero,** 33 Gran Vía (tel. 222-03-10), on the main street of Madrid. Seven other retail branches and found in the capital as well, each carrying the same merchandise. The stores feature an especially good line of suede and leather dresses and coats—custom-made, if you desire.

MADRID'S LEADING DEPARTMENT STORES: Galerías Preciados, 28 Preciados 231-35-05), right off the Gran Vía, has greatly expanded and improved in recent years. It's really two stores now, connected by an underground passageway. But it's more Macy's than Lord & Taylor, with quite presentable ready-made clothing for men, women, and children. There's a top-floor snackbar and restaurant. Some good buys I recently noted include guitars, men's suede jackets, Spanish capes for men, and women's full-length suede coats in such exciting colors as royal blue, kelly green, olive, and violet.

For men's suits, in the second-floor tailoring department, you can have a suit made to order. You're fitted with one of the basic "try-on" suits. The goodly selection of fabrics—plaids, solids, herringbones—are made into whatever style you prefer.

On the lower level is a department jam-packed with regional handicrafts, including ship models made in Catalonia, historical sword reproductions, regional dolls, tooled leather from Córdoba, damascene work from Toledo, Lladró porcelain figurines from Valencia, blown glass from Majorca, white ceramic pieces from Manises, handicrafts from Galicia, and ceramics from Gerona and Valencia.

The other big department store chain is **El Corte Inglés,** with outlets all around the country, including Málaga. At present, branches are on Calle Preciados (tel. 232-81-00), near the Puerta del Sol in the center of the city; on the Calle Goya, where it crosses the Calle de Alcalá; on the Calle Raímundo Fernández Villaverde, right off the Avenida del Castellana; plus the newest one (the fourth in Madrid) in Princesa Street. Rather than running about from boutique to tourist shop to boutique, many visitors will find it easier and often cheaper to make all their purchases in a department store. For example, at El Corte Inglés, you can buy a handsome Toledo sword or typical gypsy doll or else the well-known Spanish mantillas.

SOME BOUTIQUES: **Don Carlos,** 92 Serrano (tel. 275-75-07), is on the best street for elegant shopping in Madrid. This boutique features an excellent selection of clothing for both women and men. . .Also good is **Blanco,** 26 Velázquez (tel. 226-61-27), a most up-to-date boutique that is more popular with the younger set. . .Finally, **Berhanyer,** 25 Juan de Mena (tel. 231-41-77), is Spain's top designer, offering a wide selection of his ready-to-wear apparel in this handsome boutique. It's highly recommended for quality merchandise, but only if you can afford it.

CUSTOM TAILORING: **Valdivia,** 86 Gran Vía (tel. 247-96-40), is in the Edificio España (the Plaza Hotel building) at the Plaza de España. A tried and tested establishment, it turns out skillfully tailored suits for men. Mariano Valdivia has won the respect and patronage of many a Spanish businessman or diplomat, inheriting his skill and business from his father. His staff can produce a suit in four or five working days, if you're available for fittings. Their shop offers an excellent choice of fabrics in all weather weights. Everything is made by hand, even the buttonholes. They can give you a conservative banker's look or outfit you in more trendy clothing. A good selection of custom shirts is also available.

A HOUSE OF CERAMICS: Antiqua Casa Talavera, 2 Isabel la Católica (tel. 247-34-17), is known as "the first house of Spanish ceramics." Its wares include a sampling of regional ceramic styles from every major area of Spain, including Talavera, Toledo, Manises, Granada, and Sevilla, among other sources. Sangría pitchers, dinnerware, tea sets, plates, vases. . .everything is handmade. Inside one of the showrooms, there is an interesting selection of tiles, ranging from reproductions of scenes from *El Quijote*, bullfights, dances, and folklore, to scenes from famous paintings at the Prado. At its present location for more than 60 years, the shop is only a short walk from the Plaza de Santo Domingo and the subway station there.

ANTELOPE AND LEATHER GOODS: Boutique Shalom, 45 Gran Vía (tel. 247-17-39), specializes in antelope and leather, as well as suede. This third-floor shop will make any design you want: bring in a sketch or photograph, and the workers will turn it out within 24 to 36 hours. The shop also does work in *napalán* (sheepskin), wool, silk, and cotton. There is a variety of antelope jackets for men and women, as well as beautiful suede jackets.

HANDICRAFTS AND GIFTS: Aleixandre, 23 Gran Vía (tel. 221-29-20). At four different locations in Madrid, Aleixandre offers one of the most tasteful selections of gifts in the Spanish capital. Shopping is made even more enjoyable by the elegant, salon-like setting, combined with the flattering, personalized service. The merchandise includes a wide selection of 18th- and 19th-century fans, jewelry, costume jewelry, leather goods, perfume, mantillas, Toledo ware, and Perlas (pearls) Majorica. The other Madrid shops are at 47 Montera (tel. 221-29-20), 5 Plaza Canalejas (tel. 222-59-72), and 39 Velázquez (tel. 276-86-24).

Chapter XVI

THE ABC'S OF SPAIN

WHATEVER YOUR NEEDS or travel problems, you'll find that Madrid has the answer to them. The single question is: How do you find what you are seeking quickly and conveniently? In an emergency, of course, your hotel is your best bet. But some of the smaller hotels aren't staffed with personnel entirely fluent in English; and sometimes—even if they are—the person at the desk can be amazingly apathetic about something of vital interest to you.

What follows, then, is an alphabetical listing of important miscellany—the data that can often be crucial to a visitor. Typical queries, answered below, include: How much do I tip a porter? How do I make a telephone call? Find a doctor? etc.

AIRPORTS: Barajas is the international airport for Madrid, and it's divided into two separate terminals—one for international flights, another for domestic. A shuttle bus runs between the two. For Barajas airport information, telephone 205-40-90.

Air-conditioned yellow buses take you from right outside the arrival terminal at Barajas to the underground bus depot under the Plaza Colón. You can also get off at several points along the way, provided you don't have your suitcases stored in the hold. The cost of the service is 150 pesetas (98¢), and buses leave about every 20 minutes, either to or from the airport.

If you go by taxi into town, the approximate cost is 1500 pesetas ($9.75), and the driver is entitled to assess a surcharge (either direction), not only for the trip but for baggage handling. If you should step into a nonmetered limousine, it is important to negotiate the price in advance.

AMERICAN EXPRESS: For your mail or banking needs, the American Express office at the corner of the Marqués de Cubas and the Plaza de las Cortes (tel. 429-68-75) (across the street from the Palace Hotel) draws the visiting Yankee. The office is open weekdays from 9 a.m. to 5:30 p.m. and on Saturday until noon.

BABYSITTERS: Nearly all major hotels in Madrid can arrange for babysitters. Usually, the concierge keeps a list of reliable nursemaids or young girls and will get in touch with one of them for you, providing you give adequate notice. Rates vary considerably, but tend to be reasonable. More and more babysitters in Madrid speak English, but don't count on it. Chances are yours won't—although you can request it, of course.

BANKS: You get a better exchange rate here if you're exchanging dollars into pesetas than you do at any of the exchange bureaus around the city. Banks are open at 9:30 a.m. (but it's best to go after 10 a.m.) to 2 p.m. Monday to Friday. Banks are also open on Saturday from 9:30 a.m. to 1 p.m.

BOOKSTORES: There are many all over the city, selling both English- and Spanish-language editions, along with touring maps. **Aguilar** has three outlets: 24 Serrano (tel. 435-36-42), 18 Goya (tel. 275-06-40), and Paseo Castellana (tel. 250-36-39). Or you could try **Editorial Hernando,** 11 Ferraz (tel. 247-62-27).

BUS TERMINALS: Madrid has two principal ones— **Auto Res,** 6 Glorieta Conde de Casals (tel. 251-66-44), and the large **Estación Sur de Autobuses,** 17 Canarias (tel. 468-42-00). Buses to the environs of Madrid, such as Toledo and Segovia, leave from numerous other stations; it's best to telephone 401-99-00 for the latest information about departures.

CLOTHING SIZES: For the most part, Spain uses the same sizes as the continent of Europe. The sizes of women's stockings and men's socks are international.

For Women

Junior Miss		Regular Dresses		Shoes	
U.S.	*Spain*	*U.S.*	*Spain*	*U.S.*	*Spain*
5	34	10	40	5	36
7	36	12	42	5½	36½
9	38	14	44	6½	37½
11	40	16	46	7½	38½
		18	48	8	39
		20	50	8½	39½
				9	40

For Men

Shirts		Slacks		Shoes	
U.S.	*Spain*	*U.S.*	*Spain*	*U.S.*	*Spain*
14	36	32	42	5	36
14½	37	34	44	6	37
15	38	36	46	7	38
15½	39	38	48	7½	39
15¾	40	40	50	8	40
16	41			9	41
16½	42			10	42
17	43			10½	43
				11	44
				12	45

Warning: This chart should be followed only as a very general outline, as in the same country there are big differences in sizes. If possible, try on all clothing or shoes before making a purchase. You'll be glad you did.

CONSULATES AND EMBASSIES: The **American Embassy** is at 75 Calle de Serrano (tel. 276-36-00), and the **Canadian Consulate** is at 35 Nuñez de Balboa (tel. 225-91-19). The **British Embassy** is at 16 Fernanado el Santo (tel. 419-02-00).

CURRENCY: Spain's unit of currency is the peseta, worth about $.0065 in U.S. terms (as of this writing—subject to change). One U.S. dollar is worth about 154 pesetas. Spain also uses céntimos, units of currency so low they're almost worthless. It takes 100 céntimos to equal only 1 peseta which is worth about ½¢ in U.S. coinage.

CUSTOMS: Spain permits you to bring in most personal effects and the following items duty free: two still cameras with ten rolls of film each, one movie camera, tobacco for personal use, one bottle each of wine and liquor per person, a portable radio, a tape recorder and a typewriter, a bicycle, golf clubs, tennis racquets, fishing gear, two hunting weapons with 100 cartridges each, skis and other sports equipment.

Upon leaving Spain, American citizens who have been outside the U.S. for 48 hours or more are allowed to bring in $400 (U.S.) worth of merchandise duty free—that is, if they have claimed no similar exemption within the past 30 days. Beyond this free allowance, the next $1000 worth of merchandise is assessed at a flat rate of 10% duty. If you make purchases in Spain, it's important to keep your receipts.

DENTIST: For an English-speaking dentist, get in touch with the American Embassy, 75 Calle de Serrano (tel. 276-34-00), which has a list of recommended ones. If you have a dental emergency, you may have to call several before you can get an immediate appointment—hence, the need of a conprehensive list.

ELECTRIC CURRENT: Most establishments now have either 125 or 220 volts. Carry your voltage adapter with you and always check at your hotel desk before plugging in any electrical equipment. It's best to travel with battery-operated equipment.

EMERGENCIES: If you need the police, call 091. In case of fire, dial 232-32-32, and if in need of an ambulance as in the case of an accident, telephone 256-02-00.

FILM: As one tourist official put it, film is "expensive as hell in Spain." Take in as much as Customs will allow. I suggest you wait to process it until you return home. However, if you can't wait, and you'll be in Spain long enough to get your pictures back, you can take your undeveloped film to the leading department store, **Galerias Preciados,** 28 Preciados, right off the Gran Vía (tel. 231-35-05). There you'll find a department which will develop your film in two hours.

GAS: Gas is easily obtainable and is the normal fuel used in rented cars in Spain. The average Spanish vehicle—predominantly Seats or Fiats—gets close to 45 miles a gallon.

HAIRDRESSER: Lis is a salon offering manicures and hairdressing for women, specializing in styling and dying. It's in the Torre de Madrid (tel. 241-54-39) and is open from 9:30 a.m. to 7:30 p.m.

HITCHHIKING: This is no longer smiled upon as much as it used to be. It may be technically illegal. However, people still do it, tourists tending to pick up tourists. I don't recommend you stick out your thumb in the presence of the Civil Guard.

HOLIDAYS: They include January 1 (New Year's Day); January 6 (Epiphany); March 19 (Day of St. Joseph); Good Friday; Easter Monday; May 1 (May Day); June 10 (Corpus Christi); June 29 (Day of St. Peter and St. Paul); July 25 (Day of St. James); August 15 (Feast of the Assumption); October 12 (Spain's National Day); November 1 (All Saints' Day); December 8 (Immaculate Conception); and December 25 (Christmas). No matter how large or small, every city or town in Spain also celebrates its local saint's days. In Madrid it's on May 15 (Saint Isidro).

HOSPITAL: On the outskirts of Madrid, in the University City, stands a thoroughly up-to-date and well-run establishment, the **British American Hospital,** 1 Paseo de Juan XXIII, Ciudad Universitaria (tel. 234-67-00). Twenty-four-hour emergency care can be rendered here, and English-speaking doctors are on duty. Fees are payable in advance. They also take major credit cards. In addition, the **U.S. Embassy,** 75 Calle de Serrano (tel. 276-36-00), will present you with a detailed list of doctors in Madrid, indicating their training and whether or not they speak English.

LANGUAGE: Spanish is the official language of the land, of course, and French is also widely spoken in parts. In Madrid more and more people, especially the younger ones, are learning English. Nearly all major hotels and top restaurants are staffed with English-speaking persons. However, out in the country it is to be hoped you were a language major in school.

LAUNDRY: In most first-class hotels recommended in this guide, you need only fill out your laundry and dry-cleaning list and present it to your maid or valet. Same-day service usually costs anywhere from 25% to 50% more. If you don't have time to wait and/or you want to save money, go to the **Miele Coin Laundry,** at the intersection of Travesia del Conde Duque and Calle del Conde Duque, a short walk from the Plaza de España.

LIQUOR: Almost anyone of any age can order a drink in Spain. I've seen gypsy shoeshine boys who looked no more than 8 years old go into a *tasca* and purchase a glass of wine with their newly acquired tip. Bars, taverns, cafeterias, whatever, generally open at 8 a.m., and many serve alcohol all day until around 1 or 2 a.m. Spain doesn't have many stores devoted entirely to selling liquor and wine. Rather, you can purchase alcoholic beverages in almost any market, along with cheese and other foodstuffs.

METRIC MEASURES: Here's your chance to learn metric measures before they're popular in America.

Weights	Measures
1 ounce = 28.3 grams	1 inch = 2.54 centimeters
1 pound = 454 grams	1 foot = 0.3 meters
2.2 pounds = 1 kilo (1000 grams)	1 yard = 0.91 meters
1 pint = 0.47 liter	1.09 yards = 1 meter
1 quart = 0.94 liter	1 mile = 1.61 kilometers
1 gallon = 3.78 liters	0.62 mile = 1 kilometer
	1 acre = 0.40 hectare
	2.47 acres = 1 hectare

NEWSPAPERS: Most newsstands along the Gran Vía or kiosks at the major hotels carry the latest edition of the *International Herald Tribune.* Spain also has an American weekly, a magazine known as the *Guidepost.* It is packed with information about late-breaking events in the Spanish captial: tips on movies shown in English, musical recitals, whatever. You may also want to become a regular reader of the *Iberian Daily Sun,* an English-language newspaper containing stories and listings of interest to both visitors from North America and Britain as well as expatriates. If you're traveling south, look out for *Lookout* magazine, a quality production in English with stories focused primarily on Spain's Sun Coast, although the staff also runs articles of general interest to the traveler to Spain.

PASSPORTS: A valid one is all an American, British, or Canadian citizen needs to enter Spain. You don't need an international driver's license if renting a car. Your local one from back home should suffice.

PHARMACIES: Drugstores are scattered all over Madrid. If you're trying to locate one at an odd hour, note a list posted outside the door to any drugstore that's not open. On the list are the names and addresses of pharmacies which are in service. The Spanish government requires drugstores to operate on the rotating system of hours—thereby assuring you that some will be open at all times, even Sunday midnight.

POLITICS: In its post-Franco era, Spain now has a constitutional monarchy, and it won't disturb you unless you disturb it.

POST OFFICE: If you don't want to receive your mail at your hotel or the American Express office, you can direct it to *Lista de Correos* at the central post office in Madrid. To pick up such mail, go to the window marked *Lista,* where you'll be asked to show your passport. The central post office in Madrid is housed in what is known as "the cathedral of post offices" at the Plaza de la Cibeles (tel. 221-81-95). An airmail postcard to the United States costs 39 pesetas (25¢) if sent from Spain, and an airmail letter up to 10 grams goes for 51 pesetas (33¢).

RAILWAY STATIONS: Madrid has three major railway stations. At the **Atocha,** Glorieta de Carlos V, you can book passage for Lisbon, Toledo, Andalusia, the Levante (Valencia), and Aragon. The nearest Metro is Atocha. For trains to Barcelona and the French frontier, go to **Charmartín** in the northern suburbs, at Agustín de Foxa. The third is **La Estación del Norte** (Príncipe Pío), which is the main gateway for trains to Northwest Spain. For railway information, telephone 733-30-00.

Warning: In Madrid, don't wait to buy your rail ticket or make a reservation at the train station. By this time there may be no tickets left—or at least no desirable tickets remaining. For most tickets, go to the principal RENFE office at 44 Alcalá (tel. 247-74-00).

RELIGIOUS SERVICES: Most churches in Madrid are Catholic, and they're found all over the city. Catholic masses in English, however, are given in a church at 165 Alfonso XIII. For more information, call 233-20-32 in the morning. If you prefer a non-Catholic ceremony, the British Embassy Church of St. George is at 43 Nuñez de Balboa (call 274-51-55 for worship hours).

The interdenominational Protestant Community Church is at 34 Padre Damian (tel. 246-25-61), offering weekly services in the Colegio de los Sagrados Corazones, while the Immanuel Baptist Church offers English-speaking services at 4 Hernández de Tejada (tel. 407-43-47).

A Christian Science church is at 53 Alonso Cano (tel. 259-21-35), and a Jewish synagogue is located on the Calle de Balmes (tel. 445-98-35). It opened in the late 1960s, the first one to do so since the expulsion of the Jews from Spain in 1492. Friday night services begin at 7:30, while Saturday morning services are at 9:30 a.m.

REST ROOMS: Some are available, including those in Retiro Park in Madrid and on the Plaza del Oriente across from the Royal Palace. Otherwise, you can always go into a bar or *tasca*, but you really should order something—perhaps a small glass of beer or even a bag of peanuts.

The Spanish designations for rest rooms are *aseos* or *servicios*. *Caballeros* are for men, and *damas*, naturally, are for women.

SENIOR CITIZENS: Those traveling by rail get a 50% discount for trips exceeding 100 kilometers with the purchase of a *Tarjeta Dorada* (gold card) which is sold at RENFE ticket offices and train stations. Passport proof of age is necessary.

SMOKING: Temmie and Aubrey Baratz of Briarcliff Manor, New York, write: "Your readers should be forewarned that in Spain virtually everyone smokes. On buses. In the Metro. Everywhere. 'No Fumar' signs are ignored. With all that smoking, combined with inhaling diesel fumes, one wonders about the incidence of lung disease in Spain."

STORE HOURS: Major stores no longer take a siesta, and are open from 9:30 a.m. to 8 p.m. from Monday to Saturday. However, smaller stores, such as the "mama and papa" operations, still follow the old custom and do business from 9:30 a.m. to 1:30 p.m. and from 4:30 to 8 p.m.

TAXES: Spain has no Value Added Tax, popularly known as VAT, as it is not a member of the European Common Market. All prices in hotels, stores, and restaurants have the tax already "built into" their tariffs. However, there is a car-rental tax of 4½%, one of the lowest in Western Europe.

TELEGRAMS: Cables may be sent at the central post office building in Madrid at the Plaza de las Cibeles (tel. 221-81-95). However, the dialing number for international telegrams is 241-33-00.

TELEPHONES: If you don't speak Spanish, you'll find it easier to telephone from your hotel. Know, however, that this is often a very expensive way of doing it, as hotels impose a surcharge on every operator-assisted call. If you're more adventurous, you'll find street phone booths known as *cabinas*, with dialing instructions in English. Local calls can be made for 5 pesetas (3¢) if you don't talk more than three minutes. Some of these machines take 25-peseta (16¢) coins, giving you a chance to say a little more. However, it may be best for long-distance calls—especially transatlantic ones—to go to the main telephone exchange, **Central de Teléfonos,** 28 Gran Vía (tel. 004). You may not be lucky enough to find an English-speaking operator; however, you will have to fill out a simple form which will facilitate the placement of a call.

TELEX: You can send Telex messages from the central post office building in Madrid, Plaza de las Cibeles (tel. 221-81-95), and from all major hotels.

TIME: Spain is six hours ahead of Eastern Standard Time in the U.S.

TIPPING: It is not a problem if you follow certain guidelines, knowing that general rules are to be abandoned in the face of exceptional circumstances, such as someone performing a "life-

MADRID: AVERAGE MONTHLY TEMPERATURES

	HIGH	LOW		HIGH	LOW
January	46	34	July	91	65
February	48	34	August	90	66
March	52	39	September	76	65
April	65	45	October	65	52
May	75	52	November	55	48
June	78	58	December	50	41

saving feat." Tipping is simplified in Spain, since the government requires hotels and restaurants to include their service charges— usually 15% of the bill—in their tariffs or in the price of their food items. However, that doesn't mean you should skip out of a place without dispensing some extra pesetas.

Hotels: A porter is tipped 40 pesetas (26¢) per piece of luggage he handles, but never less than 100 pesetas (65¢) even if you have only one small suitcase. If the maid has performed some extra task for you, you might give her 50 pesetas (33¢). In front-ranking hotels, the concierge will often submit a separate bill.

Hairdressers: Both barbers and beauticians should be tipped at least 15% of the bill.

Taxis: Add about 12% to the fare as shown on the meter. However, if the driver personally unloads or loads your luggage, increase that to approximately 20%.

Porters: At airports such as Barajas and major terminals, the porter who handles your luggage will present you with a fixed-charge bill.

Restaurants: In both restaurants and nightclubs, 15% is added to the bill. To that, you should add another 3% to 5%, depending on the quality of the service.

Services: The little women who guard the washrooms get 10 pesetas (7¢) to 25 pesetas (16¢) and theater ushers—either at the bullfights or in movie houses or legitimate theaters—get from 25 pesetas (16¢) to 50 pesetas (33¢).

TOURIST OFFICE: The headquarters of the main tourist office is 50 Maria de Molina (tel. 411-40-19) in Madrid. The staff there dispenses folders and travel information not only about Madrid and its environs, but for the entire country. English is spoken.

Chapter XVII

ONE-DAY TRIPS FROM MADRID

IMPERIAL CITIES. . .El Greco masterpieces. . .a monastery considered the eighth wonder of the world. . .castles that "float" in the clouds. . .the palaces of the Bourbon dynasty. . .the snow-capped Guadarrama mountains.

Some of the most interesting, dramatic, and varied scenery and man-made attractions in Europe lie in the satellite cities and towns ringing Madrid. Each of the cities, like Segovia and Toledo, knew former glory in separate and individualized ways.

If your time is pressed, go at least to **Toledo**, which capsules the ages of Spain in miniature. Many tourists combine the tour of Toledo with a stopover at the royal palace of **Aranjuez**.

Ranking second is the day trip to **El Escorial**, the monastery built by Philip II—combined with a side trip to the **Valley of the Fallen.** This is followed up by a trek the third day to **Segovia**, with a side visit to nearby **La Granja,** the summer palace of the Bourbons.

These cities of Old and New Castile are appropriately called "monumental."

Toledo

The ancient capital of Spain looms on the horizon like an El Greco painting, seemingly undisturbed by the ages. The See of the Primate of Spain, the ecclesiastical center of the country, Toledo is medieval, amazingly well preserved. (For a preview of the city much as it is today, see El Greco's *View of Toledo* at the Metropolitan Museum of Art in New York City.)

The Tagus River loops around the granite promontory on which Toledo rests, surrounding the Imperial City on three sides like a snake.

Toledan steel, known as early as the first century B.C., has sliced its name down through the ages. Many a Mexican or Peruvian—if he had lived—could attest to the deadly accuracy of a Toledan sword. Nowadays, moviemakers call on the factories in and around the city whenever they're filming an epic.

But, except for its steel and damascene work, the lack of major industrial activity has kept Toledo a virtual museum. Many of its buildings are intact, having survived countless battles, the most recent being the bloody fighting the city witnessed in the Spanish Civil War. It is not uncommon for mansions to preserve their original coats-of-arms in their façades.

The natural fortress that is Toledo is a labyrinth of narrow and precipitous streets, decaying palaces, towers, and squares—all of them tourist-trodden.

The Spanish government has seen fit to preserve all of Toledo as a "national monument." One critic labeled the entire city "a gallery of Art," with every style represented from Romanesque to Moorish to Gothic (best exemplified by the cathedral) to Renaissance.

Essentially, Toledo is a blending of the widely diverse cultures that made Spain what it is today: Roman, Visigothic, Moorish, Jewish, Christian. Perhaps for that reason, Tirso de Molina, the 17th-century dramatist, called Toledo "the heart of Spain." He named three of his dramas *Los Cigarrales de Toledo,* which brings us to a most important suggestion:

Before you leave the Imperial City, you should—preferably in the late of the afternoon—traverse the **Carretera de Circunvalación,** that most scenic of roads across the left bank of the Tagus. Along the slopes of the hills you'll fine the *cigarrales,* the rustic houses. From this side of the river, you can obtain the best panorama, seeing the city in perspective as El Greco did. With luck, you'll be perched on some belvedere as the sun goes down. Then you'll know why Toledo's sunsets are called violet.

Toledo lies 44 miles south of Madrid. You can reach it by car, of course, although public transportation includes both train and bus. However, the train delivers you outside the city, and you must take a bus into the heart of Toledo, depositing yourself at the Plaza of Zocodover.

You can see all of the major sightseeing attractions in one day, providing you arrive early and stay late.

THE CATHEDRAL: Built at the flowering peak of the Gothic era of architecture, the Cathedral of Toledo is one of the greatest in Europe. It was erected principally between the years of 1226 and 1493, although there have been later additions. The monument is a bastion of Christian architecture, but a great deal of the actual construction work was carried out by the Moors, master builders themselves.

The cathedral witnessed many prime monents in Spanish history—such as a proclamation naming "Juana la Loca" (the insane daughter of Isabella I) and her husband Philip the Handsome heirs to the throne of Spain.

Inside, the Transparente—the altar completed in 1732 by Narcisco Tomé—is considered a landmark in European architecture. It has been called "unheard-of pomp." Lit by a "hole" cut through the ceiling, this production includes angels on fluffy clouds, a polychrome "Last Supper," and a Madonna winging her way to heaven.

Dating from the 16th century, the iron grate of the cathedral is in the plateresque style. Works of art include the *12 Apostles* by El Greco; paintings by Velázquez, Goya, Morales, and Van Dyck. El Greco's first painting in Toledo was commissioned by the cathedral. Called *El Expolio,* it created a furor when the devout saw the vivid coloring of Christ's garments. The artist was even hauled into the courts. Many elaborately sculptured tombs of both the nobility and ecclesiastical hierarchy are sheltered inside.

Don't fail to visit the Gothic colister, the Capilla Mayor, and the Renaissance-style Choir Room (elaborate woodcarvings), and you should see the rose windows, preferably near sunset. In the Treasure Room is a 500-pound monstrance, dating from the 16th century and said to have been made, in part, from gold that Columbus brought back from the New World. To celebrate Corpus festivites, the monstrance is carried through the streets of Toledo. The Mozarabic Chapel dates from the 16th century and contains paintings by Juan de Borgoña (a mass using Mozarabic liturgy is still conducted here).

The treasures of the cathedral can be visited in summer from 10:30 a.m. till 1 p.m. and from 3:30 to 7 p.m., costing 200 pesetas ($1.30) for admission. Off-season, the cathedral closes an hour earlier in the evening.

THE MUSEUM OF SANTA CRUZ: Dating from the 16th century and built in the form of a Greek cross, this plateresque hospice has been turned into a **Museum of Fine Arts and Archeology,** Calle de Cervantes. As a hospital, it was originally founded by Cardinal Mendoza. It is of such beautiful construction—especially its paneled ceilings—that it's a question of the "frame" competing with the pictures contained inside.

In the Fine Arts Museum are 18 paintings by El Greco (*The Burial of Count Orgaz* is a copy of his materpiece). El Greco's *The Assumption of the Virgin* is his most important canvas here. Other works are by Ribera and Goya. Flemish tapestries, antique furnishings, and jewelry round out the exhibit.

In the Archeological Museum, the past ages of Toledo are peeled away: prehistoric, Iberian, Roman (note the mosaics), Moorish, Visigothic, and Gothic. The museum is an easy walk from the Plaza de Zocodover.

Santa Cruz is open daily from 10 a.m. to 7 p.m., and charges pesetas 150 (98¢) for admission. The same ticket entitles you to visit the nearby **Museo de los Concilios y de la Cultura Visigoda.**

EL GRECO'S HOUSE AND MUSEUM: Happily ensconced in Toledo, the Cretan-born Domenico Theotocopuli (El Greco) settled down with Doña Jerónima, a noted beauty, who was his mistress (or wife?). Her looks inspired many of El Greco's madonnas.

El Greco moved to Toledo in 1577, living there until 1614. His house, the Casa del Greco, stands in the *antiguo barrio judío* or the old Jewish quarter of the monumental city on Calle Samuel Levi.

It is believed that in 1585 the painter moved into one of the decaying palace apartments belonging to a Marqués de Villena. The chancellor of the exchequer to Pedro el Cruel, Samuel Ha-Levi, is said to have built a home on the same spot in the 14th century. He had subterranean passages dug to hide his treasury. The house was eventually occupied by Don Enrique de Villena, a sorcerer, who is believed to have practiced black magic and alchemy in the underground cellars.

El Greco rented the main part of the palace. From the palace windows, the Greek painter could look out onto views of the Tagus, which he eventually captured on canvas.

The Villena apartments were torn down in this century, but the Marqués de la Vega-Inclán was responsible for saving El

Greco's dwelling place, a small Moorish house, probably also once the house of Samuel Ha-Levi. Eventually a neighboring house was incorporated to house the museum with 19 pictures of the Greco.

Visitors are admitted into the studio of El Greco, containing a painting by the artist. Especially interesting are the garden and kitchen. The house may be visited except on Sunday afternoon and Monday from 10 a.m. to 2 p.m. and from 3:30 to 7 p.m. in season. Off-season times are from 10 a.m. to 2 p.m. and from 3:30 to 6 p.m. The admission fee is 100 pesetas (65¢).

THE CHURCH AND CLOISTERS OF SAN JUAN DE LOS REYES: This church, 21 Calle de los Reyes Católicos (tel. 22-38-02), was founded by King Ferdinand and Queen Isabella to commemorate their triumph over the Portuguese at Toro in 1476. Its construction was started in 1477, according to the plans of architect Juan Guas. It was finished, together with the splendid cloisters, in 1504, dedicated to St. John the Evangelist, and used, from the very beginning, by the Franciscan Friars. It is a perfect example of Gothic-Spanish-Flemish style.

San Juan de los Reyes has been restored after being damaged in the invasion of Napoleon and abandoned in 1835. Actually, the national monument has been entrusted again to the Franciscans since 1954. The price of admission is 50 pesetas (33¢). You can visit the church from 10 a.m. to 2 p.m. and from 3:30 to 7 p.m. (it closes an hour earlier in winter).

THE CHURCH OF SANTO TOMÉ: Except for its mudéjar tower, this little 14th-century chapel, on the Calle de Santo Tomé (tel. 210-209), is rather unprepossessing. But by some strange twist it was given the honor of exhibiting El Greco's masterpiece, *The Burial of Count Orgaz.* Long acclaimed for its composition, the painting is a curious work in its blending of realism with mysticism. To view the painting, you have to purchase a ticket for 55 pesetas (36¢).

It is open from 10 a.m. to 1:45 p.m. and from 3:30 to 6:45 p.m. in summer, closing an hour earlier in winter. Closed on Christmas Day and New Year's Day.

THE ALCÁZAR: The characteristic landmark dominating the skyline of Toledo is the Alcázar, located on the Plaza de Zocodover. It attracted worldwide attention during the siege of the city in 1936. Nationalists held the fortress for 70 days until relief troops could respond to their plea for help, arriving on September 27, 1936.

The most famous event surrounding that battle was a telephone call the Republicans placed to the Nationalist leader inside. He was informed that his son was being held captive and would be executed if the Alcázar were not surrendered. He refused to comply with their demands, and his son was sacrificed.

The Alcázar was destroyed, and the one standing in its place today is a reconstruction, housing an **Army Museum** with a monument out front of the heroes of that 1936 siege. The price of admission is 100 pesetas (65¢).

THE TRÁNSITO SYNAGOGUE: Down the street from El Greco's museum on the Paseo del Tránsito is the once important worshipping place for the large Jewish population that used to inhabit the city, living peacefully with both Christians and Arabs. This 14th-century building is noted for its superb stucco and Hebrew inscriptions. There are some psalms along the top of the walls and on the east wall a poetic description of the temple. The building of the synagogue was ordered by the chancellor of the exchequer to King Pedro el Cruel (Peter the Cruel), Don Samuel Ha-Levi. The name of the king appears clearly in a frame in the Hebrew inscription.

The synagogue is the most important part of the Sephardic Museum (Museo Safardí), which was inaugurated in 1971 and contains in other rooms the tombstones with Hebrew epigraphy of the Jews of Spain before 1492, as well as other art pieces. The museum and synagogue can be visited from 10 a.m. to 2 p.m. and 4 to 7 p.m. Closed Monday. Admission is 75 pesetas (49¢). For information, telephone 22-36-65.

Aranjuez

On the Tagus River, 29 miles south of Madrid, Aranjuez strikes visitors as a virtual garden. It was mapped out by the royal architects and landscapers of Ferdinand VI in the 18th century. The natural setting has been successfully blended with wide boulevards and fountain- and statuary-filled gardens.

And what a setting! Surrounded in late spring by beds of asparagus and heavily laden strawberry vines, Aranjuez exudes the spirit of May. But for some visitors autumn best reveals the royal town. It is then that the golden cypress trees cast lingering shadows in countless ponds, evoking a painting by Santiago Rusiñol y Prats.

Once at Aranjuez, you can buy a ticket for 250 pesetas ($1.63), entitling you to visit the three most important sights in the town, the **Royal Palace** and the adjoining **Jardín de la Isla** (Garden of the Island), and the **Casa del Labrador** in the Jardín del Príncipe.

THE ROYAL PALACE: Since the beginning of a united Spain, the climate and natural beauty of Aranjuez have attracted Spanish monarchs, notably Ferdinand and Isabella, as well as Philip II, who managed to tear himself away from El Escorial. But the Royal Palace in its present form dates primarily from the days of the Bourbons, who used to come here mainly in the autumn and spring, reserving La Granja, near Segovia, for their summer romps. The palace was also favored by Philip V and Charles III.

Fires have swept over the structure numerous times, but most of the present building was finished in 1778. William Lyon, writing in the Madrid weekly, the *Guidepost,* called "its dominant note" that of ". . .deception: in almost each of its widely varying rooms there is at least one thing that isn't what it first appears." Among other examples, Mr. Lyon cites assemblages of mosaics that look like oil paintings; a trompe l'oeil ceiling that seems three-dimensional, although in fact it is flat; and a copy of a salon at the Alhambra Palace at Granada.

In spite of these eye-fooling tricks, the palace is lavishly and elegantly decorated. Especially notable are the dancing salon, the throne room, the ceremonial dining hall, the bedrooms of the king and queen, and a remarkable Salón de Porcelana (Porcelain Room). Paintings include works by Lucas Jordán and José Ribera.

The palace is always open in the morning from 10 a.m. to 1 p.m. However, its afternoon hours are as follows: 3 to 5 p.m., October through February; 3 to 6 p.m., March through May, and 4 to 7 p.m., June through September.

El Escorial

In the Guadarrama mountain resort of El Escorial, about 30 miles northwest from Madrid, stands the imposing **Monastery of San Lorenzo el Real del Escorial.** Many refer to it as .the eighth wonder of the world. Both a palace and a monastery, it was ordered built by Philip II to commemorate the triumphs of his forces at the Battle of San Quentín in 1557. Escorial was dedicated to St. Lawrence, the martyred saint burned to death.

The original architect in 1563 was Juan Bautista de Toledo; but after his death the monumental task was assumed by the greatest architect of Renaissance Spain, Juan de Herrera, who completed it in the shape of a gridiron in 1584.

The severe lines of the great pile of granite strike many as being as austere as the pious Philip himself. The architectural critic, Nikolaus Pevsner, called it ". . .overwhelming, moving no doubt, but frightening."

The Palace, Pantheon, Chapter House, and Library, as well as the satellite Casita del Príncipe and the Casita del Infante, may be visited in summer from 10 a.m. to 1 p.m. and from 3 to 7 p.m (till 6 p.m. in winter). The general admission ticket costs 225 pesetas ($1.46).

In the **Charter Hall** is one of the greatest art collections in Spain outside of the Prado, the canvases dating primarily from the 15th to the 17th centuries. Among the most outstanding works are El Greco's *The Martyrdom of St. Maurice;* Titian's *Last Supper;* Velázquez's *The Tunic of Joseph;* Van der Weyden's *Crucifixion;* and another version of Bosch's *The Hay Wagon* (see also a remarkable tapestry based on a painting by "El Bosco"); there are also works by Ribera, Tintoretto, and Veronese.

The **Biblioteca** contains one of the most important libraries in the world, its estimated number of volumes in excess of 50,000. The collection, started by Philip II, ranges far and wide: Moslem codices, a Gothic "Cántigas" of the 13th century from the reign of Alfonso X (known as "The Wise King"); and signatures from the Carmelite nun, St. Teresa of Jesús, who conjured up visions of the devil and of angels sticking burning hot lances into her heart.

For many sightseers, the highlight of the tour is a visit to the **Apartments of Philip II,** containing many of the original furnishings of the monarch. In the "cell for my humble self" that he ordered built, he died in 1598. He desired quarters that were spartan, and so they remain today—graced by a painting by Bosch, a copy he made of his *The Seven Capital Sins,* now at the Prado.

The **Apartments of the Bourbons** reflect different tastes and style, a complete break from the asceticism imposed by the Hapsburg king. They are richly decorated, with a special emphasis on tapestries (many resembling paintings), based on Goya and Bayeu cartoons at the Royal Factory in Madrid.

From a window in his bedroom, a weak and dying Philip II could look down at the services being conducted in the **Basilica.** As the dome clearly indicates, the church was modeled after Michelangelo's drawings of St. Peter's in Rome. Works of art include a crucifix by Benvenuto Cellini; choir stalls by Herrera; and sculptured groups of father and son (Charles V and Philip II), along with their wives, flanking the alter.

The **Royal Pantheon,** burial place of Spanish kings from Charles V to Alfonso XII, is under the altar. (The Burbon king, Philip V, is interred at La Granja; and the body of Ferdinand VI was placed in a tomb in a Madrid church.) In the octagonal mausoleum, you'll see the tombs of queens who were mothers of kings.

On the lower level rests one of the curiosities of El Escorial: A "Wedding Cake" tomb for royal children. The Whispering Hall, with its odd sound effects, is also intriguing.

The Valley of the Fallen

The Spanish call it the *Valle de los Caídos.* Inaugurated by Generalísimo Franco in 1959, it is a heroic-size monument to the Spanish dead of the Civil War, both the Nationalists and the Republicans. *"El Caudillo"* had wanted to honor only the Nationalist soldiers, but was prevailed upon to change his mind in the interest of the country's unity.

For two decades, workmen tunneled out an already existing gorge in the Guadarrama mountains, making room for a basilica and a mausoleum. Crowning the Rock of Nava is a gargantuan cross, nearly 500 feet high, stretching out its crossbars a distance of 150 feet.

Directly below the cross is the underground basilica, decorated with mosaics. The body of José António, the founder of the Falangist party, was finally interred here. His burial at the monastery of El Escorial sparked a wave of protests from the monarchists, who objected to the Spanish leader's "nonroyal" birth. To reach the basilica, you must first walk through a series of six chapels.

Segovia

In Old Castile, Segovia is one of the most romantic of Spanish cities, its glory of another day. Isabella I was proclaimed queen of Castile here in 1474. Segovians live with the memory of the time when their star was in ascendancy.

The capital of a province of the same name, it lies on a slope of the snow-capped Sierra de Guadarrama mountains, between two ravine-studded valleys and the Eresma and Clamores Rivers (actually streams). As it appears on the horizon, dominated by its Alcázar and its Gothic cathedral, Segovia is decidedly of the Middle Ages.

The city was of strategic importance to the Roman troops, and one of its greatest monuments, the Aqueduct, dates from those times. The skyline is characterized by the Romanesque belfries of the churches and the towers of its old and decaying palaces.

The Upper Town is mainly encased by its old walls; but the part outside the walls is of interest, too, especially for views of the Alcázar and visits to the Church of Vera Cruz and the Monastery of El Parral.

THE TOP SIGHTS: Many of the charms of Segovia are obvious. Merely strolling its narrow winding streets and stumbling upon a secluded plaza forgotten by time is a fit and proper reward to any traveler. More so than any other competitor, Segovia captures and maintains the pristine look of an ancient Castilian city. But the capital contains three sights which are the front rank: (1) the **Alcázar,** (2) the **Aqueduct,** and (3) the **Cathedral.**

WHERE TO DINE: One reason the Spanish go to Segovia is to dine on cochinillo asado, or roast suckling pig. Everyone from Hemingway to King Hussein has been drawn to the landmark **Mesón de Cándido,** 5 Plaza Azoguejo (tel. 42-81-02), a 15th-century inn presided over by the *mesonero mayor de Castilla.* Near the Aqueduct, the classic Castilian restaurant, the finest in Segovia, offers a choice of six dining rooms in an antique motif. Those who don't order the roast suckling pig ask for the cordero asado (roast lamb). Both seem equally good. For a complete repast, including the specialties, expect to pay from 2000 pesetas ($13) to 3000 pesetas ($19.50).

La Granja

This was the summer palace of the Bourbon kings of Spain, who imitated the grandeur of Versailles in Segovia province. Set against the snow-capped Guadarrama mountains, the slate-roofed palace dominates the village which grew up around it (nowadays a small summer resort).

The founder of La Granja was Philip V, grandson of Louis

XIV and the first Bourbon king of Spain (his body, along with that of his second queen, Isabel de Fernesio, is interred in a mauseoleum in the Collegiate Church). Philip V was born at Versailles on December 19, 1683, which partially explains why he wanted to re-create that atmosphere at Segovia.

At one time, a farm stood on the grounds of what is now the palace—hence the totally inappropriate name *granja,* meaning farm in Spanish.

The palace was built in the first part of the 18th century. Inside you'll find valuable antiques (many in the Empire style), paintings, a remarkable collection of tapestries of Flemish design and others based on Goya cartoons from the Royal Factory in Madrid.

Most visitors, however, seem to find a stroll through the gardens more to their liking, so allow adequate time for it. The fountain statuary is a riot of gods and nymphs cavorting with abandon, hiding indiscretions behind jets of water. The gardens are studded with chestnuts and elms.

Charging an admission fee of 140 pesetas (91¢), the royal palace can be visited from 10 a.m. to 1 p.m. and from 3 to 5:30 p.m. The entrance to the gardens is free, except on Thursday, Saturday, and Sunday, May through October. At those times, at 5:30 in the afternoon, the price is 60 pesetas (39¢)—little enough to pay to see the spectacular display when the water jets are turned on.

The Prado Museum, Madrid

Chapter XVIII

SPAIN IN A NUTSHELL

BEFORE LEAVING the Spanish capital, why not take the extra time at least to skim the surface of some of the most rewarding targets on the Iberian peninsula?

Central Spain

ÁVILA: One of the great medieval centers of Europe, Ávila is forever associated with St. Teresa of Jesús, the mystic Carmelite nun about whom a number of legends arose after her death. The loftiest city in Spain, Ávila is completely encircled by its 11th-century walls.

While there, visit the 17th-century **Convent of St. Teresa;** a Romanesque and Gothic cathedral that once doubled as a fortress; and the 15th-century Gothic-style **Church and Monastery of St. Tomás,** burial place of Torquemada, prosecutor of "heretics."

Ávila lies 68 miles west of Madrid, reached in about two hours by train from Madrid's North Station.

SALAMANCA: Once one of the most prestigious university centers of Europe, this golden city of plateresque buildings is wonderfully preserved. It was the home of the great Spanish philosopher Unamuno, who died there in 1936. Salamanca is a virtual museum of architectural monuments: its **Old** and **New Cathedrals;** the 13th-century **University** (oldest in Spain); the **Casa de las Conchas** (house of shells); the **Convent of San Esteban** (late Gothic, high altar by Churriguera), and the **Plaza Mayor.**

From Madrid, Salamanca is traditionally visited after a stopover in Ávila. Salamanca lies about 135 miles west of Madrid, in the direction of the Portuguese frontier. Many motorists leave

Madrid in the morning and spend the night in Salamanca. Trains bound for the city depart Madrid's North Station.

Andalusia

SEVILLE: The unofficial captial of Andalusia, Seville is the most festive city in Spain—but also one of the most dangerous. Because of high unemployment, its crime rate is among the highest in Spain. Purse-snatching is now commonplace, and cars left unguarded on the street are often broken into. Take caution whenever and wherever you travel, but be extremely careful in visiting this legendary center of Carmen.

The city is wealthy in sights, including a Gothic **cathedral,** among the largest in the world, and an **Alcázar** that was a 14th-century mudéjar palace (former tenants: Ferdinand and Isabella). The landmark of the city is **La Giralda Tower,** built as a minaret in the 12th century. But it is the city itself—especially the **Santa Cruz** district of narrow streets and bougainvillea-draped balconies—that intrigues the foreign wanderer. However, don't go wandering alone there at night. Its April Fair and Holy Week draw visitors from all over Europe.

Seville is 335 miles southwest of Madrid. It's customary for drivers to make it to Córdoba for the first night's stopover, then head on to Seville the following day, a distance of 85 miles. The fast TALGO train leaves Madrid's Atocha Station.

From Seville, the most interesting day trip is to **Jerez de la Frontera,** surrounded by its aristocratic vineyards that produce sherry. Connected by bus and rail to Seville, it lies 60 miles to the south of that city.

GRANADA: The **Alhambra Palace,** the legacy of the vanquished Moors, is the most celebrated architectural site in Spain. Stroll through its patios, past its bubbling fountains where harem girls danced, and relive Washington Irving's *Tales of the Alhambra.* The 13th-century Moslem palace stands alongside an incongruously placed Renaissance structure, ordered erected by the Hapsburg king Charles V. Isabella and Ferdinand, the "liberators" of Granada, are buried in the Gothic-style **Royal Chapel,** in back of the ornate Renaissance Cathedral of Granada.

Granada is 2200 feet above sea level, spread over two hills, the Albaicín and the Alhambra. It lies at the foothills of the Sierra Nevada and their snow-capped peaks. A gay and colorful city of

Andalusia, it attracts tourists at night to its gypsy caves of **Sacro-Monte**, where *zambras* (Moorish festivals) are staged. However, these are often unabashed tourist traps. Go if you **must**, but hang on to your valuables. Recently when one light-fingered performer couldn't pick my pocket, she chased me down the hill yelling, "Money, money, money."

Granada is 268 miles south of Madrid, a long day's drive. A fast TER train leaves Madrid's Atocha Station, the trip taking approximately seven hours.

CÓRDOBA: This Andalusian city enjoyed its greatest prosperity under the Moors when it was the seat of the Western Caliphate. In the middle of the tenth century, it was the largest city of Europe, a focal point of culture, with mosques, libraries, and palaces. Today, after much destruction and rebuilding, it is still characterized by narrow streets, flower-filled patios, white-washed houses, and Moorish, Romanesque, and Gothic sightseeing attractions.

The most important sight is the **Mezquita**, a mosque founded in the eighth century, the crowning architectural achievement of the Moselms in the West, who adorned it with peppermint-stripe pillars, a forest of jasper and marble. See also the **Alcázar** of the Christian kings, built in the 14th century, and the **Museum of Julio Romero de Torres**, a memorial to the Córdoba-born artist who delighted in painting nude women.

The distance from Madrid to Córdoba is 260 miles and can be traversed in a day's drive. You can also take a TER train from Chamartín Station, leaving Madrid in the morning and arriving at midafternoon.

Catalonia

BARCELONA: The capital of Catalonia in the northeastern part of the country, Barcelona is Spain's "second city." The largest port on the Mediterranean, it will introduce you to a way of life and culture far removed from that of the cliché-ridden Spain of mantillas and Carmens.

Barcelona is often referred to as the most European of Spanish cities; it's graced (critics say marred) by some of the most curious architecture in the world, the work of the incomparable Gaudí. See, in particular, his Catalán landmark, the uncompleted **Tem-**

ple of the **Sacred Family,** as well as his **Parque Güell,** a surrealist park on the slope of Tibidabo Mountain.

Tibidabo, a sort of Coney Island in the sky, is one of the more intriguing man-made attractions, as is the **Pueblo Español** in Montjuich Park (built in 1929 for the World's Fair). The **Gothic Quarter,** dominated by its historic **cathedral,** is the aristocratic sector of the city, characterized by narrow streets and squares.

Other sights include the **Picasso Museum** and, in contrast, the **Museum of the Art of Catalonia,** unique in the world. The denizens of Barcelona promenade up and down the Ramblas and so will you. But do so with care. One local woman confided to me that she considers the Ramblas unsafe after 12 noon!

Transportation: Barcelona is 389 miles east of Madrid. Many make-it-or-die motorists attempt to drive this long, difficult route in one day. More prudent trippers stop over in **Saragossa,** the capital of Aragón, for the night.

Iberia Airlines flies directly between Madrid and Barcelona; there is train service as well. Avoid the slow coaches that stop at every olive grove en route; instead, take the Costa Brava Express, leaving Madrid's Chamartín Station.

Excursions: Like Madrid, Barcelona is the hub for some of the most interesting excursions in Spain. Chief among them is the world-famed benedictine monastery of **Montserrat,** 38 miles to the northwest (can be explored on an organized tour). A large number of tourists are learning that it's better to visit the **Costa Brava** on a one-day excursion than to attempt to fight the French for the limited number of hotel accommodations in summer. The jagged coastline begins about 43 miles north of Barcelona at **Blanes,** a fishing village. It runs along a serpentine 95-mile trail, racing toward the French frontier. The most popular resorts are **Tossá de Mar** and **Lloret de Mar.**

Gaining in importance is the resort to the south of Barcelona, **Sitges,** on the "Gold Coast" (especially frequented by the beautiful people of Scandinavia). For historic interest, Tarragona, about 59 miles south of Barcelona, was an old Roman city (visit its "Cyclopean" city walls, its 12th-century cathedral, Roman amphitheater, and Necropolis).

The Levante

VALENCIA: Dominating southeastern Spain, known as The Levante, this Mediterranean port city is belatedly gaining recognition as a tourist center. El Cid liberated the city from Moorish domination in 1094, although the Arabs regained possession in 1101 following the death of the warrior king.

Encircling the city is the **Huerta,** studded with orange trees and rice paddies (the celebrated paella is a specialty of Valencia). The capital of its province, Valencia is Spain's third city, ranking under Madrid and Barcelona. The Valencian beach, **Playa de Levante,** is about two miles from the city proper.

In Valencia, visit the 13th-century **cathedral** (it claims to possess the Holy Grail, used by Christ at the Last Supper). See also its **Generalidad,** built in the 15th and 16th centuries in the Mediterranean Gothic style, plus the **Ceramics Museum,** housed in a Rococo and Churrigueresque palace.

The city is 220 miles southeast of Madrid, easily reached by car (one day) or by rail. If you prefer the latter, take a TALGO train from Madrid's Atocha Station.

The Balearics

MAJORCA: The largest land area in the Balearic archipelago, Majorca is the most popular tourist island in the Mediterranean. It's characterized by sandy beaches, windmills turning in the wind, olive and almond trees, mountains and winding roads, little harbors, small villages, and thousands upon thousands of visitors.

Its capital is **Palma** in the western part of the island—a big, bustling seaport with an old quarter and the greatest number of modern hotels of any city in Spain. Swimming is possible from late April through October. While on the island, you may want to take a 31-mile jaunt east to **Mancor** where the artificial Majorca pearls are made, continuing on till you reach the underground forest of stalactite and stalagmite, **Las Cuevas del Drach.** In a different direction, you can explore **Valldemosa,** where George Sand and Chopin wintered, and the artist colony of **Deyá,** long associated with Robert Graves.

Iberia Airlines and Aviaco fly to Palma from Madrid, Barcelona, and Valencia. In addition, the **Compañía Trasmediterránea** offers regular motorboat service between Palma and Barcelona, and Palma and Valencia.

IBIZA: The easy life holds forth at Ibiza, the second major Balearic island. Some 85 miles from Majorca, Ibiza is reached by boat or air. The chief center is the port of **Cuidad de Ibiza,**

although the resort of **San Antonio Abad** holds more appeal for most visitors. However, those who really want to get away from it all should head for **Santa Eulalia del Río,** five miles north of Cuidad de Ibiza.

The Basque Country

SAN SEBASTIÁN: This international beach resort on the Atlantic is the capital of the Basque province of Guipúzcoa, about 13 miles from the French frontier. In August, it becomes the summer capital of Spain, when a retinue of government officials moves here from Madrid. **La Concha Beach,** its major attraction, is one of the finest in Spain.

San Sebastián also makes a good base for excursions into the Basque country: the nearby fishing villages known as the **Pasajes,** the sanctuary of **Loyola,** the once-destroyed town of **Guernica,** subject of Picasso's most famous painting, now housed in the Prado in Madrid. Many prefer to locate in San Sebastián and commute to **Pamplona** for the week-long July festival of San Fermín, highlighted by the running of the bulls through the streets. Fifty-six miles away, Pamplona is tied to San Sebastián by rail and bus connections.

In hotels, San Sebastián never has enough in July and August. Don't arrive without a reservation nailed down.

San Sebastián is reached principally by rail or car from Madrid, a distance of 291 miles. Because the resort is such a long drive from Madrid, an overnight stopover in **Burgos,** the city of "El Cid Campeador," is recommended. Then, too, an efficient TALGO train departs from Madrid's Chamartín Station.

Galicia

SANTIAGO DE COMPOSTELA: A National Monument cathedral city, Santiago de Compostela is the most ancient—and most famous—pilgrimage city of Spain.

A university town and market center for Galician farmers, Santiago is considered the third Holy City of the Christian world. Begun in the 11th century, the **cathedral** is the most splendid achievement of the Spanish Romanesque style of architecture. The **Hostal de los Reyes Católicos,** founded by Isabella and Ferdinand, has been converted into one of the most spectacular hotels in Europe by the government.

Chapter XIX

THE COSTA DEL SOL

THE MOST POPULAR beach strip in Spain—and Europe's most spectacular real-estate boom—begins at the port of Algeciras and stretches eastward all the way to Almería. Against the backdrop of once-pagan Andalusia, the Sun Coast curves gently along the Mediterranean, studded with beaches, sandy coves, dazzling lime-washed houses, high-rise apartments, olive groves, tennis courts, golf courses, swimming pools, and hotels of every type and description.

Sun-seekers from all over Europe and North America are drawn to the mild climate and virtually guaranteed sunshine. You can bathe in the sun year round, but in January and February only the Scandiniavians dare the sea. The less hardy splash in sheltered, heated pools. The mean temperature in January, the coldest month of the year, is 56 degrees Fahrenheit. In August, the hottest month, the mean temperature is about 75 degrees Fahrenheit, as prevailing sea breezes mercifully keep the heat down.

Once the Sun Coast was only a spring to autumn affair. Now, so many shivering refugees have descended from the cold cities of northern Europe that the strip is alive year round. From June through October, however, "alive" isn't the half of it. All year, bullfights, flamenco, and fiestas crowd its calendar. Holy Week in Málaga, for example, is among the most stunning celebrations in Spain, rivaling that of Seville. And then there's Málaga's colorful winter festival, packed with cultural and sporting events ranging from horse racing to folklore songs and dances. On August fiesta days, Málaga's bullfights are second to none.

Málaga

One of the most important seaports on the Mediterranean, Málaga is the queen of the Costa del Sol and the second-largest city of Andalusia. At the foot of Mount Gibralfaro, it is marked by orange trees, flower markets, and fishing boats. The best way to see the city in true 19th-century style is in a horse-drawn carriage. If possible, visit the vegetable and fish markets.

Málaga's winter climate ranks as one of Europe's most idyllic, perhaps sufficient explanation for the luxuriant vegetation in the city's parks and gardens. Truly, **El Parque,** dating from the 19th century and filled with many botanic species, ranks among the handsomest parks in Spain.

SIGHTS 'N' THINGS: Málaga is not especially known for its art treasures, even though Pablo Picasso was born here in 1881. The **Fine Arts Museum** (Bellas Artes), 6 San Agustín, owns two of his works, an oil painting and a watercolor, both done when he was a teenager. The museum is open daily in summer from Tuesday to Sunday from 10 a.m. to 1:30 p.m. and from 5 to 8 p.m. (in winter, from 4 to 7 p.m.). Cost of admission is 75 pesetas (49¢).

The city proudly possesses a trio of historical sights, however, including the **Alcazaba,** the remains of the ancient palace of Málaga's former Moorish rulers. Towers encircle two walled precincts. In ruins, it is considered an outstanding example of Moorish-Spanish architecture. Troops loyal to Isabella and Ferdinand fought a savage battle with the Arabs to take it. When the Catholic monarchs conquered Málaga, they lodged at the castle. Right in the center of town, it offers spectacular views. Wander at your leisure through the open patios, tile-lined pools, and flower gardens. Inside is an **Archeological Museum,** containing artifacts found in prehistoric caves in Málaga province. Other exhibits document cultures ranging from Greek to Phoenician to Carthaginian. Hours are from 11 a.m. to 1 p.m. and from 5 to 8 p.m. in summer (winter hours are from 10 a.m. to 1 p.m. and from 4 to 7 p.m.). Admission is 50 pesetas (33¢).

Second Catholic monarchs conquered Málaga, they lodged at the castle. Right in the center of town, it offers spectacular views. Wander at your leisure through the open patios, tile-lined pools, and flower gardens. Inside is an **Archeological Museum,** containing artifacts found in prehistoric caves in Málaga province. Other exhibits document cultures ranging from Greek to Phoenician to Carthaginian. Hours are from 11 a.m. to 1 p.m. and from 5 to 8 p.m. in summer (winter hours are from 10 a.m. to 1 p.m. and from 4 to 7 p.m.). Admission is 50 pesetas (33¢).

Second of the historical triumvirate is the cathedral, begun in

1528. Its 300-foot tower stands as a lone sentinel, without a mate. Although never finished, the cathedral took so long to build that it's a mélange of styles, roughly classified as "Spanish Renaissance." Inside, seek out in particular its ornate choir stalls. It is open from 10 a.m. to 1 p.m. and from 4 to 5:30 p.m., charging an admission of 50 pesetas (33¢).

Finally, as the sun is setting, head for **Gibralfaro Castle,** on a hilltop over the Mediterranean bay. It, too, is what's left of an ancient Moorish fortress. Originally, it is believed, the Phoenicians built a fortress on this site, but the present castle is of Arab construction and dates from the seventh century.

So much for sightseeing. Now head back to town and do some shopping on Calle Larios and its satellite alleys, all containing stores brimming with Spanish handicrafts.

A TRAVELER'S ADVISORY: Málaga is the unfortunate winner of a recent survey which declared it to have the highest crime rate in Spain. By far the most common complaint is purse-snatching, with an estimated 75% of the crimes committed by juveniles. The related problems of reported stolen passports to the U.S. consular office in Fuengirola has become a common story in town where the pickings are rich from a floating population serviced by an understaffed police force.

As a warning to travelers, I stress that all precautions should be taken, including buttoning wallets and valuables into pockets (a money belt might be an even better idea). Drive with your doors locked and your windows rolled up (many incidents occur while motorists are waiting at traffic signals with their windows down).

In an era of changing social structures, when you are likely to be perceived as a "have" traveling in an area of "have-nots," it is wise to take special care of your valuables. Don't flaunt your possessions, especially jewelry. With the right precautions taken, you can still have a pleasant, care-free holiday, and the crime wave sweeping across Málaga need not darken the spirit of your traveling time spent there.

WHERE TO STAY: For such a large city, Málaga has a surprising lack of hotels. The best ones in all price ranges are documented below.

A Deluxe Choice

Málaga Palacio, 1 Cortina del Muelle (tel. 21-51-85), is the leading five-star hotel of Málaga, a city which, frankly, lags behind in its innkeeping. The deluxe hotel is thrust right in the core of the city, opening directly on a tree-lined esplanade, near the cathedral and harbor. The building, containing 250 rooms, is built flat-iron style, rising 15 stories and crowned by an open-air swimming pool and refreshment bar. Most of the balconies open onto views of the port. Down below you can see graceful turn-of-the-century carriages pulled by horses. In high season, a twin or double rents for 12,000 pesetas ($78), dropping to 10,000 pesetas ($65) in a single, including a continental breakfast. Rooms contain private baths, phones, bars, and piped-in music; they are air-conditioned and traditionally furnished. The street floor lounges mix antiques with more modern furnishings, not always well. Parking is available next to the hotel, and other facilities include hairdressers for both men and women, a cafeteria, boutiques, a beauty salon, and a disco in the cellar.

Upper Bracket

Hotel Guadalmar, Carretera de Cádiz, km. 238/9 (tel. 31-90-00), is a nine-story resort hotel at the edge of the city with its own private beach, about a mile from the airport. All the rooms open onto a swimming pool and garden. Each well-furnished accommodation is spaciously designed, with a private sea-view balcony. From June 21 to September 30, one person pays 6000 pesetas ($39); two persons, 8500 pesetas ($55.25). Half-board costs an additional 2500 pesetas ($16.25) per person daily. Children under 12, in addition to staying free in the same room with their parents, are provided with such extra advantages as a swimming pool and playground, plus babysitters and cribs, even a special menu. Take your meals in the dining room, La Bodega, which opens onto the sea and is decorated in a rustic theme. But for a live combo to listen and dance to, go straight to La Corrida.

Medium-Priced Hotels

Parador Nacional de Gibralfaro, Monte Gibralfaro (tel. 22-19-02), is a government-owned hotel/restaurant perched high on a hill near the ancient castle, with a view of the sea, the city, the mountains, and beaches. It's an unusual combination of taste, beauty, low cost, and comfort. To get the picture, imagine a building of rugged stone with long arched open corridors, bed-

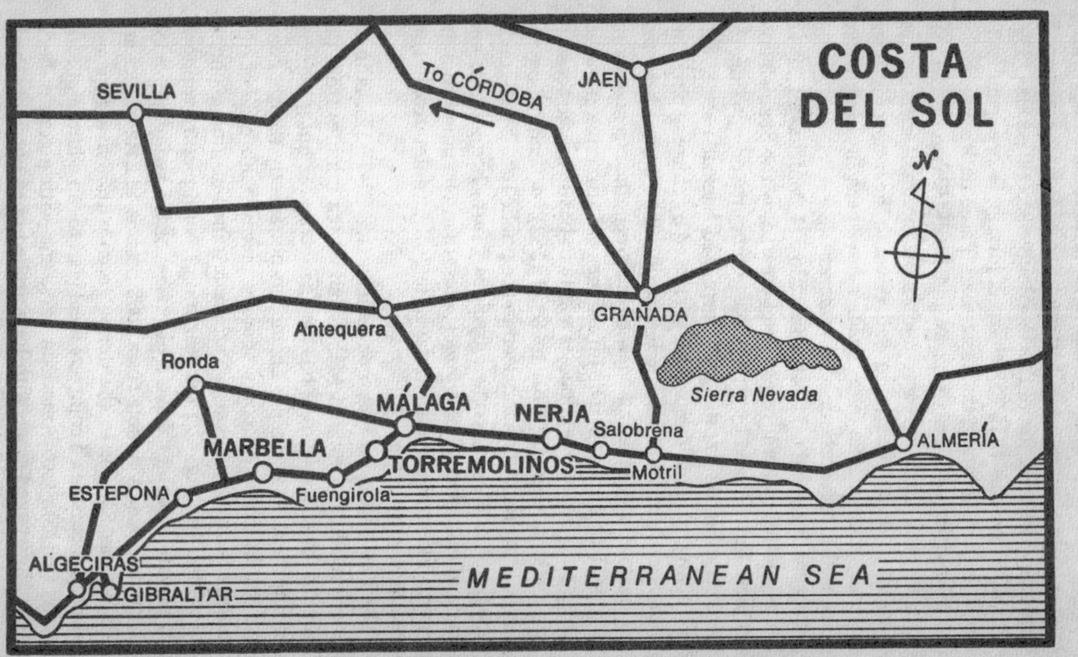
COSTA
DEL SOL
N
SEVILLA
To CÓRDOBA
JAEN
GRANADA
Antequera
Sierra Nevada
Ronda
MÁLAGA
NERJA
Salobreña
ALMERÍA
MARBELLA
TORREMOLINOS
Motril
ESTEPONA
Fuengirola
ALGECIRAS
GIBRALTAR
MEDITERRANEAN SEA

rooms furnished with cowhide upholstery and draped in hand-loomed fabrics. Moreover, each of the bedrooms comes with a private bath, a sitting area, and a terrace bedecked with garden furniture. The price for all this in a double is 6000 pesetas ($39), with 5500 pesetas ($35.75) charged for single occupancy. To reach the *parador*, take the coast road, Paseo de Reding, which becomes Avenida Casa de Pries and finally Paseo de Sancha. Turn left onto Camino Nuevo and follow the small signs the rest of the way. Do not attempt to walk down to the heart of Málaga, however. It's not safe: many readers have been mugged. (*Note:* Book well in advance for all *paradores.*)

Parador Nacional del Golf, Apartado 324, Málaga (tel. 38-12-55), is another tasteful resort hotel created by the Spanish government. Surrounded by an 18-hole golf course on one side, the Mediterranean on another, it is arranged hacienda style, with several low, tiled buildings. You're greeted by chirping birds and grounds planted with flowers. Here, too, all bedrooms have private balconies, each with a view of the green, the circular swimming pool, or the water. The furnishings are attractive, no single rooms, but you can rent doubles and twin-bedded rooms costing from 5800 pesetas ($37.70) to 8000 ($52), depending on the season. Long tiled corridors lead to the public rooms (air-conditioned, unlike the bedrooms): graciously furnished lounges and a bar and restaurant. The *parador* is less than two miles from the airport, 6½ miles from Málaga, and 2½ miles from Torremolinos.

The **Las Vegas,** 28 Paseo de Sancha (tel. 21-77-12), is in an eastern residential zone of Málaga, about ten minutes from the center of town. Its newness has long ago worn off, but it remains well kept and comfortable. The decor, not exactly stylish, combines traditional with contemporary pieces. Still, each of the spacious bedrooms has a private bath, piped-in music, phone, and central heating, and the rear rooms, with picture windows and private balconies, have a nice view of the swimming pool, garden, and sea. A double costs 5000 pesetas $32.50; singles are 3500 pesetas $22.75. In the dining room-with-a-view (Spanish and French cuisine), a complete meal goes for an additional 1500 pesetas ($9.75). Two American bars, one with a copper hood over its hearth, offer—you guessed it—good views.

Nerja

In 1959 five young men put Nerja on the map. At a point some 32 miles east of Málaga, near the hamlet of Maro, they discovered one of the great prehistoric caves of Europe. Nicknamed "the buried cathedral," the cave, about 350 yards long, is a series of intertwining galleries and passageways, reaching its highest point—about 200 feet—in what is called the Cataclysm Hall.

Paleolithic paintings of goats, deer, and horses were discovered here, as was a skeleton of a Cro-Magnon man. Rich in stalagmites and stalactites, the caves are open from 10 a.m. to 2 p.m. and from 4 to 7 p.m. in winter. Summer hours are from 9 a.m. to 9 p.m. Admission is 175 pesetas ($1.14). In August, music festivals are presented in the Hall of the Cascade, its floor the bottom of an ancient lake.

Before the discovery of the caves, the sleepy village of Nerja was known for its fabulous belvedere, the **Balcony of Europe,** commanding one of the most spectacular positions along the Costa del Sol. Nerja, perched on a cliff on the slopes of the Sierra Almijara, is a town of narrow streets and whitewashed houses. Below are plenty of hidden coves for swimming.

Medium-Priced Hotels

Parador Nacional de Nerja, Playa de Burriana (tel. 52-00-50), outside of town, takes the best of modern motel designs and blends them with a classic Spanish ambience of beamed ceilings, tiled floors, and handloomed draperies. It's built around a flower-filled courtyard with a splashing fountain. On the edge of a cliff, this government-owned hotel stands in a setting of lawns and gardens, its social life centering around a large swimming pool. There is, as well, a sandy beach below, reached by an elevator. The air-conditioned bedrooms are spacious and furnished in an understated but tasteful style. Maximum rates are charged from March 1 to October 31 and at the end of December: twin-bedded rooms with bath go for 9000 pesetas ($58.50), singles for 7000 pesetas ($45.50).

Balcón de Europa, 5 Plaza Balcón de Europa (tel. 52-08-00), occupies the most enviable position in Nerja—right at the Balcony of Europe. Reached from an entrance on the balcony plaza, it's built in a "honeycombed pueblo" style, descending to the Mediterranean below, where it has its own small beach. Most of the bedrooms have private baths and terraces overlooking the sea. The furnishings are fairly modern, meaning there's much plastic. A single costs 5000 pesetas ($32.50); a double, 7000 pesetas ($45.50). A continental breakfast at 300 pesetas ($1.95) —the only meal served—is presented in the dining room with its water-view balcony. Facilities include a sauna, a beachside grill, a disco, and a club for flamenco shows.

Inexpensive.

Hostal Fontainebleau, Calle Alejandro Bueno (tel. 52-09-39), is English-owned, directed by Peter Bainbridge and his wife Marlene, and the atmosphere is family-like. Each of the 26 pleasantly furnished rooms contains a private bath, the singles renting for 1700 pesetas ($11.05) and the doubles for 2750 pesetas ($17.88). Some family rooms, suitable for three persons (one must be a child), are offered for 3500 pesetas ($22.75). A continental breakfast is included in the rates. All accommodations open onto an attractive central patio. Weather permitting, breakfast is served alfresco. Mr. and Mrs. Bainbridge now have a chef-partner, Andrew Morris, who offers English home-style cookery served in their Beefeater Steak Bar. There is a color TV salon, and live entertainment is offered in high season. The *hostal* is about a 15-minute walk from the main beach and an eight-minute walk to the center of town, and it is open except for the month of January.

Torremolinos

On a rocky promontory in the heart of the Costa del Sol, this jet-age resort dominates a magnificent bay at the foot of the Sierra Mijas. The around-the-clock international tourist center achieved such prominence because of its five-mile-long beach, one of the finest along the Mediterranean.

If you get up at daybreak and go to the beach, you'll see the fishermen bringing in their nets. But by 10 o'clock the sun worshippers have taken over. Many never leave the beach all day, depending on vendors who come around selling snacks and drinks. The once-sleepy fishing village pulsates with life in its high-rise apartments, hotels of every hue, discos, flamenco clubs, wine *bodegas,* boutiques, restaurants, and bars, bars, and more bars—some with such unlikely names as "Fat Black Pussycat."

The original village runs along the **Calle de San Miguel,** still distinctively Andalusian despite its boutiques and restaurants. Reached past a zigzag of buildings leading down to the beach, **La Carihuela** was the old fishermen's village—it still is, if you ignore the hotels and apartments. Opposite is fashionable **Montemar,** a smart residential quarter of villas and gardens. For a slice of old Andalusia, see the **El Calvario** area, with its whitewashed houses, donkeys, and street vendors.

In the evening the sidewalk café life flourishes. Tanned blondes get inspected by retired English colonels in baggy pants —a happy melting pot of Europe (and now North America). You can spend an entire evening along the traffic-free **Calle del Cauce,** with its open-air restaurants and bars (sample predinner *tapas,* Spanish hors d'oeuvres, here).

If you want to do some shopping, you won't be disappointed: the best stores of Barcelona and Madrid operate branches in Torremolinos.

To sum up, the town has been called "Andalusian Miamic"— and.that should give you some idea of what to expect.

The Upper Bracket

Don Pablo, Paseo Marítimo (tel. 38-38-88), is one of the most desirable hotels in Torremolinos. It's a super-modern building, a minute from the beach, surrounded by its own garden and playground areas. There are two unusually shaped open-air swimming pools, with terraces for sunbathing and refreshments. The surprise is the glamorous interior which borrows heavily from Moorish palaces and medieval castle themes. Arched tiled arcades have splashing fountains, and life-size nude stone statues in niches line the grand staircase. Several of the lounges have wooden paneled and painted ceilings. Other rooms have tufted leather sofas set around Oriental rugs. At lunch a help-yourself buffet is spread before you. The 443 bedrooms have air conditioning, phones, hi-fi channels, and sea-view terraces. Facilities include a tennis center with seven courts, floodlights, and top coaching. The hotel has a full day and night entertainment program, including keep fit classes, dancing at night to a live band, and a super disco, The Caprice. Piano music is also played in a wood-paneled English lounge, and the hotel has video movies shown on a giant screen every night. Highest tariffs are in effect from July 30 until the first week of September. At that time most clients book in here on the half-board plan, paying from 6000 pesetas ($39) per person in a double and from 8000 pesetas ($52) in a single.

Cervantes, Calle de las Mercedes (tel. 38-40-33), is a four-star hotel, a short walk from the beach. It has its own garden and swimming pool (and yet another pool on the roof). The hotel is adjacent to a maze of patios and narrow streets of boutiques and open-air cafés. The Cervantes is self-contained, with many facilities, including wide sunbathing terraces. An American bar provides soft background music, and a formal dining room presents an international cuisine. In a cozy disco, generous drinks are served. The fully air-conditioned bedrooms—all with well-equipped baths—are furnished with streamlined modern. Many also contain sea-view balconies. With breakfast included, a double rents for 7450 pesetas ($48.43), a single for 4775 pesetas ($31.04). Lunch or dinner is an additional 1750 pesetas ($11.38) if you stick to the set menu. For the fatigued, there is a Swedish-style sauna with slatted wooden benches.

The Budget Range

Las Palomas, 1 Carmen Montes (tel. 38-50-00), is one of the most striking and attractive of the resort hotels built on the Málaga edge of Torremolinos. Near the coastal road, it has a formal entrance opening into spacious lounges. Tiled corridors lead to dining rooms and cocktail lounges. Public rooms often utilize ceramic collections, stone sculpture, large urns, and stylized murals in the decor. Equally stylish are the all-white bedrooms, each with balcony and private tiled bath. You pay 5000 pesetas ($32.50) in a single room, 7000 pesetas ($45.50) in a double. Lunch or dinner costs an extra 1600 pesetas ($10.40). The hotel has dancing every night to a band, and a tennis court, two pools (one heated), plus a sauna.

Miami, 10 Calle Aladino (tel. 38-52-55), near the Carihuela section, is like one of those houses movie stars used to erect in the '20s. It may even bring back memories of Vilma Banky and Rod La Rocque. Its swimming pool is isolated by high walls and private gardens. In the rear patio fuchsia bougainvillea climbs over arches. A tiled terrace is used for sunbathing and refreshments. The country-style living room contains a walk-in fireplace, lots of brass and copper. In high season, doubles rent for 3500 pesetas ($22.75), singles for 2200 pesetas ($14.30). Señora Vignale Gómez, who owns and runs it, has furnished the bedrooms with style, each traditional, each providing comfort. Every accommodation has its own balcony and private bath. Breakfast is the only meal served.

Aloha Puerto Sol, 44 Vía Imperial (tel. 38-70-66), stands on the seashore in the residential area of "El Saltillo." Away from the noise in the center of Torremolinos, it offers spacious rooms facing the sea and beach, protected by the Benalmádena Marina. One of the most modern hotels along the Costa del Sol, it contains 418 suites, each with a sitting room, a bar, and a terrace overlooking the sea. Air conditioning, radios, and telephones are provided. The highest tariff is charged in August when a junior suite rents for 9000 pesetas ($58.50) per person. In this Spanish-style resort setting, guests are given a choice of two restaurants and four bars. During the day you can lounge around two swimming pools, one heated. Spanish evenings at El Bodegón, one of the bars on the premises, last well into the early morning.

Amaragua, Los Nidos (tel. 38-46-33), is right on the beach in the middle of the residential area of Torremolinos-Montemar, with a total of 198 rooms (12 of which are suites), all with complete bath, terrace, and sea view. The hotel has lounges, television, a bar, three large swimming pools (one heated), gardens, water sports, a children's playground, a sauna, parking facilities, and a tennis court. In a double with private bath, the rate is 4500 pesetas ($29.25), 3000 pesetas ($19.50) in a single with shower bath.

Los Nidos (tel. 38-04-00) is also in the residential area of Torremolinos-Montemar next to the beach. It's in the style of a small Andalusian village, with 70 rooms and bungalows, all with bath, central heating, private entrances, and terraces. Forty have lounges and safes. Double rooms with private baths rent for 4500 pesetas ($29.25) nightly, singles for 3800 pesetas ($24.70).

Benalmádena

Where Torremolinos ends and Benalmádena begins is hard to say. Benalmádena has long since become a resort extension of Torremolinos, and it's packed with hotels, restaurants, and tourist facilities.

THE UPPER BRACKET: Tritón, 29 Avenida Antonio Machado (tel. 44-32-40), is a seafront Miami Beach-style resort hotel colony in front of the marina of Benalmádena-Costa, less than two miles from Torremolinos. It not only features a high-rise stack of air-conditioned bedrooms, but has the most impressive pool and garden area in the vicinity. Surrounding the swimming pool are subtropical trees and vegetation, plus thatched sun-shade umbrellas. The 200 air-conditioned, color-strong bedrooms have room-wide windows opening onto sun balconies, and each has a private bath. Singles cost 8500 pesetas ($55.25); doubles with breakfast, 10,500 pesetas ($68.25). Half board is an additional 3000 pesetas ($19.50) per person daily.

Among the public rooms are multilevel lounges and two bars with wood paneling and handmade rustic furniture (one has impressive stained-glass windows). For food, there's the main dining room with its three-tiered, mouthwatering display of hors d'oeuvres, fruits, and desserts; a barbecue grill, plus a luncheon terrace where ferns and banana trees form the backdrop. Not enough for you? Well, how about tennis courts, a Swedish sauna, even a piano player in the bar?

Fuengirola

This will be the Torremolinos of the future. It is already a formidable challenger. About ten miles to the west of its rival, Fuengirola and its adjacent resort village of Los Boliches are already deep into their development. Good sandy beaches against a hilly backdrop of pine woods couldn't escape attention for long—and didn't. Crowning the town are the ruins of the tenth-century **Sohail Castle,** built by the Caliphs of Córdoba and later rebuilt by Charles V as a defense against Berber pirates.

WHERE TO STAY: **Las Pirámides,** Paseo Maríitimo (tel. 47-06-00), is a skyscraper complex under pyramidal roofs favored by travel groups from the north of Europe. It's a city-like resort on the beach, with seemingly every kind of divertissement: flamenco shows on the large patio, a cozy orange bar and lounge, traditionally furnished sitting rooms, a belle epoque coffeeshop, a poolside bar, and a gallery of boutiques and tourist facilities, such as car-rental agencies. All bedrooms are air-conditioned, with slick modern styling, as well as private baths and terraces. Singles pay 6000 pesetas ($39); doubles, 8000 pesetas ($52).

Mare Nostrum, Carretera de Cádiz, km. 214 (tel. 47-11-00), was architecturally inspired by Sohail Castle on a neighboring hill. Three giant circular buildings, fortress-like in their bulk, form a self-contained holiday resort, complete with tennis courts, bowling, mini-golf, a children's park, a private beach, and two swimming pools. The lounges, dining rooms, and bars seem more geared for groups than lone travelers. Rooms are in a modified Spanish traditional style, with singles costing 5000 pesetas ($32.50); doubles, 6000 pesetas ($39).

Mijas

It's called "White Mijas" because of its bone-white Andalusian houses. Just five miles from Fuengirola above the Costa del Sol, the village is a gem, standing at the foot of a sierra. From its lofty perches 1400 feet above sea level, a panoramic vista of the Mediterranean unfolds. Along its narrow, cobblestoned streets have walked Celts, Phoenicians, and Moors. You'll do better hiring a "burro-taxi." In a park at the top of Cuesta de la Villa, you see remnants of a Moorish citadel dating from 833. Shops now threaten to inundate the village, selling everything from original art to olivewood jewelry. Incidentally, Mijas possesses the only square bullring in Spain.

WHERE TO STAY: The only hotel in town of any significance is the **Hotel Mijas**, Carretera Benalmádena (tel. 48-58-00). This is one of the special hotels along the coast, with a view of the sea and surrounding mountains. Designed hacienda style, it is perched on the side of a hill, with a semi-enclosed flower patio, a terrace with white wicker furniture and a view, a swimming pool, tennis court, and a lounge that's Castilian in decor. The Andalusian drinking tavern is pleasant, with large kegs of wine. The living room is furnished with fine antiques and inlaid chests, even a framed fan collection. All the excellently furnished bedrooms contain private tiled baths and small refrigerators. Doubles rent for 10,000 pesetas ($165); singles, 8000 pesetas ($52). Other facilities include a sauna, gymnasium, and beauty parlor. Barbecues are held in the open air or else in the Andalusian drinking tavern. Entertainment is provided (in season) in the evenings, and during the day guests can play at the 18-hole Mijas golf course.

Marbella

In the shadow of what was once an Arab fortress, Marbella is definitely chic, attracting a fashionable crowd of movie people and socialites—and "ordinary" people. Many mansions and villas are found hereabouts.

About halfway between Málaga (37 miles to the east) and Gibraltar, Marbella is at the foot of the Sierra Blanca, which keeps the climate mild. Its best beaches are the 600-yard-long Fuerta and the 800-yard-long Fontanilla. Sports, such as waterskiing, shark-fishing, and tennis, are popular. The even more athletically inclined dance till dawn.

At some point, take a walk in the old part of town, still partially enclosed by walls. The whitewashed houses, studded with potted flowers, along narrow streets make for pleasant strolling. Then stop off at a café on the Plaza de los Naranjos (oranges) for a drink.

WHERE TO STAY: Since the setting is so ideal—pure Mediterranean sun, sea, and sky, plus the scent of Andalusian orange blossoms in the air—some of the best hotels along the Costa del Sol are found in Marbella. I'll start with:

The Luxury Resort Hotels

Hotel Don Carlos, Carretera de Cádiz, km. 198 (tel. 83-11-40), is a glamorous blockbuster of a resort hotel, with every facility for a holiday right on its own grounds. It occupies a majestic beach position in a 16-acre garden setting, 10 kilometers from Marbella and 35 kilometers from Torremolinos. The main lounges are super-spacious, with high-fashion coloring. The hotel is handsomely decorated and furnished. The air-conditioned bedrooms, whether singles, doubles, or suites, are pleasantly decorated in an international-modern style. A single room costs 14,000 pesetas ($91), the tariff increasing to 18,000 pesetas ($117), in a double. For a lunch or dinner, expect to pay another 3000 pesetas ($19.50) for a set meal.

Now on to all the extras and amenities. In addition to 11 professional tennis courts, there are two freshwater swimming pools (one of them heated), surrounded by extra-wide tiled terraces with recreational facilities. Adjoining the high-rise bedroom portion of the hotel is a flower-filled, Andalusian-style courtyard surrounded by boutiques, a drugstore, coffeeshop, and sauna. Guests often take lunch at La Pergola on the terrace, preferring to have their evening meal in the main dining room, Los Naranjos. El Cid cocktail lounge is for dancing and entertainment. And a free shuttle service runs guests into Marbella.

Los Monteros, Urbanización Los Monteros, between Torremolinos and Marbella (tel. 77-17-00), is one of the most tasteful and imaginative resort complexes along the Costa del Sol. Between the coastal road and its own private beach, it attracts those seeking intimacy and luxury. No cavernous lounges here; instead, many small, tasteful rooms Andalusian/Japanese in concept. You'll find various salons with open fireplaces, a library, a bar, terraces, and four restaurants on different levels, opening onto flower-filled patios, gardens, and fountains.

The bedrooms are brightly decorated, with lightly colored lacquered furniture, air conditioning, private baths, and terraces. One is a duplex design with a stairway between the sitting room and bedroom. Half-board rates in effect from July 15 to October 15 are 28,000 pesetas ($182) for two persons; 35,000 pesetas ($227.50) for two persons for full board. Free to guests of the hotel is the nearby 18-hole golf course, Río Real. Other facilities include several swimming pools (one heated), plus a beach club, La Cabane (which has an indoor heated pool), ten tennis courts, five squash courts, a riding club and school, plus a fully equipped gymnasium with a sauna and massage.

Within the precincts, El Corzo is one of the finest grill rooms along the coast. The grill, done up in Toledo red, is on a lower level, approached by a winding stairway. Wall-size scenic murals are in the background, and tables are bedecked with bright cloths and silver candlesticks. Soft, romantic music is played nightly. The cuisine is a pleasing combination of French and Spanish.

Melía Don Pepe, Finca Las Merinas (tel. 77-03-00), is tall and impressive, occupying six acres of tropical gardens and lawns between the coastal road and the sea. Fully air-conditioned, its 218 lavishly furnished bedrooms, with private baths and wall-to-wall carpeting, face either the sea or the Sierra Blanca mountains. In high season, a single rents for 12,000 pesetas ($78), a double for 20,000 pesetas ($130). Full board per person is an additional 7500 pesetas ($48.75). The facilities are so vast you could spend a week here and not use them all. They include three swimming pools, tennis courts, a Swedish sauna, a collection of boutiques, a disco, even a bridge clubroom, along with lounges, bars, and restaurants. La Farola grill provides an international à la carte cuisine. Other facilities include a yacht harbor along the beach and a golf course.

Marbella Club, Carretera de Cádiz, km. 184 (tel. 77-13-00), is a deluxe hotel with private beach club on the road from Marbella to Gibraltar. Between the main building, with its lounges in a Spanish rustic theme, and the beach club are avenues of bungalows and garden wings housing double rooms and one-bedroom suites. These cottages and garden wings are surrounded by acres of subtropical gardens granting privacy and comfort. You may swim in the pool at the hotel or else at the seafront beach club, with yet another pool, a waterfall, and thatched huts serving meals and drinks. Bedrooms are traditionally furnished, homelike and tasteful. A standard twin-bedded room rents from 18,000 pesetas ($117) and up. The best food is in the grill, where the chef cooks imported steaks to perfection.

Golf Hotel Nueva Andalucía, Nueva Andalucía Campo del Golf (tel. 78-03-00), is a sedate golf club nestled in the hills above the sea. Its three 18-hole golf courses, considered the most exclusive along the Costa del Sol, are well sprinkled and tended. The hotel is contemporary, although the furnishings are traditional, the emphasis on good taste and comfort. The air-conditioned bedrooms are color coordinated, each with room-wide picture windows.

A single costs 10,000 pesetas ($65); a double 16,000 pesetas ($104). An open-air swimming pool and a terrace for drinks are also popular.

Andalucía Plaza, Urbanización Nueva Andalucía (tel. 81-20-40), is a resort complex on a grand scale. On the mountainside of the coastal road between Marbella and Torremolinos, twin buildings are linked by a reception lounge and formal gardens. On the sea side is the hotel's beach club. Far more than a 300-foot strip of sand, it has sunbathing terraces, a sauna, gymnasium, open-air swimming pool, even an enclosed all-weather pool. And there's a 1000-yacht marina, where you can rent one of the vessels and go deep-sea fishing. The public rooms in the hotel buildings are spacious and lavishly decorated. Equally luxurious are the 418 air-conditioned bedrooms furnished in the classic Andalusian manner, utilizing reproductions. Lone travelers pay 8500 pesetas ($55.25); two people, 10,000 pesetas ($65).

The Restaurant Sancho Panza is for more formal dining, or stop at the *tasca* in front, ordering some shrimps with garlic, washed down by a glass of sangría. Golfers take note: three 18-hole Robert Trent Jones courses are nearby.

The Middle Bracket

Estrella del Mar, Carretera de Cádiz, km. 197 (tel. 83-12-75), is a tasteful resort hotel between Marbella and Torremolinos, with its own seafront swimming pool and sandy beach. The bedrooms of Estrella del Mar, attractively furnished, have pleasant, flower-filled balconies. A single rents for 5000 pesetas ($32.50), a double for 6000 pesetas ($39). For three meals a day, the charge is 8500 pesetas ($55.25) per person. The main lounge, with its reproductions of Castilian antiques, is two stories high. Meals are taken in the informal dining room in the main building. You can try a dish created in the hotel. Called fondue Marbella, it features an assortment of Mediterranean fish served with sauces ranging from tartar to curry. The hotel is open only from March to October.

Las Chapas, Carretera de Cádiz, km. 198 (tel. 83-13-75), takes Spanish bullfight tradition seriously: most of its public rooms encircle a small bullring where mock "no-kill" fights are staged on weekends (sometimes with guests trying their skill) and matadors train with young bulls. Outside of that, it's a "regular" hotel, with air-conditioned bedrooms with private balconies and picture windows overlooking pine trees, mini-golf courses, tennis courts, and the Mediterranean across the main highway. The tone of the lounges and bedrooms is informal, with an accent on the traditional. A single room rents for 4500 pesetas ($29.25), the cost increasing to 7000 pesetas ($45.50) in a double. You can also stay here on full-board terms at a price of about 6500 pesetas ($42.25) per person. The food is good. My most recent repast included an appetizer called simply "white garlic from Málaga." It proceeded to smoked salmon from the Bidasoa River and finally fresh pineapple with Morella cherries. Two swimming pools, a children's playground, a private beach area, and that bullring make this an interesting holiday center.

Marbella-Dinamar, Nueva Andalucía, 18 Carretera de Cádiz, outside Marbella at Puerto Banús (78-05-00), is an exotic resort oasis, right on the seafront. The architecture and decor are Moorish-inspired, with stark white walls and arches. At the rear, the lounges, facing the sea, have a light, airy mood. The patio, adjoining the bar, is tropical Victorian, with ornate white wicker armchairs. The large swimming pool is oddly shaped and surrounded by a tiled terrace, lawns, and palm trees. The bedrooms, conventionally furnished, contain all the modern necessities, including radio, phone, private bath, and air conditioning. Most of them open onto a sea view. Peak-season rates are charged from July 1 to September 30: 7500 pesetas ($48.75) in a single, 9500 pesetas ($61.75) in a twin-bedded room. A more recent facility is a heated and covered swimming pool directly connected to the main building. The tennis courts are floodlit at night, and nearby is one of the best all-around golf courses along the Costa del Sol.

Hotel Guadalpín, Carretera 340 Cádiz-Málaga, km. 186 (tel. 77-11-00), is right on the rugged coast, only 300 yards from the beach (a mile from the center of Marbella). You can live at this three-star hotel for 6500 pesetas ($42.25) in a double room with private bath. For a single with a full bath, the rate is 4500 pesetas ($29.25), but only ten rooms are available in this category.

Guests spend many hours relaxing around two swimming pools, or they walk along a private pathway lined with fir trees to the Mediterranean. The dining room has large windows overlooking the patio and pool, and the main lounge has been designed in a ranch style with round marble tables and occasional leather armchairs arranged for conversational groups. The bar area of the spacious lounge is brick and natural wood, making it warm and attractive. Each room has not only two terraces, but a living room and bedroom combined. Most of the rooms are furnished in "new ranch" style. They have all the conveniences, such as telephones and central heating during the cooler months.

San Pedro de Alcántara

In a little resort suburb west of Marbella are found some of the most tranquil oases along the Costa del Sol. The Golf Hotel Guadalmina is moderately priced, the others falling into the budget categories, although they are definitely not second-rate.

Golf Hotel Guadalmina, Hacienda Guadalmina (tel. 78-14-00), is a large country club-type resort, where the first tee and 18th green are both right next to the hotel. A friendly, informal place, it is really a private world on the shores of the Mediterranean. (You reach it by a long driveway from the coastal road.) Three seawater swimming pools (one heated for children) attract those seeking the lazy life; the tennis courts appeal to the athletic. The bedrooms—most of them opening onto the pool recreation area and the sea—are attractive in their traditional Spanish style.

A single rents for 6000 pesetas ($39), increasing to 9000 pesetas ($58.50) in a double. Full board is 9000 pesetas ($58.50) per person daily. Tasty meals are served in the main dining room as well as in the woody grill, where a pianist plays nightly. The golf course is open to residents and non-residents alike. The hotel offers two excellent dining choices, one a luncheon-only, reed-covered poolside terrace overlooking the golf course and the sea, the other an interior room in the main building, with a sedate clubhouse aura. Informality and good food reign. The set luncheon or dinner is priced at 2000 pesetas ($19.20).

Pueblo Andaluz, Carretera de Cádiz, km. 179 (tel. 81-16-42), is a self-contained resort, built Andalusian village style, with many patios and gardens lined with flowering trees and shrubbery. It's right on the coastal road, five miles from Marbella and a five-minute walk to the beach. Guests congregate in the tiled bar and lounge, furnished with antiques, or else on the grassy lawn with its swimming pool. Families with children are welcomed, and there's a special paddling pool and playground. Bedrooms are consistently decorated in the Spanish style, a single costing 3500 pesetas ($22.75); a double, 4000 pesetas ($26). The regional dining room is built like a hacienda. The hotel is open from April 1 to October 30.

Cortijo Blanco, Carretera de Cádiz, km. 179 (tel. 78-09-00), is a self-contained little world of whitewashed walls, tiled roofs, fountains, courtyards, bell towers, wrought-iron balconies, and a maze of cottages linked by dozens of patios filled with tall subtropical vines and vegetation. All 162 bedrooms face the main garden, dominated by a good-size swimming pool. Rates vary according to season, the highest prices in effect from mid-July to mid-September, at which time singles range from 4000 pesetas ($26) to 4500 pesetas ($29.25); doubles, from 6000 pesetas ($39) to 6800 pesetas ($44.20), plus 2200 pesetas ($14.30) per person extra for half-board. Evening meals are a gracious affair, as you sit in high-backed, carved red and gilt Valencian chairs; lunch is quite pleasant, served around the covered pergola with its luxuriant vegetation.

Sotogrande

Sotogrande, a residential tourist development, sprawls across 4400 acres—certainly the most luxurious resort along the whole of the Costa del Sol. Across from the Rock of Gibraltar, it represents elegant Andalusia at its best.

The area appeals to the well-heeled sportsperson, one who doesn't mind crossing an ocean and/or a continent to play the three Robert Trent Jones courses. (There's a nine-hole executive course for the less energetic.)

This is a large complex, with many facilities, some of which are in the membership-only category. However, the **Tenis Hotel Sotogrande**, Carretera N. 340, km. 132 (tel. 79-21-00), is open to the general public, containing 46 handsomely furnished double rooms and two luxurious suites. The rate in a double room is from 14,000 pesetas ($91) daily, dropping to 9000 pesetas ($58.50) in a single.

The Tenis Hotel serves breakfasts, full luncheons, and dinners. Light snacks and bar service are available at the Tenis Hotel as well as at the Golf Hotel restaurant, Beach Club restaurant, and New Golf restaurant.

Next to the hotel, there are six tennis courts, a large swimming pool, children's play area, hairdressing salon, and a disco. Guests may also hire horses from nearby stables, and polo is enjoyed by players and spectators alike on Sotogrande's two polo grounds throughout the summer season.

Where to Dine

Most visitors to the Costa del Sol eat at their hotels. In fact, in high season many establishments require guests to take at least half-board (breakfast, plus one main meal). But, even so, there are many good and independent restaurants along the Sun Coast for those desiring to escape from their hotel dining room. I'll preview only a sampling of the many, many possibilities.

First, a word about the food specialties of the area. In this part of the Mediterranean, fish (such as whitebait), chopitos, and anchovies, are the major part of the banquet. Particular specialties include fish soup (sopa de pescado); a fisherman's rice dish of crayfish and clams (arroz à la marinera), and grilled sardines (espetones de sardinas). In all of Andalusia, soothing gazpacho is a refreshing opener to many a meal. Of course, everything's better when washed down with the renowned wines of Málaga, including Pedro Ximénez and Muscatel.

MÁLAGA: Antonio Martín, 4 Paseo Marítimo (tel. 22-21-13), does better with the skillets than any other restaurant in town. On the eastern edge, close to the bullring, it is a waterside restaurant favored by knowing Spanish families, local executives, and the expatriate colony. Three dining rooms are clustered under a peaked wooden ceiling with natural brick walls (try for the room on the right as you enter, the one with Valencian chairs, an open fireplace, and antique furnishings). At lunch, however, the harborfront terrace is ideal. Shellfish soup is the traditional opener, or else you might prefer the special hors d'oeuvres. A paella of shellfish, chicken, and meat is the chef's specialty. Other specialties include sirloin steak on a skewer and golden mackerel in salt. I also prefer the grilled swordfish and the stewed oxtail. Custard with whipped cream is the standard dessert. For a good, average meal, expect to pay anywhere from 1500 pesetas ($9.75) to 2200 pesetas ($14.30). Service is rapid and attentive. It's usually crowded, so reservations are necessary. It is closed Sunday night.

The **Parador Nacional del Gibralfaro**, Monte Gibralfaro (tel. 22-19-02), is preferred for its view. Government-owned, it sits on a mountainside high above the city. You can look down into the heart of the Málaga bullring, among other things. Meals are served in the attractive dining room, with a colorful ceramic plate collection, or under the arches of two wide terraces, providing views of the coast. Featured are hors d'oeuvres parador—your entire table literally covered with tiny dishes of tasty tidbits. Another specialty is an omelet of chanquetes, tiny white fish popular in this part of the country, or chicken Villaroi. If you stick to the set menu, a complete dinner will cost from 1800 pesetas ($11.70).

Another government-owned restaurant is the **Parador Nacional del Golf**, Apartado 324, Málaga (tel. 38-12-55). Its indoor/outdoor dining room opens onto a circular swimming pool, lawns, golf course, and private beach. The interior dining room, furnished with reproductions of antiques, has a refined country-club atmosphere. Pre-lunch drinks at the sleek modern bar tempt golfers and others, who then proceed to the covered terrace for their meal. A set meal costs 1600 pesetas ($10.40), although an à la carte menu is available. You can make it an afternoon, using the pool for 500 pesetas ($3.25). You'll be given a 50% discount if you order a meal.

NERJA: The **Parador Nacional de Nerja**, Playa de Burriana (tel. 52-00-50), outside of town, is the ideal choice for many diners. The dining room opens onto views of the Mediterranean at the bottom of the cliff. Good food is served in the hacienda-style beamed dining room, with wide glass sliding doors. The price for a full lunch or dinner is 1600 pesetas ($10.40). Before or after dinner, you can go for a swim, nonresidents paying 500 pesetas ($3.25) for the privilege.

TORREMOLINOS: El Caballo Vasco, Calle Casablanca, La Nogalera (tel. 38-23-36), is the best place to dine among the independent restaurants right in the heart of Torremolinos. It serves the deservedly popular Basque cuisine from the top floor of a modern building complex which is reached by an elevator. Picture windows lead to a terrace. As a prelude to your repast, you might try melon with ham or fish soup. Generous portions of tasty, well-prepared seafood are served, including prawns in garlic sauce and codfish Basque style. Also good, if you have the taste for it, is squid in its own ink, and the Basque-style hake is excellent. The meat dishes are also of uniformly good quality, and you get some imaginative interpretations, not usually found on menus along the Costa del Sol—pork shanks Basque style and oxtail in a savory sauce. For timid diners, one of the safest bets is chicken in sherry sauce. It's also one of the least expensive main courses. A complete meal will cost from 1800 pesetas ($11.70) to 3000 pesetas ($19.50). The staff takes off on Monday.

Casa Prudencio, 41 Carmen (tel. 38-14-52), is the leading seafood restaurant on the beach at Carihuela. It packs in diners like sardines, but its devotees don't seem to mind the wait. The decor is rustic, with indoor dining service. However, in summer the favored place is a reed canopy-covered open-air terrace where you dine on red-and-white-checked cloths, sitting on red chairs elbow to elbow. The owner orchestrates and choreographs the waiters to a fast and nervous pace. Service is haphazard, but friendly. For an appetizer, a soothing gazpacho is ideal. Most diners are fascinated by the specialty of the house, lubina á la sal (salted fish). Cooked in an oblong pan, the fish is completely covered with white salt which is then scraped away in front of the diner anxious to get to the well-flavored, tender white flesh inside. Other main-course dishes include swordfish, shish kebab, and a special paella. For dessert, try the fresh strawberries. A typical meal is likely to cost from 1500 pesetas ($9.75) to 2000 pesetas ($13) or more.

Hong Kong, Calle del Cauce (tel. 38-41-29), is the only restaurant along the Costa del Sol serving an Indonesian rijsttafel (literally, a rice table). You're served a large bowl of rice with a selection of highly spiced side dishes. Among the Chinese dishes offered are hot spiced pork with vegetables and chop suey. The *menú del día* goes for 1000 pesetas ($6.50). If you order à la carte, count on spending from 1200 pesetas ($7.80) to 2200 pesetas ($14.30). The Oriental restaurant is on a busy street of milling visitors, which is virtually an open-air dining room.

FUENGIROLA (Los Boliches): **Don Bigote** (Mr. Mustache) (tel. 47-50-94) was a deserted century-old sardine factory and a row of fishermen's cottages before its transformation into one of the most popular restaurants in the area. In summer, a splashing fountain in the garden patio makes the right background for the well-prepared international menu. In cooler weather, you have a choice of dining in one of the attractively decorated dining rooms, each furnished in a regional style. You might enjoy a pre-dinner drink under the rafters in the lounge bar. The chefs turn out a most recommendable Spanish and continental cuisine. Meals begin at 2500 pesetas ($16.25), and the staff serves both lunch and dinner.

MIJAS: **Club el Padrastro,** Paseo del Compás (tel. 48-50-00), is aptly named. In Spanish *padrastro* is a curious word, meaning both "stepfather" and "hangnail." However, it also suggests height, a commanding position. You'll agree after climbing the 77 steps to reach it, although it's more sensible to take the elevator at the town parking lot. After you've scaled the heights, a swimming pool and an artfully decorated restaurant await you. Before dinner, take a drink under pine trees by the pool, enjoying the view. Inside, ten picture windows on two levels also open onto the panorama, and soft music helps, too. The food is quite good. For openers, why not the pâté? Specialties include fish soup Padrastro, bass with fennel, and a special flambé Padrastro. The tab here is likely to run between 1800 pesetas ($11.70) and 3000 pesetas ($19.50).

MARBELLA: **La Hacienda,** Urbanización Hacienda Las Chapas, Carretera de Cádiz, km. 200 (tel. 83-12-67), is a tranquil choice, enjoying a reputation for serving some of the best food along the Costa del Sol. In cooler months, you can dine inside in the rustic tavern before an open fireplace. However, in fair weather meals are alfresco, served on a patio partially encircled by open Romanesque arches. The Belgian owner, Paul Schiff, features not only the fine cuisine of his own land, but of France as well. Cutlery and silverware complement the good service. He is likely to offer calves' liver with truffled butter, lobster croquettes (as an appetizer), and roast guinea hen with cream, minced raisins, and port. A baked Alaska finishes the repast quite nicely, although you may prefer an iced soufflé. For such good food, the bill isn't exorbitant, costing from 4000 pesetas ($26) for a complete meal. In summer, only dinner is served, with reservations being important. In winter, both lunch and dinner are offered. The restaurant is closed on Monday in summer and on Monday and Tuesday in winter.

La Fonda, 10 Plaza Santo Cristo (tel. 77-25-12), is run by Horchers of Madrid. The restaurant was the outgrowth of an inn, which had been created by connecting a trio of town houses in Old Marbella. Patios and colonnaded loggias are combined effectively, and the beamed ceilings, Moorish arches, checkerboard marble floors, fireplaces, and grilled windows have been retained. Considering the matchless art performed in the kitchen, the prices are reasonable. The tops in ingredients are used. You'll notice that right away when ordering an appetizer—perhaps avocado ceviche or vichyssoise. The main dishes are cooked with care and professionalism, and are a familiar array taken from an international repertoire—coq au vin, shrimp in dill sauce, veal scaloppine Don Quixote, a blanquette de veau, and chicken Kiev. A complete meal ranges in price from 3000 pesetas ($19.50) to 4000 pesetas ($26). Just as the food is international, so is the crowd. Some of the most beautiful faces of Marbella (and some of the richest) are seen here. It is closed on Sunday.

Gran Marisquería Santiago, 5 Paseo Marítimo (tel. 770-078). As soon as you enter this seaside restaurant, the bubbling lobster tanks will give you an idea of the kinds of dishes available. The orange and green decor, the standup *tapas* bar near the entrance, and the summertime patio join together with super-fresh fish dishes to make this one of the most popular eating places in town. On my most recent visit, I arrived so early for lunch that the mussels for my mussels marinara were just being delivered. The fish soup is well prepared, well spiced, and savory. The sole in champagne comes in a large serving, and the turbot can be grilled or sautéed. On a hot day, the seafood salad, garnished with lobster, shrimp, and crabmeat and served with a sharp sauce, is especially recommended. For dessert, I suggest a serving of Manchego cheese. A complete meal will cost 2200 pesetas ($14) and up.

Chez Charlemagne, Carretera de Cádiz, km. 196 (tel. 83-11-05), is a French restaurant, although you'd never know it to judge by its setting. Near an olive grove, right on the coastal road, it's a converted Spanish villa, with a regional dining room. In fair weather you dine outside under a reed canopy. Jean Charlemagne invites you to sample some of his specialties, including, just for an appetizer, snails or perhaps smoked trout. Main-dish specialties include fish soup with rouille, guinea fowl in season, and quail in raisin sauce. He also serves excellent quiches. Dinner costs about 2000 pesetas ($13) per person. In winter, both lunch and dinner are served, only dinner in summer.

It is closed on Wednesday in winter but open seven nights a week in summer.

The **Pizzeria Sanremo**, Paseo Marítimo (tel. 77-43-33), right on the beach, draws devotees of the Italian kitchen who like to sample the viands of the owner, Stefano Vella. The menu is presented in English, and most diners prefer one of the pizzas, costing from 400 pesetas ($2.60), or perhaps one of the spaghetti concoctions, averaging about 450 pesetas ($2.92) per plate. The raw carrot salad is an unusual item on menus in Spain, and the veal dishes are well prepared. For a complete meal, expect to pay about 1500 pesetas ($9.75). If you're in the resort on a Thursday, you can come here to order couscous, the North African specialty. It is closed on Wednesday.

ESTEPONA: **La Rana**, Carretera de Cádiz, km. 169 (tel. 801-055), is the "wide-mouthed frog" run by Disley Jones. Across from Camping Chimenea, it offers both continental food and such English specialties as steak and kidney pie and game in season. Mr. Jones is the chef and the host (it is necessary to call him for a table and never on Tuesday or during the month of August). He serves dinner only from 8:30 to 11 p.m.

A former theatrical designer, Mr. Jones allows you to dine in one of two rooms, one in a black-and-white theme with potted palms. Spare ribs are served Hawaiian style, and, on occasion, he'll bake a game pie. Naturally, in honor of his namesake, he offers frog legs à la Rana. His food is not only excellently prepared, it is imaginatively served. After all, Mr. Jones still retains his sense of the theatrical. Count on spending around 4000 pesetas ($26) and always ask for clear directions before heading out.

PUERTO BANÚS: **Don Leone** (tel. 781-727). Puerto Banús is becoming one of the most popular and visited spots along the Costa del Sol, and many visitors drive over just for dinner. If you decide to do likewise, you'll find this excellent Italian restaurant, run by Santi de Pablo, right at dockside. The decoration is attractive, with many luxurious touches. The waiters have been carefully screened. You can dine inside or out. The wine list is one of the best along the coast. To begin your repast, you might order the house minestrone, which is invariably good. Pasta dishes, made on the premises, naturally are featured in various savory sauces, including bolognese and a clam sauce. Lasagne is also a regular item on the menu. Veal parmigiana and roast baby lamb are among the better meat courses, and there are also some well-prepared fish dishes. Count on spending about 4000 pesetas ($26) or more for a meal. The restaurant serves both lunch and dinner seven days a week, except it is closed for lunch in summer. It tends to get crowded, so try to reserve a table.

Nightlife Along the Costa del Sol

Along the Costa del Sol, nightlife consists mainly of hopping from bar to bar, occasionally to a flamenco club or disco. Without a car and a good sense of direction, you might want to cover the top spots by organized tour: for an all-inclusive price, you're picked up at your hotel and returned there, plus given one free drink at each spot visited.

Many organizations run these tours; one such is **Viajes Alhambra,** 514 La Nogalera (tel. 38-17-20) in Torremolinos; Plaza de las Flores (tel. 21-90-80) in Málaga. Its Torremolinos night tour costs from 3500 pesetas ($22.75), 4000 pesetas ($26) if you're staying in Marbella. The tour includes two top nightclubs with flamenco shows and other attractions, plus dancing to live bands. But if you want to go it alone, here are a few suggestions.

TORREMOLINOS: Torremolinos stands in the eye of the night-time hurricane. The earliest action is always at the bars, which are lively most of the night, serving drinks and *tapas* (Spanish hors d'oeuvres). Sometimes it seems there are more bars in Torremolinos than people—so you shouldn't have trouble finding one you like.

The **Bar El Toro,** 32 San Miguel (no phone), is for aficionados (the bullfight theme is everywhere). Kegs of beer, stools, and the terrace in the main shopping street make it perfect for drinking a before-dinner sherry or an after-dinner beer. As a special attraction, the staff prepares a bullfight poster, with your name between those of two famous matadors, for 300 pesetas ($1.95).

Gatsby, 68 Avenida Montemar (tel. 38-53-72), stands on a major, traffic-choked boulevard, and, wisely, has its own private parking. Taking its theme from Fitzgerald's 1920s, Gatsby has a loud, distortion-free sound system. The illumination employs strobes and spots, as you dance to up-to-the-instant disc selections. For your first drink, you pay 600 pesetas ($3.90). The attractive clientele seeks out the romantic tables or else the tropical garden adjoining the building.

The Tivoli-World of the Costa del Sol

In what was once an olive grove, the Tivoli-World of the Spanish Riviera was inspired by its famous namesake in Copenhagen. Much has been done to avoid the Coney Island–type atmosphere, although it is a pleasure garden, with more than 34 rides and attractions such as regional folk dances staged in an Andalusian square, a Chinese pagoda, a miniature Wild West frontier town with can-can shows, and a 4000-seat theater where national and international stars perform on many special days. Among the 17 different fountains, there is one with coordinated light- and water-dancing cascades. You can eat anything from a light snack to a gourmet dinner in one of the many restaurants and snackbars or have a drink in a variety of settings. All the shows and practically all the rides are included in the entrance price, which is about $6 (U.S.) for both adults and children.

The park is open from April to October from 6 p.m. Check at your hotel before heading there, however. The Tivoli is two miles from the center of Torremolinos, about a 10-minute ride by bus or taxi. Buses and trains connect with Tivoli-World from many parts of the Costa del Sol.

Piper's Club, Plaza Costa del Sol (tel. 38-29-94), is more theatricalized, decorated tongue-in-cheek. It resembles a subterranean world, suggesting the caves at Nerja. Spread over many levels, with connecting ramps and tunnels, it has four dance floors, splashing water in reflecting pools, strobe lighting, and an aggressive set of international records to amuse its packed audience. It's very much the '60s in aura and ambience. Open nightly, it charges 1200 pesetas ($7.80) for the first drink.

The leading strictly flamenco club has been and remains **El Jaleo,** Plaza de la Gamba Alegre (tel. 38-21-50). Its *tablao flamenco* showcase of local singers, dancers, and guitarists performs nightly for a cover of 1500 pesetas ($9.75), including the first drink. Go between 10:30 p.m. and 2:30 a.m.

Finally, **La Boveda,** 8 Cuesta del Tajo (walk down a steep hill from the end of Calle San Miguel; tel. 38-11-85), is a fun spot with the accent on flamenco and South American songs. A 90-minute program is presented nightly. You sit in cavelike decor, at wooden tables, surrounded by old chests, beamed ceilings, cobbled floors, in big vaulted rooms. A flamenco show is presented at 10:30 p.m., and you can attend for 1000 pesetas ($6.50), which includes the price of your first drink. The place was a 16th-century watermill, and the word "Torremolinos" comes from it. There is dancing in a pleasant garden. You can order food here, the chef specializing in meat and grilled fish such as sea bass. A complete meal is likely to run about 2000 pesetas ($13), maybe a lot more.

MARBELLA: The best place to go for Flamenco is **Fiesta,** 8 Calle Valentuñana (tel. 77-37-43). On my latest rounds, I was treated to the talent of a performer known as "the first vedette of Spanish song and rhumba." The backup cast included some excellent *cantadores* and guitarists. It is open every night with shows from 10:45 p.m. to 12:45 a.m. and from 1:15 to 2:45 a.m. You'll be charged about 1500 pesetas ($9.75) for your first drink.

PUERTO BANÚS: **Casino Neuva Andalucía Marbella,** Nueve Andalucía, on the outskirts of Puerto Banús (tel. 81-13-44), is the most exciting nightlife complex along the Costa del Sol. To the west of Marbella, it offers about everything—including terrace dining, swimming pools, a beach, and a nightclub, as well as the gaming rooms. The casino features French roulette, American roulette, blackjack, punto y banco, craps, and chemin de fer. The club stays open all year. Winter hours are from 8 p.m. to 4 a.m., and summer hours are from 9 p.m. till 5 a.m. An admission card is available upon presentation of your passport and the payment of a fee—500 pesetas ($3.25) for one day. Everybody should dress according to the high standards of the casino.

Casino Torrequebrada, 266 Carretera de Cádiz, Benalmádena-Costa (tel. 44-25-45), is another casino in the region that offers blackjack, chemin de fer, punto y banco, and two kinds of roulette to its formally dressed clientele. On the premises are a restaurant, bar, disco, nightclub, and cinema. It is open from 8 p.m. till 4 a.m.

For a much less formal evening than the gambling clubs already previewed, you might drop in at one of the popular piano bars in the heart of Puerto Banús. The most popular is **Duques,** Local 54, Muelle Ribera (tel. 814-733). It's owned by Duke Meeks, an American with a skill for booking good acts. Drinks cost from 350 pesetas ($2.28).

NOW, SAVE MONEY ON ALL YOUR TRAVELS!
Join Arthur Frommer's $25-A-Day Travel Club

Saving money while traveling is never a simple matter, which is why, over 22 years ago, the **$25-A-Day Travel Club** was formed. Actually, the idea came from readers of the Arthur Frommer Publications who felt that such an organization could bring financial benefits, continuing travel information, and a sense of community to economy-minded travelers all over the world.

In keeping with the money-saving concept, the annual membership fee is low—$15 (U.S. residents) or $18 (Canadian, Mexican, and foreign residents)—and is immediately exceeded by the value of your benefits which include:

(1) The latest edition of any TWO of the books listed on the following page.

(2) An annual subscription to an 8-page quarterly newspaper *The Wonderful World of Budget Travel* which keeps you up-to-date on fastbreaking developments in low-cost travel in all parts of the world—bringing you the kind of information you'd have to pay over $25 a year to obtain elsewhere. This consumer-conscious publication also includes the following columns:

Travelers' Directory—members all over the world who are willing to provide hospitality to other members as they pass through their home cities.

Share-a-Trip—requests from members for travel companions who can share costs and help avoid the burdensome single supplement.

Readers Ask . . . Readers Reply—travel questions from members to which other members reply with authentic firsthand information.

(3) A copy of *Arthur Frommer's Guide to New York.*

(4) Your personal membership card which entitles you to purchase through the Club all Arthur Frommer Publications for a third to a half off their regular retail prices during the term of your membership.

So why not join this hardy band of international budgeteers NOW and participate in its exchange of information and hospitality? Simply send $15 (U.S. residents) or $18 U.S. (Canadian, Mexican, and other foreign residents) along with your name and address to: $25-A-Day Travel Club, Inc., 1230 Avenue of the Americas, New York, NY 10020. Remember to specify which *two* of the books in section (1) above you wish to receive in your initial package of members' benefits. Or tear out this page, check off any two books on the opposite side and send it to us with your membership fee.

FROMMER/PASMANTIER PUBLISHERS   Date_______________
1230 AVE. OF THE AMERICAS, NEW YORK, NY 10020

Friends, please send me the books checked below:

$-A-DAY GUIDES
(In-depth guides to low-cost tourist accommodations and facilities.)

☐ Europe on $25 a Day	$10.95
☐ Australia on $25 a Day	$9.95
☐ England and Scotland on $25 a Day	$9.95
☐ Greece on $25 a Day	$9.95
☐ Hawaii on $35 a Day	$9.95
☐ India on $15 & $25 a Day	$9.95
☐ Ireland on $25 a Day	$9.95
☐ Israel on $30 & $35 a Day	$9.95
☐ Mexico on $20 a Day	$9.95
☐ New Zealand on $20 & $25 a Day	$9.95
☐ New York on $35 a Day	$8.95
☐ Scandinavia on $25 a Day	$9.95
☐ South America on $25 a Day	$8.95
☐ Spain and Morocco (plus the Canary Is.) on $25 a Day	$9.95
☐ Washington, D.C. on $35 a Day	$8.95

DOLLARWISE GUIDES
(Guides to accommodations and facilities from budget to deluxe, with emphasis on the medium-priced.)

☐ Austria & Hungary	$10.95	☐ Cruises (incl. Alaska, Carib, Mex,	
☐ Egypt	$9.95	Hawaii, Panama, Canada, & US)	$10.95
☐ England & Scotland	$10.95	☐ California & Las Vegas	$9.95
☐ France	$10.95	☐ Florida	$9.95
☐ Germany	$9.95	☐ New England	$9.95
☐ Italy	$10.95	☐ Northwest	$10.95
☐ Portugal (incl. Madeira & the Azores)	$9.95	☐ Southeast & New Orleans	$9.95
☐ Switzerland & Liechtenstein	$9.95	☐ Southwest	$10.95
☐ Canada	$10.95		
☐ Caribbean (incl. Bermuda & the Bahamas)	$10.95		

THE ARTHUR FROMMER GUIDES
(Pocket-size guides to tourist accommodations and facilities in all price ranges.)

☐ Amsterdam/Holland	$4.95	☐ Mexico City/Acapulco	$4.95
☐ Athens	$4.95	☐ Montreal/Quebec City	$4.95
☐ Atlantic City/Cape May	$4.95	☐ New Orleans	$4.95
☐ Boston	$4.95	☐ New York	$4.95
☐ Dublin/Ireland	$4.95	☐ Orlando/Disney World/EPCOT	$4.95
☐ Hawaii	$4.95	☐ Paris	$4.95
☐ Las Vegas	$4.95	☐ Philadelphia	$4.95
☐ Lisbon/Madrid/Costa del Sol	$4.95	☐ Rome	$4.95
☐ London	$4.95	☐ San Francisco	$4.95
☐ Los Angeles	$4.95	☐ Washington, D.C.	$4.95

SPECIAL EDITIONS

☐ How to Beat the High Cost of Travel	$4.95	☐ Marilyn Wood's Wonderful Weekends	$9.95
☐ New York Urban Athlete (NYC sports		(NY, Conn, Mass, RI, Vt, NJ, Pa)	
guide for jocks & novices)	$9.95	☐ Museums in New York	$8.95
☐ Where to Stay USA (Accommodations		☐ Guide for the Disabled Traveler	$10.95
from $3 to $25 a night)	$8.95	☐ Bed & Breakfast-No. America	$7.95
☐ Fast 'n' Easy Phrase Book			
(Fr/Sp/Ger/Ital. in *one* vol.)	$6.95		

In U.S. include $1 post. & hdlg. for 1st book; 25¢ ea. add'l. book. Outside U.S. $2 and 50¢ respectively.

Enclosed is my check or money order for $_______________________________________

NAME____

ADDRESS____

CITY_____________________________________ STATE____________ ZIP__________